Jonathan Clements is the author of many books on Asia, including biographies of the Empress Wu, the pirate king Coxinga, and the philosopher Confucius. His previous writings relating to Khubilai Khan's era include *Marco Polo* (Haus, 2007), *Beijing: The Biography of a City* (Sutton, 2008) and *A Brief History of the Samurai* (Robinson, 2010). His books have been translated into French, German, Spanish, Portuguese, Dutch, Polish, Bulgarian, Czech, Estonian, Finnish, Romanian, Russian, and Korean. In a rare accolade for a British historian, his biography of the First Emperor of China was itself translated into Chinese.

OTHER TITLES IN THIS SERIES:

A Brief Guide to Charles Darwin Cyril Aydon

A Brief Guide to the Greek Myths Stephen Kershaw

A Brief Guide to Islam Paul Grieve

A Brief History of 1917 Roy Bainton

A Brief History of the Birth of the Nazis Nigel H. Jones

A Brief History of British Kings and Queens Mike Ashley

A Brief History of Christianity Bamber Gascoigne

A Brief History of the Crusades Geoffrey Hindley

A Brief History of the Druids Peter Berresford Ellis

A Brief History of the Dynasties of China Bamber Gascoigne

A Brief History of the End of the World Simon Pearson

A Brief History of Florence Nightingale Hugh Small

A Brief History of Globalization Alex MacGillivray

A Brief History of Infinity Brian Clegg

A Brief History of Italy Jeremy Black

A Brief History of Japan Jonathan Clements

A Brief History of Life in Victorian Britain Michael Paterson

A Brief History of Magna Carta Geoffrey Hindley

A Brief History of the Martial Arts Jonathan Clements

A Brief History of Medieval Warfare Peter Reid

A Brief History of the Middle East Christopher Catherwood

A Brief History of Misogyny J. Holland

A Brief History of the Normans Francois Neveux

A Brief History of the Private Life of Elizabeth II Michael Paterson

A Brief History of the Private Lives of the Roman Emperors Anthony Blond

A Brief History of the Samurai Jonathan Clements

A Brief History of Science Thomas Crump

A Brief History of Secret Societies David V. Barrett

A Brief History of Stonehenge Aubrey Burl

A Brief History of the Vikings Jonathan Clements

A Brief History of the Wars of the Roses Desmond Seward

A BRIEF HISTORY OF

Khubilai Khan

Jonathan Clements

ROBINSON

ROBINSON

First published in Great Britain by Robinson,
an imprint of Constable & Robinson Ltd, 2010

This edition published by Robinson in 2019

Copyright © Jonathan Clements, 2010

1 3 5 7 9 10 8 6 4 2

The moral right of the author has been asserted.

A CIP catalogue record for this book is available from the British Library

ISBN: 978-1-47214-320-4

Printed and bound in Great Britain by CPI Group (UK) Ltd, Croydon CR0 4YY

Papers used by Robinson are from well-managed
forests and other responsible sources

MIX
Paper from
responsible sources
FSC® C104740

Robinson
An imprint of
Little, Brown Book Group
Carmelite House
50 Victoria Embankment
London EC4Y 0DZ

An Hachette UK Company
www.hachette.co.uk

www.littlebrown.co.uk

For David Lei

Now am I come to that part of our Book in which I shall tell you of the great and wonderful magnificence of the Great Kaan now reigning, by name CUBLAY KAAN; *Kaan* being a title which signifyeth 'The Great Lord of Lords,' or Emperor.

– The Travels of Marco Polo, c.1307

In Xamdu did Cublai Can build a stately Pallace, encompassing sixteen miles of plaine grounde within a wall, wherein are fertile Meddowes, pleasant Springs, delightful Streames, and all sorts of beasts of chase and game, and in the middest thereof a sumptuous house of pleasures, which may be removed from place to place.

Hakluytus Posthumus, or Purchas His Pilgrimes, 1613

CONTENTS

Maps   xi

Family Tree   xiv

Introduction: Rise of the Mongols   1

Chapter 1   Conquered by Wine: The Reign of Ogodei   13

Chapter 2   Voices Prophesying War: The Sons of Tolui   29

Chapter 3   In Xanadu: Khubilai in the Reign of Mongke   46

Chapter 4   The Revolution of Fate: The Battle to be
            Khan   62

Chapter 5   A Plague upon the Throne: The Yangtze
            Campaign   81

Chapter 6   Beginning: The Yuan Dynasty   100

Chapter 7   Samurai: The First Mongol Armada   114

Chapter 8   The Miscellaneous Aliens: Khubilai's
            Cosmopolitan Empire   137

Chapter 9   Dragons in the Water: The Second Mongol
            Armada   152

Chapter 10 The Accursed Doctrines: Political Intrigues
            and Religious Persecutions   169

Chapter 11   Death to the Mongols: The Annamese
             Resistance   192

Chapter 12   Down to a Sunless Sea: Last Years   207

Chapter 13   The Romance of the Grand Khan:
             Khubilai's Legacy   219

Chronology   231

Notes on Names   236

Sources and Further Reading   238

Notes   247

Index   261

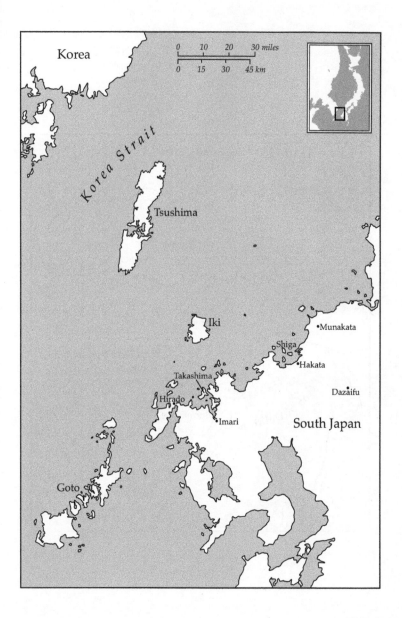

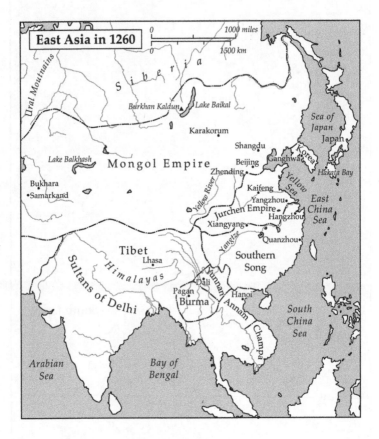

East Asia in 1260

0   1000 miles

0   1500 km

Ural Mountains

Siberia

Burkhan Kaldun   *Lake Baikal*

Karakorum

Shangdu

Lake Balkhash   Mongol Empire   Beijing   Ganghwa

Zhending

Korea

Sea of Japan

Japan

Bukhara

•Samarkand

Yellow River

Kaifeng

Yellow Sea

Hakata Bay

Yangzhou

Jurchen Empire

East China Sea

Xiangyang•

Hangzhou

Yangtze

Quanzhou•

Tibet

Lhasa

Southern Song

Himalayas

Sultans of Delhi

Dali

Yunnan

Pagan

Hanoi

Annam

Burma

Champa

South China Sea

Arabian Sea

Bay of Bengal

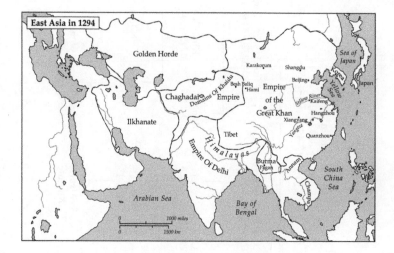

East Asia in 1294

Golden Horde

Sea of Japan

Karakorum   Shangdu

Chaghadai Empire
Domains Of Khaidu
Besh Baliq
•Hami

Beijing•

Korea

Japan

Empire of the Great Khan

Yellow Sea

Yellow River
•Kaifeng

Ilkhanate

Tibet

Xiangyang•

Hangzhou•

Yangtze

Quanzhou•

Himalayas

Empire Of Delhi

Burma
Pagan

Annam

Champa

South China Sea

Arabian Sea

Bay of Bengal

0   1000 miles
0   1500 km

The Descendants of Temujin
(highly simplified)

Temujin
(Genghis Khan)
1167–1227

Jochi
1184–1227

Batu
d.1255

⟹ The Golden Horde →1360

Chaghadai
1185–1242

⟹ The Chaghadai Khanate →1347

Ogodei = Toregene
1186–1241   d.1246

Guyuk
1206–1248

Qashi
d.1236

Khaidu
1230–1301

Aiyaruk
(Khutulun)

Tolui = Sorghaghtani
1190–1232   1198–1252

Mongke
1209–1259

Khubilai
1215–1294

Zhenjin
1243–1285

⟹ Later Emperors of the Yuan dyanasty →1368

Nomukhan

Hulagu
1217–1265

⟹ Persian Ilkhante →1335

Arigh Boke
d.1266

(many birthdates estimates only)

INTRODUCTION

RISE OF THE MONGOLS

They were composed of many races from the east – mainly Mongols, but others including the Keraits, Turks, Uighurs, Naimans, Tatars. This last word caught the imagination of Christian authors, who added an extra letter to allude to hell itself. These unstoppable hordes of warriors were now often called *Tartars*, demons from Tartarus, vengeful terror unleashed upon a sinful world.

In 1260, Pope Alexander IV issued a proclamation to all civilized nations:

> There rings in the ears of all . . . a terrible trumpet of dire forewarning which . . . proclaims with so unmistakable a sound the wards of universal destruction, wherewith the scourge of Heaven's wrath in the hands of the inhuman Tartars, erupting as it were from the secret confines of Hell, oppresses and crushes the earth . . .[1]

The Pope had reason to be afraid. The Mongol advances in Eastern Europe were redolent of the conquests of Attila the Hun or the Visigoths of antiquity. Mongol savagery was widely known; entire cities had perished at their hands after refusing to surrender. The speed of their advances was astounding; their ability to integrate vassal populations turned them into an ever growing, ever more dangerous enemy, sure to descend upon Europe at any moment.

In fact, at the time that Alexander wrote his call to arms, the Mongol world was changing forever. Temujin, *the* Genghis Khan, had been dead for thirty-three years. The hordes that ravaged Poland, Hungary and Bulgaria were the last flotsam of the tide of invasion. Temujin's grandchildren were arguing about the future of the Mongols, and Europe was not on the top of their agenda. In the Middle East, one grandson, Hulagu, was invading Persia, while another, Batu, sired a son who would convert to Islam and 'avenge' this deed by turning on his own. Meanwhile, in Mongolia itself, another grandson, Arigh Boke (Arigh the Strong), favoured the old ways, living on the wide grasslands, and occasionally stealing whatever the Mongols might need from the rest of the world. His forty-five-year-old brother, Khubilai, was more interested in an eastward-directed empire, the adoption of elements of Chinese culture and society and the transformation of the Mongols. Either of them might present a threat to Europe in the future, but for the moment, they were a far greater danger to each other. Ultimately, Khubilai would become the Khan, leader of all the descendants of Temujin. The Mongol drive westwards slowly faded, while inquisitive missionaries from Europe headed east, wondering with relentless optimism whether they might convert the Mongols to Christianity.

Temujin, leader of the Mongols, better known by his title of 'Great Leader' or 'Genghis Khan', had been far from impressed with his new grandson, Khubilai. A good Mongol child, as far as Temujin was concerned, needed to take after his father.

'All our children are of a ruddy complexion,' said Temujin in 1215, 'but this child is swarthy like his maternal uncles.' True to his background as a herder, Temujin thought that the new arrival merely required the right sort of milk. He ordered Khubilai's mother Sorghaghtani to make sure that her son found a good wet-nurse; taking the hint, she picked a heavily pregnant woman of the Naiman people, a Turkish steppe race, sure to impress the crotchety grandfather with their similarity to hearty Mongol folk.[2]

The story of the baby Khubilai is the oldest tale about him, and is followed in the historical record by almost two decades of silence. Understandably, nobody took much interest in the childhood and teenage years of yet another Mongol princeling, one of many dozens born to Temujin's unruly brood of sons. In later life, he would be blessed with two superb storytellers, who would record many anecdotes from his life. The first, the source of the above story, is Rashid al-Din, the Persian author whose *Compendium of Chronicles* is one of the great works of Middle Eastern history. The other was a man who may have once met Rashid, but who would later write his own account of Khubilai's realm: Marco Polo, whose *Description of the World* has fascinated readers for centuries. Khubilai appears in many other places. The *History of the Yuan*, the chronicle of the dynasty he founded in China, includes many quotes and decrees. Similar annals in Japan, Annam (Vietnam) and Korea also record the acts of Khubilai where relevant to those countries. To put together a history of Khubilai himself, we must use all of these documents and more.

As with many famous figures from the past, there is a surfeit of both uncritical hagiographies and demonizing smears. Khubilai's own subjects did not dare to describe him in anything but the most glorified of terms, whereas comments attributed to him in later manuscripts, particularly from the Koreans and the Ming dynasty that ousted his descendants, may be later interpolations that make him seem like a clueless thug. Then again, it is his own chroniclers who gingerly record that Khubilai the great leader once charged pell-mell into the desert in pursuit of his rebellious brother Arigh Boke, only to flee on horseback when his supplies ran out, abandoning thousands of his own footsoldiers to a burning death in the sands. Khubilai Khan, about whom not a bad word could be said, is that same Mongol prince who invented an excuse to run home as soon as he had received the surrender of the ruler of Dali, leaving his underlings to undertake a mop-up operation that lasted for decades. It was also Khubilai Khan, emperor of the world, who was swindled by a double agent into personally funding the fortification of a border city that was then handed to his enemies.

Accounts of his middle years are those of an earnest, serious leader, who curtly orders Korean vassals to stop using gold in their tribute dishes – a world away from the portly, scowling despot painted by Liu Guandao in 1280. Many Chinese sources focus on Khubilai's enculturation, breathlessly arguing that the supposedly savage Mongol prince was tamed, charmed and invigorated by the civilizing influence of China itself.[3] He arrived in China as a conqueror, but died as an emperor. Marco Polo describes a man of wisdom and diplomatic openness to other faiths, although more cynical observers have suggested that Khubilai only entertained multiple religions in order to keep all parties guessing. Khubilai was truly stuck in the middle between the Mongols and the Chinese, and struggled his whole life to unify these mutually antagonistic societies. He is remembered as the last of the Great Khans, but his Mongol realm was already fragmenting when he came to power, and he enjoyed a mere three years of peace before facing a tedious thirty-year civil war with one of his own relatives.

Khubilai endures as a symbol of transformation, as the brutal, savage conquerors of his grandfather's generation gradually died out, leaving descendants with very different priorities. The conquests of Temujin, *the* Genghis Khan, were embittered, hateful despoliations of the farm-centred, city-dwelling way of life that the Mongols found so despicable. In the aftermath of Temujin's early assaults, conquered farmland was left fallow – in other words, transforming back into the pasture so beloved of the nomadic Mongols, and the former citizenry of conquered towns was often arbitrarily divided between Mongol leaders as slaves. It was only with Khubilai's uncle Ogodei (r.1229–41) that the new rulers began to regard their subjects as anything other than corpses-in-waiting. This is not necessarily a sign of enlightenment among the Mongols; perhaps it is better regarded as a glimmer of recognition that a smarter thief leaves his victim alive and prosperous, all the better to steal from him again. Nor is it merely a case of taxation, or of the restoration of civil order or the adoption of native accoutrements. The Mongols notoriously thrived on the contribution of local collaborators and assimilated subjects – the *semuren*. But they also excelled at getting others to do their dirty work for them. By luck or by design, the bulk of the occupation administrators, law-enforcers and tax collectors were Muslims from Central Asia, a handy buffer zone between the conquerors and conquered, and one which often took the blame for mismanagement and corruption. Meanwhile, when 'Mongol' armies thrust into Korea, southern China, Japan and Vietnam, they were arguably not Mongol at all – the force that toppled the Song dynasty largely comprised conscripts and turncoats from northern China. The force that then pushed south to Burma and east to Japan comprised large numbers of men from the fallen Song dynasty.

The recurring theme in the story of Khubilai Khan, among friends and enemies alike, is one of 'going native'. Raised and groomed to be the overlord of China, he was soon accused by rival princes of losing touch with his Mongol roots. He inherited a mandate born of conquest and atrocity, but was often swayed by the suggestions and ideas of his foreign advisers. It was a Jurchen minister who talked the young Khubilai into behaving like a Chinese emperor; it was a meddling Korean interpreter who tipped him off that Japan lay just beyond the horizon. For emissaries of the Muslim and Christian faiths, Khubilai was a tantalizing prospect – a terrifying former foe that let it be known that he might consider converting to their religion.

However, while many writers, Marco Polo included, presented Khubilai as a wise, syncretic ruler, there is ample evidence to suggest that he was still a Mongol at heart. Khubilai and his fellow khans often seem to be the innocent dupes of obfuscation and deflection, repeatedly confused by the cunning excuses of their vassals. In particular, Khubilai never really appears to have appreciated the intricate politics of Japan and Annam (north Vietnam), where his blunt, direct demands to deal with someone in charge were often given the runaround, fobbed off and misdirected. One wonders whether he ever realized that the Shōgun's *Regent* was the true ruler of Japan, or that the 'retired' Emperor of Annam continued to manipulate his successor from behind the throne? There is an element of Alexander the Great in Khubilai's earnest pursuit of a way to cut through such Gordian knots, and an element of oriental tragicomedy in his constant failure to do so. More than once, Khubilai – the great emperor of the world – is presented instead as a deluded dictator, trading on the military reputation of his forebears, but periodically surprised when his far-flung 'vassals' choose to disobey him.

Another powerful element of Khubilai's era is the tyranny of distance – the awesome and, to modern readers, alien prospect that Khubilai's realm was so large it could take years to cross. Despite immense Mongol achievements in the use of post-riders and letters of transit, Khubilai still had to face the prospect that a simple message to his field commanders could take weeks to arrive, and that he might wait months for a reply. Marco Polo writes of embassies and responses with immediate results, as if Khubilai were on the other end of a telephone, largely obscuring the fact that his dealings with rebels and vassals on his borders could stretch over years. Our own geographically inclined habit of treating his conquests separately – China, *then* Annam, *then* Japan – rather forgets the untidier elements of Khubilai's rule, such as the sequence of events in the 1270s, when his reign was undermined by institutional corruption, and his rule challenged by upstarts. When he first boasted to the Japanese that he was the Emperor of China, his armies had yet to take the Chinese capital at Hangzhou, and he was facing fierce resistance in what is now Vietnam; his own Yuan dynasty was proclaimed in pretence, not in victory, and only legitimized after the fact. No wonder, perhaps, that the Japanese at first regarded him as a braggart and a fool. It is for this reason that this book includes a chronology, setting the events of Khubilai's reign into a straightforward timeline in order to unite elements whose relation might not otherwise be immediately obvious.

The very words that we use to describe 'civilization' demonstrate our agrarian bias at work. For the Chinese in the east, and the Europeans in the west, civilization is a way of life that, by definition, requires living in cities. Our culture demands that we stay in one place, constructing our hearths and homes of solid material, wandering out to the fields to tend our crops. But history is also littered with cultures where this did not work. Even in medieval Europe, it was understood that the land could not withstand constant farming, and that fields would periodically have to be left fallow. All over the world, there are the ruins of sedentary civilizations that woke up one day to discover that the nearest timber was now more than a brisk walk away, that nearby mines now took too long to yield any resources and that the wells had run dry. Ancient China itself had many ghost towns and ruins, attesting to forgotten cultures that moved on. Further to the west, in Central Asia, there are the wastes of the Gobi and Taklamakan Deserts, now known as the Sea of Death, but once the centre of a flourishing Dark Age civilization. In all such cases, we might observe that all humans are ultimately nomads, although the farming cultures cling for longer, sometimes too long, to the ideal of staying in one place.

When our word 'civilization' itself is rooted in Roman concepts of cities and citizenship, it can be difficult to appreciate the world of the nomads. The Chinese also wrote off all cultures beyond their own as 'barbarians'. Nor did the nomads do themselves any favours in the long run, often lacking monuments, literature or many lasting artefacts apart from the occasional items of jewellery and weaponry found in their graves.

Tribes of the Mongols, Tatars, Keraits, Naimans and others migrated seasonally, like many of the birds that would fly over the distant farming communities. Their herds grazed where there was good grass, and moved on, heading north for the summer and south for the winter, usually rotating inside a set area that was understood by other tribes to 'belong' to its residents. Nomadic dwellings were hence designed to be mobile. A Mongol 'tent' could be a surprisingly solid construction, with walls made of a free-standing wooden trellis, weighted down by an outer layer of sturdy animal skins or felt, which also kept out the cold.

When the time came to move on, after a few days or months, the dwelling could be swiftly dismantled and loaded onto pack animals. Among the Mongols, it was usually placed aboard a large ox-drawn wagon, driven by the wife of the family. The wagon would lumber along at a slow pace, matching the speed of the grazing sheep and cattle.

William of Rubruck, a European traveller who visited the Mongols when Khubilai was in the prime of life, took the trouble to measure the size of Mongol homes and transport:

> These houses they make so large that they are often thirty feet in breadth. Measuring once the breadth between the wheel-ruts of their carts, I found it to be twenty feet over: and when the house was on the cart, it stretched over the wheels on each side five feet at least. I counted twenty-two oxen in one team, drawing a house upon a cart, and eleven more before them: the axletree of the cart was of huge size like the mast of a ship. And a fellow stood in the door of the house, upon the forestall of the cart, driving the oxen.[4]

The Mongols carried their possessions in other carts, safely packed in chests made from wicker and covered in waxed sheepskin. On the move, a lone woman would often drive a train of up to thirty carts, with the ox-team of each linked to the back of the cart in front. This method, crawling along at slower than walking pace, would be used on the wide, flat steppes. On tougher ground, the train would be split up into its component parts, and each would try to find its own way across. When the Mongols made camp, each wife would have her own main tent with satellite tents for her servants and supplies, and each woman's 'court' would be separated from her fellows' by a distance of 'a stone's throw'. William of Rubruck, attending the court of Khubilai's wealthy cousin Batu, noted that each of Batu's wives had an entourage of some 200 carts.

The Mongols had some odd superstitions, some of which could cost unwary visitors their lives. As the hearth fire was the heart of Mongol life, it was considered bad luck and a gross insult to one's host to touch the fire with a knife, or to use a knife to spear food from the central pot. Nor was it deemed appropriate to use a hatchet close to the hearth. Treading on a man's threshold step was punishable by death – a superstition that seems cognate with a similar proscription in China, where one is not supposed to touch the threshold step of a temple.

Some Mongol customs seem rooted in the careful conservation of resources. Mongols were discouraged from killing young birds, and spilling of one's drink was considered a capital offence if done deliberately. So, too, was urinating inside a tent, although it seems that there were enough inadvertent cases of this for an 'inadvertent' transgression to be punishable with a fine. If a man was given food by another, was unable to eat it and instead spat it out, he was to be dragged out of his tent and executed. Strangely, despite this, Mongols seemed to allow themselves to vomit – one Christian observer noted that Mongols who had drunk too much were welcome to puke their dinner back up again, so as to make space for yet more.[5]

The Mongols had their own word for the world they lived in – *ordo*, meaning variously tent, camp or herd on the move. An *ordo* was the impression left in the ground by one of their tents when it was moved on – a sign to other tribesman that someone had made this part of the steppe their home only recently, and a sign that perhaps the newcomer was not welcome. An *ordo* was the land around oneself, one's home and one's family. Thanks to the predations of the Genghis Khan Temujin and his descendants, the word made its way into many European languages with more sinister connotations. In Russian, it became *orda*. In Polish: *horda*. In the West, including French and English: *horde*.[6]

The antagonism between settled, agricultural cultures and wandering, pastoral cultures is a recurrent theme in human history. Invariably, the nomads get the blame, since it is usually they who are perceived to be wandering across an unknown border or into a farmer's territory. After all, a settled farming community does not habitually pick itself up and move twenty miles over. Nomads make such journeys all the time, and European history is littered with the results. The steppe is wide and long, but inevitably narrows as it reaches the European peninsula or the Chinese heartland. It is then, when times are hard and nomads move a little further than usual, that the friction turns into conflict. The boundary line between such cultures is perilously close. Since prehistoric times, the edge of the *ordos* culture has been a mere 300 kilometres from the site of modern Beijing.

While the women drove the wagons, the men rode on horseback. They marshalled the straggling herd animals, hunted on the outskirts and rode ahead to check the land. The nomads' way of life favoured the creation of a class of accomplished horsemen, accurate with a bow and arrow, experienced at scouting. Whereas cavalry was a rarity and a privilege in the cultures built around farmland, for the nomads it was part of everyday life. In a farming culture, the word for horseman came to be a reflection of wealth and power, a rarity like the English 'knight' or the Roman *equites*. In Mongolia, the men were trained their whole life in a skillset that could be readily repurposed to armed conflict.

The nomads were by no means unaware of the sedentary cultures. During the rotation of the year, they would invariably come into contact with civilizations on their borderlands, and offer items for trade. The nomads would always have leather goods, animal skins, wool, milk and meat. They might even try to trade their chosen beverage, a fermented horse milk they called *airag*, although it is usually known as *koumiss*, from the Turkish. From the sedentary populations, they could barter bread, honey, metal goods. Such a relationship worked well for both sides, for most of the time. Except, invariably, when times were hard, and a group would then take something that did not belong to them.

The history of China is peppered with clashes between the farmers and the nomads. The Great Wall (or rather, walls), a defining monument of Chinese civilization, was a failed attempt to draw a definite line between the two cultures. A large zone of northern China can be used for either agriculture or herding, and it is this area that has always been the source of conflict between these ways of life.

Stories of the rise of Temujin start off as little more than cattle rustling. But when the herds were vast in number, the wealth at stake was similarly great. In a series of broken alliances and pledges of faith, Temujin hunted down the enemies of his clan, and somehow welded the tribes of Mongolia into a massive host of warriors. At least in part to prevent the Mongols turning on each other, he directed their violence outwards.

The swift succession of ensuing military victories persuaded Temujin that he was not merely the Genghis Khan, but a man with a divine destiny, chosen by the fates to become the ruler of the entire world. In 1206, Temujin's army destroyed the Xixia, an empire in the west of China ruled by the Tangut people.

They did so secure in the belief that the Jurchens (Manchus) who ruled north China as the Jin dynasty would not come to the aid of the Xixia. In 1211, Temujin turned on the Jurchens, in a campaign that saw abortive peace negotiations, and then a resurgent invasion. By 1215, the Jurchen capital (now known as Beijing) had been destroyed, and the administration relocated south to the interim capital of Kaifeng. The second decade of the thirteenth century found Temujin's armies entering Manchuria and east Persia. By the 1220s they were rounding the Caspian Sea and heading for Europe.

In 1227, Temujin died, leaving instructions for his sons to divide the realm between them as khans subordinate to a single leader. The Mongol hordes would carry their conquests even further over the next generation. It was their duty to Temujin. It was their duty as Mongols.

I

CONQUERED BY WINE

THE REIGN OF OGODEI

Khubilai Khan did little to attract the attention of writers or poets in the first half of his life. He was in his forties when he became the Great Khan, and in his mid-fifties when he proclaimed himself to be the Emperor of China, a position that was not truly his until his early sixties. For Khubilai as a young man – as an idle princeling, an industrious noble and then a scheming power broker – we must look to asides in earlier chronicles of his uncles and grandfather. *The Secret History of the Mongols*, a rambling account of the lives of Temujin and his children, comes to an end when Khubilai was still in his mid-teens, but there are other accounts and biographies that allow us to piece together at least some incidents from Khubilai's first three decades. Partly, this job is easier because of the wide-ranging fame of his mother, Sorghaghtani. She left a deep enough impression on the world around her that, several decades after her death, she was still a famous enough figure to attract the attention of Marco Polo.

She was the niece of Toghrul, the leader of the Kerait steppe people, who at the beginning of the thirteenth century had been a more powerful warlord than Temujin himself. Toghrul, however, had refused to give his daughter in marriage to a son of Temujin. Although explained in such romantic terms by later chroniclers, this was far from a tale of star-crossed lovers. It is more likely that Temujin's offer was a 'peaceful' offer to take land by dynastic alliance that he would otherwise conquer by force. When Toghrul refused, the Keraits were plunged into war, and ultimately defeated by Temujin and his allies. Knowing which way the wind was blowing, one of Temujin's allies was Toghrul's brother – Sorghaghtani's father – who had no qualms about marrying off his daughters to the new authority. Temujin 'married' Sorghaghtani's elder sister, in the sense that she shared his bed for a while before he grew tired of her and handed her on to one of his generals. The teenage Sorghaghtani was given to Temujin's youngest son Tolui, and subsequently became his chief wife:

> And if he has more wives than one, she with whom he slept the night before sits by his side the day following: and all his other wives must that day resort to her house to drink: and there the court is held for that day: the gifts also which are presented that day are laid up in the chests of that wife.[1]

Since Sorghaghtani bore Tolui four sons, including Khubilai, she appears to have spent a lot of time at his side. This, in turn, will have put her in the right position to receive a lot of the treasures and tribute received by Tolui during the high point of the Mongol conquests. This put her in a powerful position after the death of her husband, particularly when she refused to ally herself by remarriage to any of the other descendants of Temujin.

Sorghaghtani's family were Nestorian Christians – and she remained a devout believer for the rest of her life. In later years, garbled accounts of their belief led some commentators to assume that her uncle had been the legendary Prester John, whom European Christendom was expecting to attack the Muslims in the rear. For decades, there had been stories of a Christian king in Asia, called variously David or John, and even during Khubilai's lifetime, it was widely understood among European visitors to his realm that his mother had been from the family of this fabled king.

However, European hopes of a Christian king in the east were unfounded. Prester John's reputation had been newly fostered by a fake letter that caused a minor stir in Europe at the beginning of the thirteenth century, and may have been responsible for several of the missions sent by the popes into the wilds of Central Asia. But despite his association with Prester John, Sorghaghtani's uncle was unlikely to have ever considered marching south to help out in the Crusades. Nestorians were deeply unwelcome in Christendom, and the founder of their sect had been responsible for a schism in the Church. In the centuries that followed, Nestorian belief had drifted steadily eastwards, although many of its adherents, facing hostility from the Christian world, converted to Islam, which has several similarities with it, including the daily prayer routine, and a god called Alohe. Further east, Nestorianism took on attributes of Chinese religions, with many saints reassigned the names of Buddhist deities. When Catholics from Europe eventually came into contact with Nestorian believers in the presence of the Mongols, they regarded them as braying drunks and deluded heretics, and spent longer enumerating their differences of belief than the shared fundamentals that might have united them.[2]

Matters of succession created powerful difficulties for the descendants of Temujin. The elephant in the room was Temujin's eldest son, Jochi. Circumstantial evidence suggested that Jochi was not Temujin's son at all, but had been fathered by a Mongol rapist during the brief period that Temujin's chief wife had been in captivity as a young woman. Temujin had never once said a word to disown or otherwise marginalize

Jochi, but the pair of them had been increasingly estranged in Temujin's later years. It was, perhaps, a mercy that Jochi predeceased his father by a few months, thereby allowing the rest of the clan to discuss only his brothers as potential successors. While the sons of Jochi and their descendants would be powerful kingmakers in the Mongol world, none dared to make a bid for Great Khan for themselves.[3]

Before his death, Temujin decreed that succession should be in the direct male line, through his third son Ogodei. Nevertheless, true to the Mongol idea of the survival of the fittest, he foresaw that the time might come when none of that branch of family was fit to rule:

> Set one of my seed as governor, and you shall not be disobedient. Destroy it not, and you shall be right and true. But if the seed of Ogodei is born [so worthless that] even if wrapped in green grass, an ox would not eat it; even if soaked in fat, a dog would not eat it, then surely there would be among my descendants even one that is suitable.[4]

Temujin's words were sure to cause trouble later. During a war, Mongols had a high turnover of manpower, and diligently kept their tribe resupplied by mating with multiple wives and concubines. The attrition of warfare and disease took care of many such offspring, but even so, by the time Temujin died, he already had over 100 living descendants. His surviving sons were similarly fecund, such that his 'seed' presented future kingmakers with literally hundreds of candidates.[5]

The reference to 'one of my seed' was enough to disqualify the sons of Jochi – never spoken of, but sure to come out in deliberations, and hence never permitted to come up as a topic. But issues of interpretation did not end there. In resorting to the quaint, rather facetious imagery of animal fodder, Temujin's decree failed to suggest *what* would make a candidate 'worthless'. Consequently, Temujin's sons and grandsons would fight several wars over whether or not a would-be ruler was a worthy successor to his legacy, and these conflicts only petered out when the legacy itself had faded and was largely forgotten.

Notably, the 'legacy' of Temujin was disbursed solely in the realm of Mongolia and the Turkic tribes. In other words, Temujin's brothers and sons, under the new Great Khan Ogodei, split a region comprised entirely of grassland, steppes and sandy wastes. The settlement of Temujin's estates did not involve any areas where Mongols could not live as Mongols – the mountains toward Persia, the green hills above the Gobi Desert, the farmland of north China, the forests of eastern Europe. Hence, in the generations after Temujin, we see his descendants holding relatively small areas in their homeland, but leaning for support on vast stretches of territory on their borders. This was how disputes between herders in Mongolia suddenly involved quests for manpower, resources and wealth far beyond the Mongol realm. This need among the feuding Mongols would radically change the lands on their borders; it would also change the Mongols themselves.[6]

It is with the accession of Ogodei, for example, that we see the Mongols adopting ideas from their newly conquered Jurchen subjects. Ogodei is seen having a series of supposedly brilliant ideas after he has been taken to one side by the turncoat official Yelu Chucai (1189–1243). The men of Yelu's family were excellent survivors. His surname came from that of the founding family of the earlier Liao dynasty. Somehow, his ancestors had clung onto their status when the Liao were ousted. Yelu served as a minister in the new Jurchen government, and managed to cling to his position after the predations of Temujin, largely because he stood up to the barbarian ruler when Temujin bragged that he had rescued Yelu from an ancestral conflict.

'Liao and Jin [the Jurchens] have been enemies for years. I have taken revenge for you,' bragged Temujin, only for the towering, long-bearded minister to curtly disagree. Yelu Chucai did not accept Temujin's version of events, noting that his father and grandfather had both faithfully served the Jurchen regime, and that he was not about to congratulate anyone about the dynasty's fall. People had been summarily executed for less in Temujin's presence, but Yelu was not only permitted to live, but to serve as an administrator and, eventually, the governor of north China.

Reading between the lines of Yelu Chucai's behaviour, we should give him the benefit of the doubt. True enough, he kow-towed to the new regime, although nobody else managed to stand up to them and keep their head. In later life, Ogodei was heard to taunt Yelu Chucai, asking him: 'Are you going to weep for the people again?' In just those few words, we are permitted a glimpse of Yelu's impossible, forgotten victories of diplomacy – unspecified occasions when he had put all thought of his own safety aside in order to plead for mercy on behalf of anonymous Chinese subjects. Now little more than a footnote to history, in his heyday he may have saved millions of lives.

Yelu and men like him taught the younger generation of Mongols that there was more than one way to loot outsiders. Traditionalists among Ogodei's family demanded that the Mongols sweep away the unsightly towns and farms of the civilized world, returning them to the featureless, sweeping plains that nature must have surely intended. For such members of the old guard, wealth could only truly be measured in cattle and pasture. The hapless peasants could be left to rot, and China would be brutally returned back to basics.

In the interests of the aforesaid peasants, Yelu pleaded a different cause. Of course, he told Ogodei, it was only natural for a man of nomadic birth to want to see the world look more like the steppes of Mongolia. But the world was clearly different. What the conquerors had perhaps failed to see was that their new chattels could be made to produce wealth for them. The Mongols could go about their business, live all their lives in tent if they wished, but for as long as they were the rulers of a territory, they could extract tribute and tax from its inhabitants. A Mongol need not even go on a raid to extract such largesse. Instead, the mere *threat* of retribution should be enough to ensure donations of treasures, food and fine silks. Accordingly, argued Yelu, the Mongols should try to avoid despoiling their conquests any further. Indeed, the conquered peoples were now slaves, little more than cattle – in one illuminating incident, the Mongols had to be talked out of literally branding their Chinese subjects so that they could be identified if they fled.[7] But what a wonderful world it would be if the 'cattle' would put meat on the Mongol table without being asked; how wondrous if the cattle brought new clothes, wives and wine for their masters. The Mongols were now ready to reap the rewards of Temujin's conquest – they could raid by proxy, through taxation.

Hence, with the accession of Ogodei the legacy of the Mongols took on a new, more 'civilized' form. In 1229, we see the establishment of the post-rider system that made communication across the empire quick and efficient; we see granaries installed to supply food in times of need instead of simply taking it from the nearest victim. Conspicuously, we also see the institution of property taxes – the Mongols turning away from the disenfranchised, destroyed peoples they conquered, and instead seizing wealth from the collaborators and profiteers who had been the first to offer their support.

Thanks to the likes of Yelu Chucai, Ogodei confronted the issues that his father had largely avoided. Many among the Mongol old guard would prefer to keep rolling ever onwards, taking whatever they wanted, pushing the boundary of Mongol culture out ever further. But even in the days of Temujin, some had dimly apprehended that there would come a day when a conqueror would need to rule lands that did not fit the steppe stereotype. Temujin himself had marked out a valley in the Orkhon river basin which he thought would make an admirable Mongol capital. It even had a name: Karakorum ('Black Rock'). But Temujin had done little with it, and it was left to Ogodei to set up a static town with four walls of rammed earth, each with a gate, and an inner palace for the Mongol royals.

Karakorum seemed at first to be designed less as a town and more as a fortress. The outlying grounds beyond the walls were dotted with silos and storage bunkers for supplies and treasure. William of Rubruck, a Franciscan friar who visited Karakorum in its heyday, thought it to be an unassuming cluster of buildings, and belittled it by comparing it to a village outside Paris. Karakorum was built where it was because the Mongols of Temujin's generation still thought of it as home. Their children and grandchildren, spreading farther afield, were sure to find more lavish 'homes' elsewhere. Khubilai himself, in later years, would move first to Shangdu, and ultimately to Beijing.

Nevertheless, Karakorum was a fixed point around which the wandering nomads could gather. Tents sprang up in its outskirts, including, according to legend, one massive creation on wheels. This was Ogodei's mobile palace, a wagon ten metres wide, drawn by twenty-two oxen in a ponderous, rumbling procession across the flat ground of the steppes. It was an odd halfway house between palace and tent. Karakorum itself largely became a place of civil servants and religious administrators.

Ogodei was adept at appointing able administrators. In 1229, he made Yelu Chucai the official with responsibility for all of conquered north China, effectively creating him as a prime minister to rule his own people in Ogodei's name. He tried something similar with a Muslim official in Persia – not only delegating, but also deftly hiding the face of a foreign conqueror behind a familiar local mask. Yelu proved his worth the following year, when he delivered 10,000 silver ingots in tax income to Karakorum without having to fire a single arrow or besiege a single town.[8]

As a sign of the relentlessly nomadic, outward-facing nature of the Mongol mindset, it was customary for the youngest son to watch the family hearth. Ogodei himself, seemingly referring to a tradition from the nomadic days, decreed that it was the duty of eldest sons to ride out to war:

Let the princes that govern peoples send to war the eldest sons
of their sons. And let the princes that govern not peoples . . .
make the eldest of their sons to go a-warring.[9]

A European or Chinese sense of primogeniture might have
favoured the eldest by giving him the homeland, but for
Mongols, for whom mere land was everywhere for the taking,
the concept of a hearth seemed more mobile, and less desirable.
Eldest sons were expected to range the furthest from their
father (hence the location of the sons of Jochi, far away at the
edge of Europe), while custom presumed that the youngest
would still require maternal care. Hence, even though Temujin's
youngest son Tolui was a full-grown man in his thirties, a
veteran of the wars against the Xixia and the Jurchens, as the
'baby' he was left in charge of the homeland while the other
Mongols sallied out on further conquests.

Tolui hence retained the area around Karakorum. Perhaps, as
implied by their drinking and whoring, his elder brothers had
already decided that the action was elsewhere, but the decision
to leave Mongolia in Tolui's hands left him not so much with
the oldest, over-grazed heartland, as with the first secure
Mongol city and administration. His brothers, meanwhile,
faced lands that were largely still under dispute, with wars to be
fought and rebellions to be put down. Nor did they have a fully
efficient organization, whereas Tolui inherited a generation of
officials and underlings – as Karakorum transformed from a
patch of waste ground into the centre of Mongol affairs, it was
young Tolui who sat at the heart. 'Civilization', in the literal
sense of living in a city, was not something that had attracted
the Mongols before, but it was Tolui and his sons who reaped
the first benefits of it in education and simple security.

Ogodei continued his campaigns. He launched an attack on
mountainous Korea, the first of many that would wrack the
land for decades without a decisive victory. He sent a force into
what is now Iran, routing the remnants of the Seljuk Turks and
establishing one of the most enduring Mongol dynasties. He

also embarked once more on the conquest of north China, returning in 1231 to complete the job that his father had left unfinished.

Soon after he recommenced his campaign against the Jurchens, the forty-five-year-old Ogodei was left incapacitated by a terrible affliction that sounds, when reading between the lines of the *Secret History of the Mongols*, like a debilitating stroke, 'losing mouth and tongue'.[10] His soothsayers, having consulted an unspecified number of entrails, decided that he was subject to a curse, sent by the lords of the Jurchen people as the first shot in a spirit war.

The shamans of the Mongols did not believe in, or perhaps accept, the concept of alcohol abuse. Observing their ruler's unstoppable shakes, they observed that the 'spirits of earth and water' contended within him, and arranged futile rituals and sacrifices to put the internal conflict to rest. When this failed, they considered the unthinkable – that some sort of human vessel could be found into which the angry spirits could be lured and contained. This was a chilling form of living sacrifice, since whatever raged within Ogodei was plainly killing him, and was sure to kill the host.

Much to everyone's surprise, Tolui volunteered for the suicidal mission. In a gesture framed as the love of a brother for a brother, and the duty of a subject to a loyal sovereign, he agreed to let the shamans hurl Ogodei's demons into his own body. Seemingly the only brother then present, and hence the only candidate, Tolui is reported accepting immediately, noting that if a deadly fate befell Ogodei: 'The many Mongol people would be orphans, the Jurchen people would rejoice.'[11] Notably, however, the 'sorcery' practised by Ogodei's shamans appears to be a form of sympathetic magic. Tolui is made to drink the 'waters of conjuration', which are described in terms little different from those of massive quantities of alcohol. In fact, he appears to drink himself into a ritual stupor, in imitation of the sprees that put the 'curse' on Ogodei in the first place.

The bare facts of the case, stripped of portent and poetry, suggest a far more prosaic end – that Tolui died as the result of a drinking binge – somehow spun by the author of the *Secret History* into a bold sacrifice by a loyal subject. Ogodei lived on for another decade, and somehow recovered enough to continue making the rambling and indistinct proclamations that characterize his chapters in the *Secret History*. However, in appearing to have died in Ogodei's place in 1231, Tolui ensured that his own descendants would be highly praised and rewarded by the Mongol regime. Although Tolui's eldest son Mongke was old enough to take over his responsibilities, Mongke was already serving on Ogodei's campaigns. Consequently, Tolui's wife Sorghaghtani was put in charge of Tolui's estates, and effectively made acting queen of Mongolia for the next decade.

Hoping to keep everything within the family, Ogodei suggested that his own son, Guyuk, then just about to leave for the invasion of Europe, should marry Tolui's widow Sorghaghtani, thereby linking the two most powerful branches of Temujin's descendants. When Ogodei eventually died, this would ensure that a large part of his wealth remained directly in the hands of his son and grandson. Sorghaghtani, however, politely refused this request, with the excuse that her duty remained to her sons.

It was a strange thing for a Mongol woman to say. It was considered normal for a widow to remarry to a relative of her husband – an act that kept wealth and property within the family. The Mongols took the remarriage of widows very seriously, and even saw fit to impose it on their subjects. In an infamous incident that occurred during Khubilai's youth, a Russian duke was executed by the Mongols on suspicion of having spirited some of their horses out of their territory. When his widow and younger brother arrived in the court of Khubilai's cousin, Batu Khan, to plead to be left their lands, the Mongols told the widow that it was her duty to marry her late husband's younger brother. She refused, saying that she would rather die. The Mongols, however, had other ideas. 'Carrying them to bed,' wrote a shocked Christian author, 'they compelled the youth, who was lamenting and weeping, to lie down and commit incest with his brother's wife.'[12]

This, however, was another Mongol way of showing their victims who was boss. Among their own kind, 'remarriage' was only consummated for those younger widows who might have been decades younger than their late husband. For older wives, it was merely a symbolic act, and amounted to the reassignment of her entourage to a new group of travelling carts within the same clan. As a woman in her early thirties, Sorghaghtani was still of marriageable age in Mongol eyes, but as the mother of a young son, Khubilai's youngest brother Arigh Boke, she had better reasons than most to claim to have other duties. She was certainly powerful enough to make her case and get away with it.

'Of all the others,' noted one missionary, Sorghaghtani 'was most honoured among the Tartars, except the emperor's mother [Toregene], and mightier than any subject except [Jochi's son] Batu.'[13]

At the time that these events took place, her son Khubilai was in his mid-teens. While earlier Mongol children had been raised on the move – forged, like Temujin, in the fires of raid and counter-raid, fighting from an early age merely to stay alive – Khubilai was raised amid previously unknown comforts. Of course, he was encouraged in Mongol pursuits: hunting, in particular, seems to have been one of his favourite occupations. Like his father and uncles, he appears to have been fond of 'fine' living, and the first mentions of gout on his record appear as early as his thirties. But Khubilai was also given the best education that Sorghaghtani could arrange in the middle of nowhere. Illiterate herself, she hired Tolochu, a Uighur from Muslim Central Asia, to teach Khubilai how to read the Turkic script used by the Mongols.

In 1236, she officially requested that Ogodei let her extend her domains into China's Hebei province. Despite his respect for her, Ogodei took his time answering, leading Sorghaghtani to remind him that Hebei had been conquered by her late husband, and that asking Ogodei's permission was merely a gesture of respect. She may have had other reasons – Ogodei was muscling in on parts of Sorghaghtani's fief, and she seems to have preferred to move her centre of operations away from him rather than risk open conflict. When Sorghaghtani and her sons travelled to their new territory to survey it, they found a land left in ruins. The massive loss of life during the Mongol invasions had been bad enough, but millions of survivors had then preferred to move south to Song China rather than endure Mongol rule. A further exodus had fled south after the imposition of ever-rising Mongol taxes – a region that once had an estimated population of 40 million had been reduced in a single generation to something closer to 10 million.[14]

Sorghaghtani chose to settle in Zhending, some 200 kilometres south-west of Beijing. Zhending had surrendered to Temujin and hence avoided the worst depredations of the original invasion. It had attracted refugees from less fortunate population centres, and had become a burgeoning territory of some half a million people. The small town at its heart remained a centre for Buddhist pilgrimage and it was here that Sorghaghtani set herself up as the local authority. In doing so, she was taking over an estate that was already running smoothly, largely because the Mongols had left it alone.

In what was surely a stirring example to the young Khubilai, Sorghaghtani honoured all religions in her area. She was a Nestorian Christian, and made no secret of that, but she also offered donations to the Buddhists, Taoists and Muslims. Many mosques and temples included her in their lists of donors, and she was credited with funding the foundation of a *madrasa* (Muslim college) as far away as Bukhara in what is now Uzbekistan.

Perhaps largely because she was *not* a Mongol, Sorghaghtani was more than ready to follow the suggestions of Chinese ministers such as Yelu Chucai. She regarded the continued rape of the land as a short-term Mongol folly, and seems to have genuinely desired to keep things running as they had been in the days of the defeated Jurchens. As far as Sorghaghtani was concerned, it was better for everyone if life in the farming regions went on as it had done before. She had no time for the philistine Mongol policy of 'returning' the farmland to pasture; nor did she want to see the Chinese population subjected to any further indignities. Zhending was her great experiment, not at conquest, but at managing the region's way out of its earlier troubles.[15]

Khubilai, still a mere twenty-one years old, was given Xingzhou, a nearby estate of his own. By Chinese reckoning, which rates ten houses as a village, Khubilai's sector encompassed 'ten thousand households' – not all in one place, but in the form of a thousand villages, scattered throughout the farmland. Predictably, Khubilai does not appear to have cared about it in the slightest. Instead, he stayed in Mongolia, busying himself with whatever hobbies occupy a young Mongol prince – hunting, drinking and sex.[16] Khubilai left the day-to-day running of the estate in the hands of his cronies, and the result was a disaster. Left unsupervised, his Mongol underlings and Central Asian tax farmers preferred to line their own treasure chests with the takings from Khubilai's region. The peasantry were variously bullied, assaulted or simply scared off, leading to more abandoned villages, and a further decline in revenue.

This disaster is glossed over in most accounts of Khubilai's life but its effect may have been underestimated. On discovering the ruin he had inadvertently unleashed on Xingzhou, the young Khubilai did everything in his power to put it right. In imitation of his mother, or perhaps under her orders, he drafted in Chinese officials to sort out the mess. Notable among them was Shi Tianze, the son of the local warlord who had originally surrendered to Temujin. Just like Sorghaghtani, Khubilai rejected the Mongol way in favour of a more acceptable, local tradition. He adopted a policy that he would use on a wider scale later in life, appointing 'pacification commissioners' (*Ancha-shi*) from the local population, on the understanding that they would have a better grasp of the way to keep the state running smoothly. Over the next few years, as his Chinese assistants abolished the most crushing taxes and left the farmers to work their land, the population of Xingzhou noticeably increased again, not through childbirth, but through the return of refugees to the homes they had once fled.

From that point on, Khubilai seemed to be doing a better job in his little corner of the Mongol empire than the Mongol emperor himself. Whatever the 'curse' that had afflicted Ogodei and been apparently lifted by the death of Tolui, Ogodei continued to drink. Fermented mare's milk, the chosen beverage of previous Mongol generations, gave way to wine from conquered Persia and stronger grain alcohol from China. His doctors, sure that the drinking was damaging his health, began to keep a careful count of the number of goblets he got through in a day. Ogodei, ever the enterprising alcoholic, began using bigger goblets.

While Great Khan Ogodei staggered through each day in a drunken haze, his relatives quarrelled. His brother Batu and his son Guyuk, partway through their conquest of Muscovy, got into a pointless squabble about seniority at a banquet – Batu was the elder, but Guyuk the supposed heir apparent. In the aftermath, with Guyuk calling Batu little better than a bearded lady, and Guyuk suggesting that he had practically conquered Persia single-handed, an angry Ogodei disowned Guyuk, and nominated Guyuk's nephew Shiremun as his new successor.[17]

As 1241 drew to a close, Ogodei remained sober enough to organize a grand hunt with some of his drinking buddies. Chasing after deer and wolves in a purpose-built enclosure many miles across, he ended the day with yet another binge – this one finished him off. *The Secret History of the Mongols* preserves his rambling summary of his reign – a dreary set of mumbled reminiscences about the good old days under Temujin, and self-pitying speculation about whether he had lived up to Temujin's legacy.

And then, being made to sit on the throne of my father, the Great Khan, following his passing, I shouldered the great burden of many subjects, and yet was I conquered myself by grape wine. This was one of my wrongs.[18]

Ogodei enumerated some other half-remembered failings, mainly to do with family members he had sinned against. He even expressed his shame at the nature of his last great hunting trip. What kind of hunter, he slurred, what kind of Mongol employed armies of beaters and scarers to push the prey towards him in a killing ground? What kind of hunt was that? The older Mongols were right, he whispered. Fencing things in was contrary to the way of Mongol life. Walls were a crime against nature. It was not clear whether he was now talking about hunting or about the drift towards settling in cities. But there was no means to seek clarification. Ogodei was dead.

As with the 'collaboration' of Yelu Chucai, this seemingly insignificant event, the addled passing of a lone drunk, saved uncountable lives. When the news reached the Mongol horde in Europe, the army retreated from Hungary – in the words of one authority, saving the West 'from the gravest danger it had faced since Attila'.[19] The question of who would follow Ogodei as Great Khan now had to be resolved, or rival Mongols would turn their armies upon each other.

2

VOICES PROPHESYING WAR

THE SONS OF TOLUI

In the struggle over Ogodei's successor, the late Temujin's fateful words about 'worthless' candidates came into play. Ogodei had chosen his grandson Shiremun as his heir, but Ogodei had been a laughing stock, dead in a heap after a day spent hobbling around after wild deer. Was it necessary to place such value on his wishes?

Ogodei's widow Toregene was certainly ready to challenge her late husband's last few decrees. She did so by reminding the assembled nobles about Mongol tradition: a khan's legacy had to be decided by a public council. In the olden times, this would have been easy to convene, and might have taken weeks, or perhaps a couple of months, calling in the widespread tribes from whatever pastures they had drifted onto. Now, with Mongol princes commanding armies all over the continent, it was sure to take years to get everyone together. Maybe the new heir should be Shiremun, but maybe Guyuk had been robbed of his rightful throne by a few angry words. Toregene refused to let the fate of the Mongol rulership rest on whether or not Ogodei had been in a bad mood on the day he disowned Guyuk. Such a question required a *kurultai* – a full Mongol council – and until such time as a *kurultai* could be convened, Toregene would remain as regent.

Her unofficial reign would last for four years. Within months, she undermined the authority of her supposed superior, another of Ogodei's wives whom he had himself inherited from Temujin. She dismissed or reassigned many of her late husband's advisers, replacing them with officials of her own choosing. Abd al-Rahman, a Muslim who had been Ogodei's greatest drinking partner, was put in charge of tax collecting in northern China. Fatima, a Shi'ite lady who excelled as Toregene's chief adviser, was also delegated to bring in revenues for Karakorum. Toregene was of Naiman Turk descent, which meant that while she may not have been a Mongol, she was still a steppe dweller, and seems to have had little sympathy for the plights of land-bound, sedentary populations. Although the Mongol old-timers grumbled about Toregene's use of so many foreign officials, she was still an old-school nomad, and gave little thought to the effects that her demands might have on the still recovering peasantry of the farmlands.

Despite her legendary wisdom, Toregene made a mistake when it came to administering tax collection. She ignored Yelu Chucai's subtle admonitions about leaving the peasantry enough money to be able to tax them another day. Instead, she allowed parts of her realm to succumb to the dangerous practice of tax farming. Instead of appointing a local official, Toregene allowed locals to bid for the right to collect taxes on behalf of the Mongols. In the short term, this provided superb revenue for Karakorum, as established Muslim entrepreneurs such as Abd al-Rahman and Fatima handed over large sums to Toregene. However, by the later years of her realm, this had created an awful crisis in north China, as the collectors hiked up rates in order to reclaim their initial investments. Tax percentages in the former Jurchen kingdom soared as high as 100 per cent.

The regency of Toregene was accompanied by religious tensions. Yelu Chucai was pushed aside, and died soon afterwards – some said of a broken heart. Meanwhile, the ascent of Muslim advisers and officials seemed to come at the expense of positions once held by prominent Nestorian Christians. It is difficult to say, eight centuries later, how much of this apparent Christian–Muslim tension was inferred after the event – straightforward geography and personal connections may have played far more important roles than religious faith. But it is conceivable that Toregene swiftly made enemies among the Christians in her domain, including Khubilai's mother Sorghaghtani.

Such problems, however, did not trouble the inhabitants of Khubilai's personal fief. He had already learned the lesson that Toregene still faced, and had already turned his territory around. Some of the new arrivals in Khubilai's prosperous realm might even have been refugees from Toregene's tax farmers. Khubilai had learned his lesson well, and continued to seek help from the Chinese. Once again, in apparent imitation of his mother, he surrounded himself with advisers from the conquered culture. In 1242, he invited the Buddhist monk Haiyun to speak at his court, and even asked him to choose a name for his second son. The monk chose Zhenjin, 'True Gold', a name loaded with portents of great fortune, suggesting that one day the child might be destined to achieve great things in China.[1]

As Toregene's interregnum stretched on, it became plain that several Mongols knew what she was up to. Batu, whose quarrel with Guyuk had caused him to be disowned in the first place, spent several years refusing to come to the *kurultai* at all, on a variety of pretexts. Meanwhile, the septuagenarian Temuge, youngest brother of the long-departed Temujin, gruffly suggested that if nobody could make up their mind, perhaps he should take over – as a brother of the great Genghis Khan, he would surely not even require a *kurultai*.

It was Sorghaghtani who broke the impasse by throwing in her lot with Toregene, offering the support of the sons of Tolui for Guyuk's bid for power. At last there was a majority, and the *kurultai* was convened in 1246. It was a shaky vote, and support for Guyuk's candidacy was barely quorate – involving only the sons of Tolui, Khubilai among them, and the sons of Jochi, including the powerful Batu. Among the other princes, there was a silent community of very reluctant subjects.

Although the *Secret History of the Mongols* comes to an end before the accession of Guyuk, and other sources largely gloss over it, we are fortunate enough to have the account of a European eyewitness, Friar John of Plano Carpini (1180–1252). Arriving with letters from the Pope, Friar John was admitted into Guyuk's entourage as he arrived for the *kurultai* in July 1246:

> After five or six days, he sent us to his mother [the Regent Empress Toregene], under whom there was maintained a very solemn and royal court. When we came there we saw a huge tent of fine white cloth, which was, in our judgement, so great that more than two thousand men might stand within it, and around about it there was set up a wall of planks, painted with diverse designs.[2]

Toregene's 'tent' had a base wall of giant wooden slats, broken in two places by massive ceremonial gates. Both stood open and guarded, but one remained tantalizingly unused by any of the attendants. The first gate was for regular subjects; the second could only be used by a Great Khan, and the *kurultai* had been convened to decide who that Great Khan would be.

Unable to follow the ceremonies that went on around him in Mongol, Friar John was only able to report the sights and sounds. The assembled lords from all over the Mongol realm, including Khubilai himself, had arrived at Toregene's court with all their entourages. The deliberations, or ceremonies – there seems to have been a bit of both – took four days. On the first, the throng were dressed in white; on the second, everyone wore red; on the third, blue; on the fourth, richly embroidered brocades. Only the chiefs, barons and princes were permitted inside the tent itself. Their entourages lurked in rowdy antici- pation outside, maintaining a respectful distance from the armed guards, who were ready to beat anyone who approached too near.

Friar John and his companions were dragged into the celebrations, which started at noon with a drinking binge of fermented mare's milk. When the priests cried off, complaining that it disagreed with them, some kind soul among the party- goers found them some mead instead, which they politely drank until they felt ill. Perhaps because, as an Italian, he had come the furthest, Friar John was given a place of honour among the celebrants, and found himself rubbing shoulders with a Russian nobleman, the ruler of a vassal state:

> Without the door stood Duke Yaroslav of Susdal in Russia, and a great many dukes of the Cathayans, and of the Solands. The two sons also of the King of Georgia, an ambassador of the Caliph of Baghdad, who was a Sultan, and we think, more than ten other Sultans of the Saracens beside.[3]

According to Friar John's fellow revellers, there were some 4,000 envoys presents, some as representatives of tribute- paying nations, and others of an indeterminate, more allied status that entailed them to bring mere 'gifts'. Amid the clash of races and languages, with no common tongue amongst them – communication clattering between Latin, Persian, Arabic, Chinese and Mongol – not everyone seemed to appreciate what was going on. In hindsight, Friar John realized that Guyuk had been chosen as the new leader inside the great tent:

> Guyuk came forth out of the tent, he had a noise of music, and was bowed to, or honoured with inclined staffs, having red wool

upon the tops of them, and that, so long as he remained, which service was performed to none of the other chiefs.[4]

It was only a few days later, when the entire carnival upped stakes and relocated ten or so miles to a nearby riverbank, that Friar John understood the implications. A second, even more lavish, tent, the 'Golden Orda', was set up; its pillars decorated with golden plates, and mundane planks fixed with golden nails. The congregation was informed that Guyuk was to be officially enthroned, but on the appointed August day it was called off due to a hailstorm. It was a disastrous omen, in which 'there fell such an abundance of hail, that, upon its sudden melting, more than one hundred and sixty persons were drowned. Many tents and other things were carried away.'[5]

The coronation did not get underway until over a week later, on what was identified by Friar John as St Bartholomew's Day (24 August). Bewildered as ever, Friar John stood among the attendant throng, watching Mongol shamans on their knees conducting a ritual facing towards the southern steppes. Only after this unknown ceremony, which went on, Friar John archly informs us, 'for a long time', did the Mongol nobility officially enthrone Guyuk – at which point the entire congregation, stretching across the plain, bowed down before him. 'Except ourselves,' boasts Friar John, 'for we were not his subjects.'[6]

Within the great tent, hidden from commoners such as Friar John and his drinking companions, Khubilai and his fellow princes performed an act of ceremonial submission to their new leader. They took off their hats, loosened their belts, and waited as Guyuk was placed on a golden throne, built with looted riches, by enslaved artisans. The assembled princes bowed before Guyuk nine times, in a ritual that extended outside the tent, as even those who could not see Guyuk were exhorted to kneel to the ground, rise up, and repeat. It is this part of the ceremony that Friar John appears to have recalled.[7]

Friar John was also entirely unable to perceive the fervid politicking behind the scenes. Few of the assembled Mongols really rated Guyuk all that highly. Sorghaghtani's eldest son, Khubilai's brother Mongke, was widely regarded as a better candidate, but since Sorghaghtani had backed Toregene, the point was largely moot, at least for now. But Sorghaghtani was no fool. There were many scores to be settled by the new Khan, and by proclaiming her support for Toregene, Sorghaghtani kept her sons out of the inevitable putsches that followed. Mere days after Guyuk's coronation, when the great party still had many hundreds of merry stragglers, the new ruler instituted a witch-hunt against the 'murderers' of his father.

It may seem surprising that Ogodei's death had been declared as murder – but now that Guyuk was in charge, he proclaimed that his father had been poisoned by his sisters and aunts. After a show-trial, in which nobody dared claim that Ogodei had brought about his own demise, the women were killed. Guyuk, it was claimed, was angry that the women's intrigues had forced him to put aside his warring in Hungary to return to Mongolia for the *kurultai* ceremonies. However, many guests suspected that it was Toregene at work behind the scenes, settling personal scores in the name of her husband and son. Among the doubters was Friar John, who noted that his new acquaintance, the Russian Duke Yaroslav, was invited to dinner with Toregene before he left for the long journey home:

> Immediately after the banquet, he fell sick, and within seven days he died. After his death, his body was of a strange blue colour, and it was commonly reported that the duke was poisoned.[8]

Recriminations continued in the months that followed. Guyuk's uncle Temuge was accused of plotting to take the throne for himself, and he was executed. One of Guyuk's brothers complained that Toregene's assistant Fatima was practising witchcraft against him. When the brother died under suspicious circumstances, Fatima was immediately suspected of engineering his demise – there was, after all, ample evidence that dining with Toregene and her cabal could seriously damage one's health. Toregene refused to hand Fatima over, only for Guyuk to flex his newly acquired royal powers. He sent in his own men to seize her, and Fatima was put to death. Toregene herself died soon afterwards, in circumstances never really explained.

Despite Guyuk's appointment as the Great Khan, resentment still simmered between him and his brother Batu, who remained supreme in the distant west. Guyuk ordered Batu to attend an audience, but both assembled large armies, for an 'audience' that was likely to turn into a battle. Risking everything, Sorghaghtani sent a warning to Batu that Guyuk was planning to double-cross him.

In April 1248, less than two years after being proclaimed Great Khan, Guyuk died near the shores of Lake Balkash. He was forty-two years old, and his death has been attributed either to the alcoholism that also killed his father, or to the poison of an unknown assassin. One European observer claimed that Guyuk had died in a drunken brawl with one of Batu's envoys:

> [Guyuk] had invited Batu to come to render him homage and Batu set out in great state, but not without great fear, he and all his men. He sent on ahead his brother named Stican, who when he had arrived in the presence of [Guyuk] and had to present him the cup, a quarrel then arose between them and they killed each other.[9]

Father William of Rubruck, who repeated this story in his report to the Pope, did so with the implication that he had heard it at the household of Stican's widow, for whom he was asked to pray. Nonetheless, even he seems to doubt this all-too-convenient accident, and instead notes that he had heard from another missionary that Guyuk 'lost his life following the taking of a certain medicine which was administered to him by order, one believes, of Batu'.[10]

Hence there was no need for the forces of Batu and Guyuk to rush into open conflict. Instead, Guyuk was gone, and Batu was in the neighbourhood at last, with an army behind him. Now the most senior member of the Mongol royal family, Batu had every opportunity to proclaim himself Great Khan. However, he does not appear to have wanted such a poisoned chalice, particularly not with the unspoken question of his father's paternity. Happy with his life on the borderlands of Europe, Batu initially left matters in the hands of Guyuk's widow. When he eventually convened a *kurultai* of his own, he held it controversially outside the Mongol heartland. It was hence boycotted by many of the surviving notables of the old guard. Guyuk's family demanded that the leadership be given to Shiremun, Ogodei's chosen heir. Batu, instead, suggested that Sorghaghtani's eldest son Mongke should be the new Khan. Representatives of the other sons of Tolui, Khubilai included, supported this suggestion, although others questioned its provenance, as far too many of the key figures of the Mongol world were absent. It was not until 1251, at a second *kurultai* – also boycotted by many relatives – that Mongke was officially proclaimed as the new Great Khan.

Even then, there were ructions. William of Rubruck, who travelled through the realm of Batu to convey a letter to Mongke, noted that it was an open secret that Batu had the upper hand: 'The subjects of Batu are stronger and show not so much courtesy to the subjects of [Mongke] Khan as is shown to them.'[11] Meanwhile, Shiremun still regarded himself as the rightful heir of Ogodei, and seemed reluctant to accept that his birthright was about to snatched away from him by yet another relative. Accordingly, he set out with his army, towards Mongke's last known location, intent on taking the khanship for himself. He was, according to William of Rubruck, encouraged in this by Guyuk's widow, who blamed Mongke for her husband's premature death.

Unfortunately for Shiremun, one of his wagons threw a wheel during the long exodus. Impatient to kill Mongke,

Shiremun left the cart and its outriders to conduct repairs, and continued on ahead with the rest of his retinue. As the men struggled to repair the broken wheel, fellow Mongols approached and offered to help them get back on the move. A grateful driver thanked his unexpected assistants, only to reveal the nature of his journey. The good Samaritans, who were of course some of Mongke's men, immediately rode off at full pelt for a day and a night, outstripping Shiremun's forces, who had been forced to proceed at the pace of their slowest ox cart. They reported Shiremun's plans to Mongke, who was able to have his men at battle stations by the time Shiremun showed up.

Shiremun's excuse was that he was coming to pay homage to Mongke. However, sufficient evidence soon arose for Mongke to believe the stories of his own spies. Dragged before Mongke, Shiremun confessed, also giving up Guyuk's oldest son as a co-conspirator, along with 300 leading Mongols. 'Messengers were sent to find the women, who were whipped with red-hot brands in order to obtain from them a confession. And after they confessed they were all killed.'[12]

Only Guyuk's youngest son was spared, inheriting the accumulated wealth of his disgraced father and elder brothers, becoming the ruler of a fiefdom shunned by other Mongols. When travelling close to what had once been Guyuk's personal territory on the journey back towards Europe, William of Rubruck was cautioned not to approach too close, for 'the mistress of nations sat in sorrow, and there was no one to console her.'[13]

In the aftermath of Shiremun's 'revolt', there was another round of revenge killings. Guyuk's widow, stripped and interrogated by Sorghaghtani in her tent, was adjudged to have played an instrumental role in the unrest. She was rolled in felt and thrown into a river, where the wet, ever-tightening fabric was sure to leave her helpless as she drowned. She was, said Mongke gracelessly in her memory, 'more contemptible than a bitch.'

Shiremun himself briefly sought refuge with Khubilai, who gave him sanctuary until Mongke ordered the young man to be handed over and executed. Mongke's path to power was accompanied by hundreds of similar killings. He became the new Great Khan, determined to prevent the legacy of Temujin from decaying any further into another round of squabbles. As far as Mongke was concerned, the only way to ensure this was to direct Mongol destructiveness outwards once more, initiating a new wave of conquests at the edge of his realm. For as long as the Mongol men pushed outwards, they would spare the heartland and leader any further butchery.

Chinese advisers surrounded Khubilai by this point, including one, Liu Bingzhong, who made a point of questioning the latest round of warfare. Quoting a famous epigram from the ancient Han dynasty, Liu cautioned Khubilai: 'One can conquer the world on horseback, but one cannot govern from horseback.'[14] If the Mongols continued to act like thieves fighting over stolen goods, there would never be an end to the violence.

There is no record of what Sorghaghtani thought of this opinion. Sorghaghtani's victory was short-lived: she had lasted long enough to see a son of hers proclaimed as the ruler of all the Mongol tribes, but fell ill a few months after his succession, and died in her early fifties. However, amid all the poisonings and executions of the Mongol aristocracy, Sorghaghtani's death does not seem to have met with any suspicion. Her sons regarded it instead as an unfortunate tragedy, and she was buried, as per her wishes, in a Nestorian church in north-west China.

Mongke's reign continued in a fashion not unlike those of his predecessors. It began with Mongke as unified ruler in name only, entirely unable to challenge the authority of Batu west of Lake Balkhash. However, Batu died in 1255, and his two successors swiftly met with suspicious ends, likely to have been the result of further intrigues among the sons of Jochi. As a result, Mongke's rule remained free of further direct challenges, and he was free to pursue his new policy of outward expansion.

The westward advance of the Mongols was largely over. The late Batu's 'Golden Horde' had established cordial tributary relations with the nations on its border, and would eventually turn southwards to war on its relatives in Mongol-occupied Persia. Although there would be further battles with the Europeans, the Europeans would regain their strength and improve their tactics by the time the Mongols returned. In the meantime, the memories of the awful damages inflicted by the Mongols continued to reverberate among the kingdoms of Europe. Europe's counter-attack on the Mongols during this period became more cerebral, as several missionaries arrived in an attempt to convert leading khans to Christianity.

The Christian envoy William of Rubruck – eventually admitted, shivering and barefoot, to Mongke's winter court after elaborate security procedures – reported a preoccupied, idle despot, who would periodically drift away to play with his falcons before returning to listen to more of the foreigners' messages. Although William graciously refused the alcohol offered to him, *koumiss* and mead soon rendered many of the attendants incoherent, although Mongke did regain clarity long enough to say, through an interpreter: 'Even as the sun scatters its luminous rays everywhere, so does my power and that of Batu's spread everywhere.'[15]

William was not quite sure how to take this information, and noted wryly that Mongke was 'staggering a bit' when he said it. A wily Armenian missionary had already told Mongke that converting to Christianity would ensure that he would become the ruler of the world. However, not even Mongke seems to have been drunk enough to believe this.

Mongke and his brothers were already part of a cosmo-politan world. Even though Karakorum sat in the middle of nowhere, it had attracted huge throngs of hangers-on. Some of them were there through no choice of her own, such as Paquette, a woman from Metz in eastern France, who had been snatched in Hungary as part of the spoils of conquest, and somehow ended up on the other side of Eurasia. But despite her travails – William of Rubruck draws a discreet veil over her 'unheard-of misery' – she had somehow survived and prospered. For some reason, Paquette was no longer among the slave girls of a Mongol warrior: she had instead been co-opted into the entourage of one of the Mongol Christian princesses. She had married a fellow émigré, a Russian carpenter, and the couple had three children in Karakorum. Mongke's favourite goldsmith was William Bouchier, a Parisian, similarly snatched from Europe in the last campaigns, and put to work at the head of a workshop of some fifty artisans.

The extent of foreign residents in Karakorum is difficult to ascertain. William of Rubruck himself complains that the artisans were scattered throughout the encampments, and only saw each other if they were called by chance to the same audience. Nor do many of them appear to have returned home to tell their stories. The displaced Europeans, dragged to Karakorum by the Mongols returning for the *kurultai*, either perished there or migrated with their masters to points even further east, dying far from home.

Mongke regarded China as the most crucial part of the Mongol advance – not the least because, in the intervening years, the Chinese had regained several scraps of lost territory. Khubilai, already strongly associated with matters Chinese in the eyes of his family, and already successfully administering part of Chinese territory, was given the right to rule a much larger swathe of the region, stretching, at least on paper, from the Yellow River to the Yangtze, and extending east as far as 110 degrees of longitude. This effectively made Khubilai responsible for conquering Sichuan, and Yunnan to the south.

Khubilai was chosen for this mission because he had already demonstrated a masterful grasp of the different rules required in China. Just as he had successfully turned around the refugee disaster in Xingzhou, he could be expected to grapple with the very different problems that a military campaign would face. Khubilai's advance would take him out of the comfort zone familiar to both nomads and farmers. There would be no long wagon trains of Mongol carts here – the Mongols were out of the steppe, in the heartland of farmers, but also facing forests and mountains. Moreover, the Chinese heartland was dotted with fortified cities. Although Mongols were no strangers to sieges, they would have to recognize that simply surrounding a town and waiting for the defenders to run out of food was a much more difficult enterprise if a massive city had months of supplies and neighbours close by ready to ride to its reinforcement.

The western edges of China proper had been utterly despoiled by their own inhabitants, creating a zone of destruction in which no living thing could be found. This had been carefully calculated to ensure that a traditional Mongol horde, lumbering along from food source to food source, would have to cross a region entirely devoid of fodder for horses and cattle. Hence, the opening steps of Khubilai's campaign against the south took the form of massive incentives to put peasantry to work in farms under Mongol control. Khubilai not only offered seeds and tools to anyone who might want to farm in his domain, but also sent many of his soldiers into the fields. These men were not Mongols, but Chinese conscripts, who were surely much happier being back on the land than forced to march south as soldiers.

As one of Khubilai's incentives, he did as his brother had done, and authorized the printing of paper money. Mongols had little use for actual money, but were intrigued by the concept that a roundel of copper might be traded for something more than its intrinsic value, simply because of the number it bore on its face. It was a short step from this discovery to money made out of paper, bearing values that bore no relation to the cost of the paper itself. In the early stages, such chits allowed the Mongol Pacification Bureau to draw huge numbers of workers into their realm, and to keep them there, as the paper money was worthless outside Mongol territory. In time, of course, the temptation was irresistible to simply print more money if times were hard, as inevitably happened, creating inflation that would threaten later periods of Mongol rule.

The tantalizing target of the Mongol conquest remained the Song dynasty, still clinging to southern China. However, Khubilai's scheme for the Southern Song would require him to flank them from the west, by first advancing into the mountain kingdom of Dali.

Dali was a Buddhist state, crossed by the upper reaches of the Yangtze, Mekong and Salween rivers, straddling the trade route from India to Annam (modern Vietnam). It was often claimed that the inhabitants were so devout that ten of its twenty-two rulers had given up the throne to become monks – though this concealed a more pragmatic fact, that power was often vested in the hands of Dali's chief minister, and many kings of Dali were mere figureheads.

In 1253, the thirty-eight-year-old Khubilai commenced his operations, marching across the difficult, mountainous terrain of Sichuan, through the autumn rains and impenetrable fog, into Dali itself. As he approached, he sent three envoys to offer Dali's ruler, King Duan Xingzhi, the usual Mongol terms: to spare his life if he agreed to submit to the rule of the Grand Khan Mongke, in whose name Khubilai was advancing. The envoys reached the true ruler of Dali, the king's minister Gao Taixiang, who made the fatal error of executing them.

Any hopes Khubilai may have had of peacefully annexing Dali were now ruined. Mongol custom was very specific about the sacrosanct nature of envoys, and about the cataclysmic punishments to be unleashed on anyone who did not recognize this. In October 1253, Khubilai launched a three-pronged assault on Dali, with himself approaching from the north, the experienced general Uryangkhadai attacking from the west, and a group of lesser Mongol princes approaching from the east.

Khubilai found himself facing Gao Taixiang's army on the opposite banks of a river, in a state of stalemate. Fortunately for the inexperienced Khubilai, his army included Bayan of the Baarin (1236–95) the young scion of a family of military leaders, who had recently returned from the campaigns of Khubilai's brother in Persia. Bayan was put in charge of requisitioning the army's vast supply of sheepskin bags, in order to make flotation devices to get across the river. It was also Bayan who led the night-time raid that followed, crossing the river under cover of darkness. The attack caught the Dali forces entirely off guard, and cost thousands of lives, although Gao Taixiang and a group of his men managed to flee the field and run for the capital.

Chinese sources are keen to stress that Khubilai was taken to one side by his language teacher, the scholar Yao Shu, who told him an old story about a general of the early days of the Song dynasty, who made his soldiers swear that they would not massacre or plunder a town under siege. As a result, the story went, the city the general was besieging fell the next day, but life went on exactly as before, and the markets opened for trade as if nothing had happened. Supposedly, this little parable was sufficient to persuade Khubilai to give the inhabitants of Dali one more chance, despite the Mongol custom of massacring entire cities if they resisted.

Perhaps, in this case, Khubilai was prepared to listen to the argument that a corrupt minister had acted falsely in the king's name. If so, it is remarkable that Khubilai would have been so wise in Dali, when similar chain-of-command fudges in Annam and Japan later in life would often elude him. Whatever the rationale behind it, he besieged Dali's capital, and sent bannermen parading before the walls with large notices in Chinese, promising to spare the inhabitants of the city if it surrendered. It is not even clear if anyone in Dali could even read Chinese, but someone was presumably found, and the king duly surrendered.

Gao Taixiang made a run for it, but did not get far. He remained defiant before Khubilai, who ordered for him to be beheaded at the city's south gate. The men who had carried out Gao's orders to kill the Mongol envoys were also killed. The corpses of the envoys themselves were given a proper burial, and the king's first act as a Mongol vassal was to deliver their eulogy, which he was made to write himself. Satisfied that Dali was now in good hands, Khubilai left the king nominally in charge, but with the real power now in the hands of a new prime minister, one of Khubilai's appointees. He had successfully overseen the transfer of the Kingdom of Dali into what would eventually be known as the Mongol province of 'Yunnan': 'South of the Clouds'.[16]

3

IN XANADU

KHUBILAI IN THE REIGN OF MONGKE

Having apparently proved his worth as a general, Khubilai returned to the north. The continued conquest of the south would never be quite so easy thereafter, and he appears to have taken the sensible decision to report to Mongke with an impressive victory. The messier business, of carrying the Mongol conquest to hundreds of recalcitrant, and doubtless rather poor, hill tribes, was left in the hands of Uryangkhadai, who would continue to campaign in Tibet and south-east Asia for several years.

Back in his northern estates, Khubilai continued his drift towards a Chinese model of statesmanship. He continued to appoint Confucian scholars to his entourage, and left them in charge of much of the day-to-day operations, legislation, and education. He authorized a campaign to register Confucian scholars in order to keep them from suffering at the hands of Mongol bullies, and backed a campaign to hunt down fortune-tellers. In this, he was marching in step with Confucian orthodoxy – Confucius never had any time for superstitions, while soothsayers among the Chinese were unlikely to have anything positive to say about the Mongol conquerors.

Prominent among Khubilai's advisers was Liu Bingzhong, the man who had reminded him of the dangers inherent in trying to 'rule from horseback'. Liu was of a similar age to Khubilai, but a dedicated man of letters. Like most other Confucian scholars, he valued history and precedent, and particularly enjoyed citing either moments of great wisdom from history, or awful errors that might have been avoided if only a ruler had listened to his advisers. Liu seems to have been particularly good at this, and Khubilai a willing listener. Whereas many of Khubilai's relatives seemed to only keep scholars around as a form of entertainment, Khubilai's youthful problem solving had reinforced his belief that the advisers were genuinely useful. Already very much a Sinophile, he leaned increasingly on the customs and practices recommended by advisers such as Liu. This led to vast improvements in relations between ruler and ruled in Chinese territory, although it continued to cause friction back in Mongolia. As far as some of Khubilai's relatives were concerned, a happier Chinese population was only happier because it was paying less tribute to the Mongols. Back in Karakorum, there was a growing sense that Khubilai was pandering to the Chinese at the expense of wealth to which the Mongols felt they were entitled.

Notably, however, there were two suggestions that Khubilai still vetoed. Liu and his fellow Confucians were keen to recommence the old civil service examination system. At first glance, this would seem to have been precisely the sort of thing that Khubilai was likely to encourage – a three-tiered system of classical education, instructing new students in the history of China, the quotations of eminent philosophers and the construction of poetry and essays in an approved, Chinese style. The examination system had been the acceptable means of entry into public service for centuries in China, and served, as did Latin and Greek in Europe, to create an elite class with shared cultural heritage and points of reference. Reinstating the examination system in Khubilai's realm would have seemed like a smart decision that would hardly require any thought, but Khubilai surprised his advisers by rejecting the idea.

For his advisers, it was an unwelcome reminder that Khubilai the Sinophile and statesman was not himself Chinese. While he made unabashed use of scholars' knowledge of Confucius, Chinese history and Chinese thought, he saw no need to raise a new generation of like-minded figures. The Chinese education system was not merely a set of academic disciplines, it was an ideological apparatus of the state, designed to turn all its graduates into acceptable members of Chinese society. It had worked its magic on many previous conquerors – the Jurchens of the north had been successfully Sinified within a couple of generations, and were now barely distinguishable from the Chinese that they had conquered. Khubilai, however, baulked at the idea of reinstating a system of learning that placed 'Chinese-ness' at the centre of all things. The return of the civil examinations would shut out all non-Chinese officials, and Khubilai was ever the syncretist. If the Chinese examination system were reinstated, Khubilai would be unable to appoint Muslim tax collectors or Nestorian engineers. Khubilai himself was unlikely to have ever mastered Chinese beyond the halting fragility of a second language, and it is possible that he was reluctant to approve reforms that would exclude even him from intricacies of Chinese politics.

For some time, Khubilai's officials had allowed themselves to believe that life was going on as per usual. As in the recently incorporated state of Dali, the old guard were still in charge, and while tax monies might eventually end up in different places, the old system was more or less unchanged. Khubilai's refusal to endorse the examinations was a blunt reminder that life had changed more than people recognized. Khubilai's domains were occupied territory, the Mongols were a race of conquerors, and the Chinese system only proceeded as before under their sufferance.

Furthermore, it seemed presumptuous in some quarters for Khubilai to act as if he were the ruler of all China. The Southern Song regime still laid claim to all the Chinese lands below the River Yangtze, and until such time as it was incorporated within the Mongol realm, it would be a logistical nightmare to run a set of 'Chinese' civil structures while a rival China still operated across the border.

Ever since the Jurchens had encroached into the territory of the Song, there had been two Chinas. Beyond a few geographical differences – local produce, a few customs – the Jurchen north and the Song south became very similar with the Sinification of the invaders. However, for 300 years, there had been two emperors, two sets of rituals and two Chinas, with an ever-present sense that the country had been split in two, and yearned to be reunited.[1] Khubilai's policy, mirroring that of his grandfather Temujin, was to present himself as the grand unifier, glossing over the likely warfare that such a unification would require.

For this reason, Khubilai vetoed another of his advisers' suggestions. It was considered normal for a new dynasty to gather the court records and diaries of its predecessor and then to write its history. This, too, was a spin-off of the Confucian education system: with the emphasis on learning from the mistakes of the past, it was considered to be a wise act for the new order to analyse whatever errors may have led to the downfall of the old. However, the authorship of one's predecessor's history rather required one's predecessors to be demonstrably gone. As some of Khubilai's advisers would have surely already been thinking, it was not only presumptuous to commence such a job so soon after the fall of the Jurchens, but also a doomed enterprise when so many of the records and archives of the Jurchens had been spirited away to the domains of the Southern Song. Were Khubilai to commission some eager young scholar to compile the story of the Jurchens in a *History of the Jin* [dynasty], he was sure to face the embarrassment of large pieces of missing data. Meanwhile, he would also have to deal with the political issue of why there had not yet been a *History of the Liao*, the dynasty that had preceded the Jurchens in the north. Confucian scholars of the time regarded the ousted Liao as barbarian nomads, unworthy of being legitimized after the fact by being incorporated into the official histories of other Chinese dynasties. The Jurchens plainly could not be bothered with the task, so any compilation project would have to encompass the preceding Liao dynasty, as well. And here was the real problem – if the Liao and the Jurchens were mere barbarians, what did that make the Mongols in the eyes of the Chinese?

Khubilai preferred to keep away from all such debates, not the least because it was not his right to order the writing of such histories. His rulership of much of what had been Jurchen territory was merely a matter of luck and inheritance from Tolui. It was his brother Mongke who was the Great Khan of the Mongols, and hence only Mongke who possessed anything like the correct authority to give such an order. All these things considered, the histories of the Liao, the Jin (Jurchens) and the Song would not be written until the 1340s, long after Khubilai's death.

Instead, Khubilai occupied himself after the conquest of Dali with a much lower-key project. In 1256 he decided to build a new residence in the old Jurchen territory, and asked Liu Bingzhong to find a location that sat at ease with the Chinese requirements for geomancy – in other words, somewhere with suitable feng shui. Liu came back with a location that he thought ideal, about 170 miles north of modern Beijing. Planned to be a mile square, it would be a miniature replica of a traditional Chinese capital. An inner palace area was designed for Khubilai's personal use, while the walls offered ample protection for the followers, merchants and inevitable hangers-on that such an illustrious resident was sure to attract. It was originally known as Kaiping, 'open and flat', presumably describing the ground, but by 1263 it would be renamed Shangdu, or 'upper capital'. In the hands of European observers, the name would soon be mangled into many variations, including Chandu, Ciandu, Xamdu and the one by which the world is most likely to know it today: Xanadu. Marco Polo visited the site when its construction was complete, and when it functioned as a place for an older Khubilai to while away the hot summer months:

> There is at this place a very fine marble Palace, the rooms of which are all gilt and painted with figures of men and beasts and birds, and with a variety of trees and flowers, all executed with such exquisite art that you regard them with delight and astonishment.
>
> Round this Palace a wall is built, inclosing a compass of 16 miles, and inside the Park there are fountains and rivers and brooks, and beautiful meadows, with all kinds of wild animals (excluding such as are of ferocious nature), which the Emperor has procured and placed there to supply food for his gerfalcons and hawks, which he keeps there . . . Of these there are more than 200 gerfalcons alone, without reckoning the other hawks. The Kaan himself goes every week to see his birds . . . and sometimes he rides through the park with a leopard behind him on his horse's croup; and then if he sees any animal that takes his fancy, he slips his leopard at it, and the game when taken is made over to feed the hawks . . .[2]

Polo's description mixes up 'miles' with Chinese *li*, since Khubilai's inner sanctum was four *li* on each side, but otherwise tallies with other accounts. Shangdu was built as a defensive bastion, with six large watchtowers observing the surrounding plains, and enough space inside for a thriving population of perhaps 100,000. Placement of temples within the city followed the lines prescribed within the ancient *Book of Changes* (*Yijing*), and hence was sure to meet with the approval of Khubilai's Chinese subjects.

The land was not quite as perfect as Liu might have suggested. The area was boggy and riddled with springs, and

Khubilai's own palace was built on a rocky platform that lifted it out of the local water table. It is unclear how long Khubilai planned to reside at Shangdu – in later life it was always his summer residence, although he would build an even bigger city, now known as Beijing, further to the south. Shangdu's most unusual feature was the hunting preserve – a massive walled area that formed a third of the city. Earlier monarchs of China, particularly those with ties to equestrian clans, had often had hunting grounds of their own, but Khubilai's was a truly vast park, with an earthen wall and a protective moat, where the Mongol prince could exercise his falcons and shoot deer.

As during his youth, Khubilai's main interest appears to have been hunting, and he would spend many happy days in a genteel imitation of Mongol heaven, living in a luxurious tent. Built in imitation of the yurts of the Mongol steppes, it was described by European observers, whose readers lacked the necessary understanding of how a Mongol 'tent' might be more richly appointed than a palace, and yet still be mobile:

> At a spot in the park where there is a charming wood he has another Palace built of cane. It is gilt all over, most elaborately finished inside and decorated with beasts and birds of very skilful workmanship. It is reared on gilt and varnished pillars, on each of which stands a dragon entwining the pillar with its tail and supporting the roof on outstretched limbs. The roof, like the rest, is formed of canes, covered with a varnish so strong and excellent that no amount of rain will rot them . . . The construction of the Palace is so devised that it can be taken down and put up again with great celerity; and it can all be taken to pieces and removed whithersoever the Emperor may command. When erected, it is braced by more than 200 cords of silk.[3]

Polo, like other European writers, has trouble finding a way of expressing the ornate nature of the greatest Mongol dwellings. It is not enough to merely call it a 'tent' – we might, like Friar John of Plano Carpini, call it a 'tabernacle' in an attempt to distance it from our own concept of what a tent might be. Polo takes the opposite tack, and prefers instead to describe it as some kind of portable 'palace'. There were many attempts by later commentators to describe Khubilai's leisure yurt. The vaguest, but also most enduring, seems to have been born as a pun that might appeal to a classical scholar, in Samuel Taylor Coleridge's judicious term that plays on *domus*, the Latin for 'house', and the hemispherical shape of the traditional yurt: 'pleasure dome'.[4]

But Khubilai's high life attracted jealous grumbles from Mongke's officials. There were whispers in Karakorum that the Great Khan's little brother had gone too far in his acceptance of Chinese ways. Despite Khubilai's own refusal to pursue certain areas of Chinese practice, his detractors in Karakorum saw only a Mongol prince who was ignoring traditional Mongol ways, and instead pandering to the conquered locals. The grandson of Temujin was going native, to the extent that he had now even built himself a city to live in – a fixed point at Kaiping, perhaps even intended as a rival to Karakorum itself.

In 1257, Khubilai bore the consequences. Two stern auditors arrived from Karakorum, under orders to check Khubilai's accounts. After a cursory inspection of Khubilai's records, they claimed to have found numerous irregularities. A bunch of Chinese officials were dragged in for questioning, briefly interrogated, and executed. Pointedly, the auditors steered clear of long-standing associates of the Mongol heartland, targeting only those with strong ties to China. When the bodies had been dragged away, the Mongol official Alandar announced that he was founding a new institute, whose job was to scrutinize tax collection in the area. Notice had been served on Khubilai's private fief.

The arrival of the auditors was suspiciously confrontational. In Chinese terms, Khubilai lost face. In Mongol terms, his brother had all but accused him of treachery and corruption. It would have been entirely in keeping with the Mongol character for Khubilai to take umbrage and strike back, with an army.

However, in consultation with his advisers, he resolved that such an action would be unwise. The auditors' behaviour was certainly provocative, but there was no guarantee Mongke masterminded it.

In an attempt to go over the auditors' heads, Khubilai sent emissaries directly to his brother at Karakorum, to plead that he was being wrongfully accused. They returned empty-handed, with reports that Mongke was indeed angry with Khubilai for something. Khubilai risked everything by going to see Mongke himself, carefully taking an entourage small enough that it could not be mistaken for an army. Their reunion was described in the Chinese annals as a tearful embrace, with all thoughts of enmity forgotten. Suddenly, with one hug and a big party, everything was back to normal again.

Few historians believe this explanation. It has been suggested that Mongke and Khubilai had a definite falling-out, and that their reconciliation in the early months of 1258 was a pragmatic decision – a recognition that they needed to cooperate, despite their differences. There are subtle indicators of a rift to be found in the writings of Rashid al-Din, who notes that Mongke had decided to commence a new assault on the Southern Song, and did so without Khubilai. Pointedly, Mongke 'decreed that since Khubilai had gout and had previously fought a campaign and subjugated a hostile country he should now repose at home.'[5] This implies that Khubilai's time at Shangdu was something of an internal exile, shunted aside after his service in Dali because of some unrecorded sleight or failing. Then, suddenly, Rashid's Khubilai sends a message to Mongke to the effect that he was feeling much better now, and somewhat jealous that everyone else was off on a military campaign when he was stuck at his Shangdu retreat. In Rashid's history, the next proclamation from Mongke directly quotes Khubilai's statement of a return to health, and puts him in charge of 100,000 men for the next attack.

We know that Khubilai was fond of food and drink, and that gout ran in his family. He would certainly suffer from it in old age, but would he really have already succumbed to it at the age of forty-two, only to make a miraculous recovery a year later? No clue is offered in the main body of the Chinese annals, although there is a tantalizing possibility to be found in their appendices. Tucked at the back of the *History of the Yuan*, in the accounts of the Mongols' relations with other countries, there is a chronology of communication with the far southern state of Annam – dealt with in much greater detail in Chapter 11. During the period of Khubilai's dispute with Mongke, some might argue that his rightful place was not in Shangdu at all, but back in the south, leading the army that he had left behind after the conquest of Dali. Khubilai had returned to Mongolia in triumph from Dali, taking the credit for a victory that was largely the work of the real military men, the generals Uryangkhadai and Bayan. However, Khubilai had returned home just as the going became genuinely tough. Uryangkhadai had been stuck in the south for the years that followed, and had recently suffered an embarrassing retreat before an Annamese counter-offensive. By 1258, the Mongols had been pushed all the way out of Annam and back into Yunnan, hence achieving remarkably little in the period since Khubilai had headed home and boasted of his victories.

News drifting in from Annam – of Mongol warriors having to flee for their lives – may have led to the accusations against Khubilai. While he played in his new mountain retreat, the army he had left to mop up in the south was in deep trouble, and threatened the hard-won reputation of the Mongols all over Eurasia. If this were the cause of friction between him and Mongke, highlighted by what may have been a sarcastic exchange about a supposed 'gout' affliction keeping Khubilai out of action, it also offers a possible explanation for the sudden thaw in relations.[6]

Around the time that Khubilai set out to confront his brother directly, Mongke received an unexpected new update on the war in the south. It took the form of a communiqué from the King of Annam, acknowledging Mongol suzerainty, offering tribute, and essentially agreeing to everything that the Mongols had wanted. This missive was sure to confuse the Mongols; indeed, it had been intended by the Annamese to do just that. In the short term, it would give the impression that reports of Mongol defeats in the south were gross exaggerations, and that all was suddenly well. Khubilai was not a failure at all – he now appeared once more to be a general who had rightly left his theatre of operations when he deemed it appropriate. The commanders to whom he had delegated authority had completed their tasks adequately.

Meanwhile, the assault on the Southern Song was going badly for Mongke. It was only now that he called up Khubilai to take to the field, as if acknowledging that Khubilai was not a military dilettante, but an unbeaten general. It is certainly only after the brothers' reconciliation that there is a sense in the sources that Khubilai's service in Dali was no longer just a quota that had been fulfilled: it was now a success that he was ordered to emulate.

However, there is another possibility regarding the brothers' reconciliation. Mongke's sudden decision to rekindle his friendship with Khubilai seems to have come at a time when Mongke realized that he genuinely needed someone with experience of the Chinese to help with the conquest of the Southern Song. Khubilai was already plugged in to the institutions and philosophies of the Chinese, and would be able to supply officials and experts to smooth the progress of Mongke's campaigns in the Southern Song realm. Ironically, he would not be able to supply as many officials as he might have managed earlier, because Mongke's auditors had killed many of them. However, Mongke faced another cultural problem within his realm – a religious dispute between adherents of a religion he regarded as 'Chinese', which threatened to escalate into all-out civil war.

In an irony that the Mongols failed to appreciate, it was partly their fault. The expansion of the Mongol realm towards the south had encouraged travel and resettlement across what had once been inaccessible borders. During Mongke's reign, Mongol troops had managed to incorporate Tibet within their sphere of influence. This had in turn brought a large number of Tibetan Buddhists into the north, bringing with them their magical and divinatory practices.

The Tibetan-influenced Buddhists were soon at odds with local Buddhists, although their showmanship and conjuring tricks proved to be much more popular with the Mongol overlords. Meanwhile, they crowded out more modest sects such as the quiet, contemplative Chan Buddhists (known today as Zen Buddhists), and irritated the sorcerers and alchemists of a growing number of Taoist sects.

As recorded by William of Rubruck, Marco Polo and many others, the courts of the Mongol leaders were constant proving grounds for religious debate. Christian missionaries, Muslims, Taoists, Buddhists and itinerant conjurors all vied for the attention of princes and the Great Khan, with not only the favour of the new rulers, but material rewards and political appointments at stake. The early winner had been Chang-zhun, a Taoist whose powers had so impressed Temujin that he had granted his sect freedom from taxation. In a time of crushing Mongol taxes, such status had allowed the Taoists to flourish like never before, and within a generation they had accumulated massive wealth.

The Taoists courted controversy in the 1250s by dismissing Buddhism as nothing more than a sect of their own religion. They did this with the aid of the *Book of Barbarian Conversions* (*Huahu Jing*), an 800-year-old scroll about Laozi, founder of Taoism and author of the *Daode Jing* (*Book of the Path and the Power*), who had legendarily left China by walking towards the west, beyond the Great Wall. However, it went on to claim that he had neither died nor ascended to heaven. Instead, he had supposedly walked all the way to India, where he regenerated into the figure known as Buddha. According to the *Book of Barbarian Conversions*, Buddhism was hence only a foggy reflection of Taoism, and the many

Buddhists in Mongke's realm were deluded fools who could only be saved by returning to the true faith.[7]

Chan Buddhists, with their emphasis on meditation, were in for a drubbing. 'Do you think you can clear your mind by sitting constantly in silent meditation?' asked the book. 'This makes your mind narrow, not clear.' The text also spoke disparagingly of 'extremist religions and ideologies' and ridiculed the Buddhist concentration on enlightenment: 'Greed for enlightenment and immortality is no different from greed for material wealth. It is self-centred and dualistic, and thus an obstacle to true attainment.'[8]As a guaranteed temptation to the Mongols, the book contained prophecies and warrior analogies, as if the Taoists and the Mongols were destined to become allies:

> Those in future generations who study and practice the truth of these teachings will be blessed. They will acquire the subtle light of wisdom, the mighty sword of clarity that cuts through all obstruction, and the mystical pearl of understanding that envelops the entire universe.[9]

The titular 'barbarians', at least originally, were the ancient Indians. But the term was also readily applied to the Mongols themselves, at least out of earshot – were they the next barbarians to be converted, and to Taoism? It was, to be sure, merely the claims of one particular sect of Taoists, but it angered the Buddhists. They soon struck back by claiming that everyone's books were wrong, and that Buddha had actually been born 500 years earlier than previously thought. This, in turn, rendered the Taoists' claims for Laozi ludicrous, since Buddha now predated *him* by several centuries. In fact, Laozi and Confucius (and, while they were at it, Jesus and Mohammed as well) could now be said to be little more than imitators of the Buddha. Buddhism was hence the true religion, and all others merely its shadows.

There was more along the same lines, and matters of theory, belief and conjecture soon affected real-world events. Buddhist proselytes printed and distributed copies of the *Book of Barbarian Conversions*, which travelled far within the Mongol realm. Meanwhile, Taoist vandals desecrated Buddhist temples, or took them over, either by force or by leaning on Mongol officials.

The religious conflict pointed to unrest within areas that the Mongols already regarded as pacified and obedient. It offered the prospect, however small, that Mongke was somehow squandering his grandfather Temujin's legacy. Since Temujin regarded it as the destiny of his descendants to rule the world, Mongke's failure to keep order could be seen by some as a sign that he was 'worthless', which could lead to another succession dispute. Mongke was also completely at a loss on how to deal with the rival claims of different sects, many of whom were quibbling on minor points within impenetrable dogma. With tensions between dozens of sects rising fast, Mongke called upon Khubilai to deal with the problem.

Suddenly, Khubilai's close association with the Chinese was no longer a liability. Khubilai was a member of the ruling aristocracy, known to have strong sympathies with the conquered peoples, which made him the perfect candidate to convene a great debate between Buddhists and Taoists, and decree once and for all who had power over whom. The result was a great conference at Khubilai's Kaiping retreat in 1258, attended by 300 leading Buddhists and 200 Taoists, with Khubilai as the presiding judge. Such religious free-for-alls would continue in Khubilai's presence intermittently for the next three decades, but the first carried the greatest political implications.

Unfortunately, only Buddhist accounts of the event survive, so we only have a one-sided version of events. Khubilai, despite his avowed love of China, was already leaning towards the Buddhist side, and counted prominent Tibetans in his entourage. One was Drogön Chögyal Phagpa, also known as the 'Phags-pa Lama (1235–80), a charismatic priest in his mid-twenties, whose uncle had legendarily cured a Mongol prince of a life-threatening disease, and who had berated the Mongols for taking Chinese lives. Drogön Chögyal was favoured by Khubilai's favourite wife, Chabi, and had already become, to all intents and purposes, Khubilai's personal guru. As the debate got underway, it became clear that the Tibetans had little ammunition apart from two documents – the aforementioned *Book of Barbarian Conversions* and a second work, *Depictions of the Eighty-One Conversions (Bashiyi Huatu)*, which listed eighty-one incarnations of Laozi, including one image that clearly showed him as Buddha.

That was all very well, argued Drogön Chögyal, but since the Taoists were relying on literary evidence, perhaps they would like to prove that it was genuine. After all, there did not appear to have been any mention of these works in any biography or bibliography of Laozi, and the acknowledged Chinese classics were strangely silent on any alleged late-life trip to India for the famous sage. All things considered, Drogön Chögyal argued (and modern scholars largely agree) that both books were later forgeries.

There is no record of how the debate proceeded against the Buddhists. It would appear that whatever outrageous claims for revised dates may have been made in the heat of the moment, the Buddhists in the debate itself saw no need to fiddle with their own history. As a result, the burden of proof was dumped firmly at the feet of the Taoists, who had little to add after Drogön Chögyal had demolished their claims of document authenticity.

Khubilai, who had taken an active part in the debate, offered the Taoists a last chance, and suggested that if their superior religion gave them magic powers, they might like to demonstrate a few to the assembly. When the Taoist sorcery supply came up empty, Khubilai ruled in favour of the Buddhists. The Taoists were made to shave their heads like Buddhist monks, and 237 temples were returned to Buddhist control. Carefully, Khubilai avoided any intimations of revenge or reprisal – the Taoists were simply reduced to a status like that of any other holy men within the Mongol realm, and not accorded any special concessions. The offending texts were banned within the Mongol khanate, in an attempt to prevent further unrest from developing.

With religious order somewhat restored, Khubilai Khan set out on the next mission that Mongke had for him. This was also a form of unification, albeit a much more temporal and widespread one. The time had come for the Mongols, and their vassals from the Jurchen north, to head across the Yangtze River to take on the Southern Song. Mongke would lead an army personally, to attack China from the west. Khubilai would advance from Shangdu towards the south, at the head of 90,000 men.

As Khubilai set off in the late winter of 1258–9, he asked the Taoist stragglers at his court for a prophecy. The answer came back: 'Within twenty years, all below heaven will be united.'[1]

4

THE REVOLUTION OF FATE

THE BATTLE TO BE KHAN

Mongke was determined to conquer the Southern Song. The late Genghis Khan had, after all, suggested that it was the destiny of the Mongols to rule the world, and outward expansion often seemed to be the only way to stop the Mongols turning on each other. Discussion of the project danced around the fear that it might be impossible. The embarrassment in Annam was still fresh in the minds of some of Mongke's advisers, and it seems that many had a healthy mistrust of the ambassadors who had arrived to proclaim that the war with the Annamese was over. The real enemy of the Mongols in Annam, far deadlier than the Annamese, was the climate. Mongols died in their thousands from disease and dehydration, and it was widely understood that conditions in many parts of southern China would be unpleasantly similar.

Mongke rejected such doubts, even though his advisers repeatedly voiced them. He had other worries, largely to do with the very different terrain of southern China, which was sure to call for siege warfare and infantry over the habitual Mongol reliance on cavalry. For such tactics, Mongke would need to rely on non-Mongols, particularly Muslim experts in the construction of siege engines, and northern Chinese who knew something of the lay of the land in the south.

The cities would be the greatest obstacles that the Mongols faced, as Chinese conurbations were the largest in the world at that time. Hangzhou, by the sea, was the 'temporary capital' of the Southern Song, although it had enjoyed that distinction for over a century, and had a population estimated at one and a half million people. Such a city, and its attendant satellite suburbs, farmlands and fishing fleets, could present a massive logistical threat to the Mongol war machine, far from home and relying on its own supply lines.

Mongke hoped that the name of the Mongols would still carry enough fear into the hearts of their enemies. He decided to send four armies into China, the better to split the defensive forces of the Southern Song. He would concentrate the best of his own efforts on the cities of western China, in the hope that news of swift victories there would encourage the Southern Song bastion in Hangzhou to surrender without a fight.

Khubilai was part of the grand scheme, advancing from the north-west with 80,000 borrowed troops and his own personal army of another 10,000. Uryangkhadai would arrive from the south-west, setting out from Yunnan with a similar force. A fourth force would start out from the north-east, sure to push rumour ahead of it that the Mongols were approaching from that direction, too. By the time the four armies met at a pre-arranged point on the Yangtze, the Southern Song headquarters would have been inundated with panicked reports of Mongol armies advancing from 'all sides'.

Mongke also left his youngest brother, Arigh Boke, holding the fort back at Karakorum. In doing so, he was acting admirably within the bounds of Mongol tradition, which always left the youngest son minding the hearth. However, Mongke appears to have already forgotten that his own father had been the youngest son of Temujin, and that leaving Tolui and Sorghaghtani in Karakorum had been the beginning of their own rise to power.

Ordered to rendezvous with another Mongol force deep in Southern Song territory, Khubilai did not waste time besieging the large metropolis of Xiangyang – an odd choice, since it would surely leave hostile Song loyalists to his rear. However, this seems to have been part of the plan. The emphasis on speed was designed to give the impression that the Mongol frontline was considerably closer to Hangzhou than it really was. Accordingly, Khubilai marched south as fast as he could, covering 500 miles in just a week – the news of his advance surely deemed to be more valuable to the Mongol propaganda machine than any actual battles fought or cities won. His general Bahadur Noyan was leading an advance force, riding ahead of the main column with orders to secure supplies for the approaching hordes, and to spread the word of the coming Mongols. Bahadur Noyan's men were under strict orders from Khubilai to show mercy to the Chinese; Khubilai was very specific – anyone killing the Chinese without reason would be subject to the death penalty themselves, all part of Khubilai's scheme to win the Chinese over without a fight. This was particularly important to Khubilai as the territory he was in bordered directly on his own fief. It was perfectly reasonable to assume that he would end up administering whatever he won.

In August 1259, Khubilai reached the Huai River, beyond which he faced true Southern Song territory. He peeled off a small force under the Uighur official Lian Xixian, who was sent on a subsidiary mission to order nearby towns to submit.

Khubilai was still ten days away from the rendezvous objective when news arrived of a drastic change in circumstances. Out in the west, Mongke had enjoyed early successes, but had become bogged down during the spring of 1259 in a long siege. Reminded by his generals of the danger of disease, Mongke had ignored any such objections, and doggedly camped out, waiting for the Chinese to crack.

As the summer heat piled on, Mongke lost 3,000 of his men to disease. Although the siege limped on, Mongke himself retreated to higher ground to escape from the heat. He drank large quantities of wine, but succumbed to a condition that sounded like cholera. Just over a week later, Mongke died. He was fifty-one years old.

Mongol tradition was very clear on what should happen next. Any Mongol armies should cease their advance and return to the homeland. After a suitable period of mourning and the correct funeral rites, there would be a new *kurultai* convened, and the selection of a new Great Khan. Khubilai, however, broke with tradition. Rashid al-Din's chronicle has Khubilai on the banks of the Huai River (the watershed of the Yangtze basin) – several days into Southern Song territory, but also at the symbolic dividing line between north and south. According to Rashid al-Din, Khubilai consults with his advisers, and notes that the news of Mongke's death is far more useful to the Chinese than it is to the Mongols: 'We have come hither with an army like ants or locusts: how can we turn back, our task undone, because of rumours?'[1]

The moment Khubilai turned for home, he would lose all of his momentum in Chinese territory. It might be years before the Mongols were organized enough to make another attack, and in the short term, he would be abandoning his advance parties to suffer the consequences of an inevitable Southern Song counter-attack. His claim that the news of Mongke's death was a 'rumour' was facetious in the extreme, since he had heard the news from a trusted Mongol relative. But even as the late Mongke's forces ground to a halt, and their brother Hulagu cancelled his own campaign in the Middle East to begin the long return to Mongolia, Khubilai took the decision to forge on ahead. It is unclear how long he was planning on ignoring the news of Mongke's death, but his decision to cross the Yangtze itself implies that he was determined to take on the entirety of the Southern Song.

It was a daring move, quite out of character for the prince who had played it safe in Dali. Nonetheless, Khubilai may have been thinking strategically – as long as he propelled his army ever onwards, the chance remained that the news of Mongke's death would fail to reach the Southern Song. Instead, they would continue to hear of the multi-pronged Mongol advance, suspect the worse, and perhaps even surrender after minimal resistance. As long as that was a possibility, Khubilai stood to gain territory on his borders at an unprecedented rate, and it was a risk that he readily took.

A storm brewed on the Yangtze, and Khubilai was advised to delay his crossing. Instead, he pushed on, brandishing a birch-bark amulet that was supposed to have the power to quell troubled waters. Nothing else is known about this charm or who may have supplied it – presumably one of the Taoists or a Mongol shaman. As Khubilai's army reached the far bank of the Yangtze, they ran into the first heavy resistance from the Southern Song. The skies cleared, mockingly, as the two armies threw themselves at each other, but, despite heavy casualties, Khubilai maintained his beachhead on the southern side.

His main objective was a city called Ezhou, a suitable stronghold and crossroads that would allow the Mongols to dig in for the long term. However, the city held out, and initial claims that Khubilai had the city 'surrounded' were prove to be unreliable when a brigade of reinforcements was able to sneak through Mongol lines and into the city to help defend it. Soon afterwards, Uryangkhadai arrived, at the head of his own forces. He, too, had studiously ignored the news of Mongke's death, and seemed to have similar plans to Khubilai – a last-ditch rush against the Southern Song, on the assumption that it was now or never. Emissaries arrived from a prominent minister of the Southern Song, Jia Sidao, who made a great show of offering the Mongols tribute.

Jia Sidao's offer was unappealing, and clearly a desperate measure. Citing a 'precedent' from 1005, Jia offered to pay the

Mongols an annual sum of silver, carpets, fine silks and brocades, if they agreed to pull back to the north. The ill-fated Northern Song had tried something similar with nomad tribes in the distant past.

Meeting with little progress, Jia Sidao instead suggested that the Chinese hand over the scrap of territory between the Huai and Yangtze rivers, fixing the borders between the Southern Song and the Mongols at the mighty Yangtze River.

'Now, after we have already crossed the Yangtze,' laughed Khubilai's negotiator, 'what use are these words?' Typically, the Southern Song were trying to sell the Mongols land that they had already seized. The siege of Ezhou stretched on, with both sides refusing to budge, until Khubilai's hand was forced by a letter from his favourite wife, Chabi, who had been left in charge of Khubilai's home ground at Kaiping.

Chabi's message simply stated that agents of Arigh Boke had arrived on a recruitment drive, seeking soldiers for an unspecified war. Considering that all wars were supposedly cancelled while the *kurultai* was convened to choose the new Great Khan, his intentions seemed obvious. Unwilling or unable to state what everyone must have been already thinking, Chabi finished with a cryptic comment: 'The heads of the big fish and the little fish have been cut off. Who is left but thou and Arigh Boke? Is it possible for thee to return?'[2]

Two days later, while Khubilai and Uryangkhadai still puzzled over this message, messengers arrived from Arigh Boke himself, supposedly to 'enquire after Khubilai's health'. In fact, Arigh Boke had learned of Khubilai's suspicions and had sent a series of ostentatious gifts, including falcons, on the advice of one of his most prominent accomplices, Ogodei's grandson Dorje. Dorje had suggested that such gifts would ensure that Khubilai would 'feel secure and grow careless'.[3]

They were unprepared for the news that Khubilai had already learned what their master was planning, and had nothing to say when Khubilai asked them to explain how Arigh Boke was planning on using his new troop levy.

'Therefore,' Khubilai comments sagely in Rashid al-Din's account, 'it may be a matter of deceit and treachery.'

In distant Mongolia, Arigh Boke had attracted a powerful coterie of supporters, including Mongke's most influential widow, many of Mongke's sons, and descendants of Ogodei and Jochi. He also strongly implied, without much evidence, that he had the blessing of the leaders of the Mongols in the far west, who were too far away to come in person. The old arguments from generations before were dragged up again, along with the old quotes of Temujin, and debates over 'worthlessness'. Khubilai, it was true, was a natural candidate to take over from Mongke, but seniority was no longer enough, not when both he and Arigh Boke were the sons of Temujin's youngest son. Arigh Boke pandered to the traditionalists among the Mongols, citing, as ever, that Khubilai had practically gone native among the Chinese. With every year, Khubilai became less Mongol – building his palaces, surrounding himself with foreign advisers, trusting in alien religions. Arigh Boke, meanwhile, was the candidate for traditional Mongol values – dwelling in Karakorum, clinging to old Mongol ways.

In the aftermath of the dispute, as with the argument between the Buddhists and the Taoists, we only have the words of the winners, but it is plain to see how Khubilai could have easily characterized Arigh Boke in similarly negative terms. Rashid al-Din's history of Khubilai's reign contains unlikely passages where Arigh Boke cackles with his cronies, plotting deeds that they bluntly call their 'treacheries'. Chinese accounts are less stereotyped, but still present Arigh Boke as a scheming mastermind, brought down by the heroic Khubilai.

Had matters been ever so slightly different, history may have described the hateful Khubilai, who disregarded Mongol family values for his own self-advancement, and who rebuked the peace offerings of his innocuous, pure-hearted younger sibling. Instead, Khubilai's great reluctance to set aside his campaign in China is portrayed, with his slow realization that Arigh Boke was hell-bent on destroying him. Accordingly, he pulled back from Ezhou, leaving a token army under Bahadur Noyan.

If Arigh Boke had survived to write his version of history, he would have perhaps noted that Khubilai had no need to take the main body of his army back to the north with him unless he already suspected trouble at home. Several hundred miles on the retreat, Khubilai received more emissaries from Arigh Boke, who reassured him that reports he had heard of troops being drafted for a civil war were gross exaggerations.

Khubilai gave two answers to these pleasantries. 'As you have explained those unseemly words,' he said to the messengers, 'everyone's mind is at rest.' However, he then immediately followed this with a second message to the remainder of his army in Southern Song territory: 'Abandon the siege of Ezhou at once and come back, for our mind, like the revolution of Fate, has changed.'[4]

Arigh Boke put out an innocuous-sounding decree: 'In order to mourn for Mongke Khan it has appeared necessary that [Khubilai] and all the princes should come.' However, Khubilai and the surviving generals of the China campaign were now all in agreement – the decree was a trap, and Arigh Boke's group already planning to murder their rivals. If this sounds paranoid, the intrigues over the succession of Guyuk and Ogodei – with their executions, show-trials and poisonings – should be remembered.

With neither side trusting the other, there were two rival *kurultai* conferences in 1260. At the first, held in Kaiping in May 1260, Khubilai was proclaimed as the new Great Khan by all the 'progressive' princes of the Mongols who favoured increased communication with other cultures. A month later, a second *kurultai*, this time at Karakorum, proclaimed Arigh Boke to be the true ruler. Khubilai had been announced first, but as Arigh Boke's supporters would argue for years to come, a *kurultai* that was not held in Karakorum was no *kurultai* at all.

In the far west, Hulagu, leader of the khanate of Persia, and Berke, leader of the Golden Horde, declared war on each other.

Hulagu might have offered support to Khubilai; Berke largely favoured Arigh Boke, but the war over borderlands and religion (Berke had converted to Islam) largely isolated the west from the struggle between Khubilai and Arigh Boke.

Khubilai's propaganda war against Arigh Boke was conducted in pointedly Chinese terms. Largely drafted by Khubilai's Confucian advisers, his decrees presented him less as a khan of the Mongols and more as a putative emperor of China. He cited his great achievements in administration and keeping the peace, and called for countrywide loyalty in the interests of the 'empire'. A few days later, he adopted a Chinese reign title 'Zhongtong', or 'Moderate Rule'. Carefully chosen for him by his adviser Wang E, this appears to have been an allusion to one of the chapters in the *Book of Changes* that referred to a dragon arising in the fields – an imperial candidate from unexpected origins, who would be somehow able to steer a moderate, middle course between unspecified, contending opposites.[5] The claim is historically interesting because, in choosing a reign title, Khubilai implied that he had a reign! It was the moment in Khubilai's life when he first suggested, even obliquely, that he was not so much a Mongol khan, but a Chinese emperor. There may even have been an intentional message in his choice of title as he was quite literally stuck in the middle. After all, he faced a rival claimant on Mongolia in the north, and a rival claimant on China in the south.

The Southern Song took advantage of Khubilai's retreat to seize back the lands he had invaded. Jia Sidao reported to the Emperor that he had chastised the barbarians, rather omitting to mention that the Mongol army had largely left of its own accord. Khubilai sent some emissaries in an attempt to hammer out a deal with Jia Sidao that retained some semblance of the previous Mongol gains, but a freshly confident Jia Sidao arrested the envoys and kept them in confinement.

However, it was not all bad news for Khubilai. He had put out feelers in all directions, and received support from an entirely unexpected direction. In May/June 1260 one of Khubilai's envoys had arrived in Korea, with a polite, plaintive message attempting to work out whose side the Koreans were on:

> Of all beneath Heaven who have not surrendered, there is only your nation and [the Southern Song] . . . At the time when the Emperor had not yet ascended the throne, we heard that the King had arrived in the Western Capital, and remained there eight or nine days. We suspected there was a calamity therefore we bestow this letter.[6]

The 'Western Capital' was the fortified island of Ganghwa near modern Incheon, where successive Korean rulers had held off many Mongol attacks since the time of Ogodei. However, in this case, a faction among the Koreans had sent their heir apparent, Prince Wonjong, to pledge allegiance to the 'ruler of the Mongols' after Mongke's death. Presumably, the Koreans had sent their prince on his way without actually knowing who the real ruler of the Mongols was, but by either luck or judgement, the prince and his entourage ran into Khubilai as he marched towards Mongolia.

Hence, even as Khubilai headed north for the confrontation with Arigh Boke, he received a royal embassy en route that proclaimed Korea's submission. The news was a massive morale boost to Khubilai's entourage, and was greeted with breathless enthusiasm by his Chinese advisers.

'Although Korean is a small country,' noted the Jurchen minister Choyonpil, 'due to its perilous mountains and seas, our nation has used troops [against them] for over twenty years and they are still not our vassals.'[7]

Khubilai reportedly could not contain his excitement, and noted that Korea had been an impregnable fortress for centuries, and that not even the great warrior-emperor Taizong of the glorious Tang dynasty had been able to conquer it.

> Korea [is] a nation 10,000 *li* [distant], Tang Taizong himself led an expedition [against them] and was unable to obtain their

submission. Now their Heir Apparent himself comes to me.
This is the will of Heaven.[8]

The Koreans' proclamation of fealty was a happy accident
that Khubilai would never forget. He could (and did) boast
that he had conquered an unconquerable territory without
even setting foot in it. Surely this was precisely the sort of
charisma that the joint ruler of Mongolia and China would
require? Agreements were made with the Koreans that
Ganghwa, the 'Western Capital', would have its defences
dismantled, since there was no longer a state of war between
Korea and the Mongols. Mongol officials would set up post-
stations to ensure speedy communications, and all would
presumably be well.

The reality was not quite so neat. Although Khubilai was
proud for the rest of his life of the 'submission' of the Koreans,
he was now mixed up in a difficult situation. The winter of
1259–60 had been harsh, followed by a terrible drought during
the summer of 1260. In Korea, 'there was a great famine in the
capital . . . and . . . many officials starved to death.'[9] The prince's
father, King Gojong (r.1213–59), died in July while the prince
was still away, and a faction in Korea planned to put a younger
son on the throne in the place of the rightful heir. Hence, before
Khubilai could really capitalize on any 'support' from the
Koreans, he was obliged to support them instead, returning the
prince to his homeland with Mongol support, proclaiming him
as King Wonjong (r.1260–74).

King Wonjong returned home accompanied by an honour
guard of Mongols loyal to Khubilai, and headed straight for the
capital, Gaeseong. While his relatives waited in vain to welcome
him on Ganghwa, King Wonjong reached the capital, broke
open a government granary, and distributed rice to the
surviving inhabitants. The food problem dealt with, at least for
now, he began dishing out appointments in his administration
to many of the officials who had followed orders and gone to
the capital instead of the old resistance base at Ganghwa, which

continued to support guerrilla operations against the Mongols in the hinterland.

King Wonjong was accompanied by Shulita, a Mongol 'adviser' whose role was actually that of *darughachi* – the viceroy of Khubilai himself. There are intimations of trouble between them, with Shulita testing Wonjong's loyalty by ordering him to ride on for longer than he wanted. Wonjong appears to have called Shulita's bluff and done just that, to the point where Shulita pitched his own camp in a sulk. Nevertheless, Shulita was sure to get his own way. While the new King was the official ruler, and would soon be crowned as such on Ganghwa Island, Wonjong's son was a hostage with Shulita's forces. The hostage prince would soon be married to a daughter of Khubilai, and King Wonjong's grandson would also be Khubilai's. Although Khubilai would not live to see it, his descendants would rule Korea for the next century.

Meanwhile, Khubilai had a succession dispute of his own to handle, in the form of Arigh Boke. In an ironic strategy that he must surely have appreciated and enjoyed, his first assault on his wayward brother took the form of economic sanctions. While Arigh Boke bragged about his old-fashioned Mongol ways and his homespun traditional values, Khubilai cut him off from all access to trade goods and supplies from the despised, sedentary, agrarian south. It soon became very plain that, despite Arigh Boke's claims to the contrary, the reliance of the Mongols on their vassal states had already been grossly underestimated. Karakorum was not only a city itself, but one with a newly increased population of soldiers loyal to Arigh Boke. It hence required a steady supply of food that could only really be met by grain caravans from the southern farmlands. To be sure, the Mongols could subsist for a while, as their ancestors had done, on meat and milk from their herds, but the herds themselves would need to keep moving in order to graze. If Arigh Boke did not deal with Khubilai swiftly, he would be forced to quit Karakorum and wander the steppes like his ancestors.

Khubilai already controlled the former Jurchen territories, and his machinations in Korea shut off the north-east – it is possible that some of the Korean actions against 'Mongols' in 1260 went unpunished because they were targeted at men from Arigh Boke's faction, not Khubilai's. Khubilai also sent emissaries to his cousin in the largest section of Uighur territory and secured a promise of support, cutting Arigh Boke off from any supplies from the south-west. Mongolia was suddenly, grimly isolated, with the lords of the west still preoccupied in their own war with each other, and Khubilai's faction walling off most other directions. Arigh Boke's only remaining avenue was the north, in the forbidding wastes of Siberia.

By the winter of 1260, Arigh Boke was relying solely on supplies from the north, namely the limited farming and herding capabilities of the upper Yenisei valley, a river system that wound its way towards the Arctic Circle. Lake Baikal might have kept him supplied with fish for a time, but was now frozen over.

Over the months that followed, Arigh Boke and Khubilai attempted to hammer out an agreement between them. It was a game of deadly bluffing, with Khubilai neglecting to mention his losses in China as the Southern Song took back their land. Meanwhile, Arigh Boke made no mention of the awful deprivation in his realm, and instead made several attempts to imply that help had arrived from Hulagu and Berke in the west. This was patently not true. In fact, while Arigh Boke, 'at his wit's end', had been bragging of support from Hulagu, Hulagu himself had sent envoys to Arigh Boke berating him for his revolt.[10]

Eventually, Arigh Boke made overtures of peace to Khubilai, claiming that he would 'fatten up his horses' over the spring, and then come to Khubilai to offer grudging tribute. Khubilai did not believe this claim for a moment, and busied his own men in preparation for the inevitable conflict once the snows had thawed.

In the summer of 1261, one of Khubilai's best generals arrived, dusty and exhausted after crossing a desert, with news of a defeat at the hands of Arigh Boke's men. As expected, the rebel leader had appeared with claims that he was surrendering, only to fall upon Yesungge's forces in a crushing rout. Yesungge appears to have left his entire army on the other side of the desert, and was hence not a participant in the rematch between Khubilai's forces and those of Arigh Boke, fought beside a midge-infested, brackish lake at the edge of the Gobi Desert. This time, the battle went in Khubilai's favour, and Arigh Boke's men were soon in retreat. True to the merciful form he had shown in China and Dali, Khubilai reined in his troops from hounding the fleeing forces: 'Do not pursue them, for they are ignorant children. They must realize what they have done and repent.'[11]

However, the 'children' had not yet learned their lesson. Ten days later, Khubilai's forces were engaged in another battle, this time against a son of Mongke, coming to blows 'after midday on the edge of the sand desert called Elet'.

The blunt recitation of the facts in most chronicles draws a gentle veil over the consequences. The fight was indeed 'at the edge of the desert', but during the week after the first battle both sides seem to have been drawn far deeper into the sands that that might imply. One wing of Arigh Boke's army collapsed, but the rest held on; as night fell, Khubilai's forces withdrew. Both sides must have known the awful consequences – it was possible, just within the realm of chance, that mounted riders might be able to make it out of the desert in the cool of the night. For anyone on foot, or deprived of their horse, the following dawn would be a lingering death sentence, marooned in the badlands, with no remaining supplies. Rashid al-Din's history offers what at first appears to be a contradictory statement: 'Both princes now *retired with their armies* and went to their own ordos, while *most of their troops perished* because of the great distance and their being on foot.'[12]

In other words, both Khubilai and his rival made their getaway with their cavalry – that is, with their personal Mongol entourages. The footsoldiers – in Khubilai's case, mainly comprising some 15,000 conscripts from north China – were left to their deaths.

Arigh Boke's desperation was to prove his undoing. He sent agents to grab supplies from Prince Alghu, a descendant of Temujin's second son Chaghadai. When Alghu tried to stop them taking quite so much, they unwisely snapped that it was of no concern of his, and that it was his duty to uphold the will of Arigh Boke, his ruler.

Whatever happened in the course of the argument, Alghu went too far, so much so that his own advisers were recorded telling him that he had insulted a princess (someone's mother – it is not clear whose), disobeyed Arigh Boke and undoubtedly incurred the wrath of his former ally. Believing, for some reason, that there was no way he could make amends with Arigh Boke, Alghu instead executed the arrogant emissaries, and announced he was defecting to Khubilai's faction. That at least is the official story – though it makes a lot more sense if we assume that Alghu killed the envoys, and *then* realized that he had gone too far.

Arigh Boke was furious, executing the messenger that brought this news, and turning instead on the Muslim and Christian communities at Karakorum, demanding that they donate supplies to his war effort. Coming up fairly empty-handed, he scornfully told the foreigners that he was counting on their prayers for victory, but that if Khubilai won the next battle, he was sure his enemy could count on their 'support'.

Arigh Boke marched off against Alghu, partly to chastise him for his supposed treachery, but largely because he had nowhere else to go. Alghu was a weaker foe than Khubilai, and Arigh Boke was now reduced to taking the path of least resistance and simply stealing supplies. Khubilai retook Karakorum, and Arigh Boke's support gradually dwindled as he reached the edge of the steppes.

By the end of 1263, more bad weather had caused many more defections from Arigh Boke's cause. One of Mongke's surviving sons asked Arigh Boke if he could have his father's precious jade seal and, on receiving it, marched off to join Khubilai's camp. By the end, the horses were starving along with their riders, and Arigh Boke was not even able to drink in his tent in peace:

> One day Arigh Boke was carousing and making merry when a whirlwind suddenly sprang up, ripped the thousand-pegged audience tent, and broke the supporting pole, with the result that a number of people were hurt and wounded. The ministers and emirs of his court took this occurrence as an omen predicting the decline of his fortune. They abandoned him altogether and dispersed on all sides . . .[13]

The Mongol sanctity of one's hearth had been directly challenged. If Arigh Boke could not even feel safe under his own roof, what protection could he offer his subjects?

By 1264, Arigh Boke faced battle on two fronts, with Khubilai in the east and a resurgent Alghu in the west. He literally had nowhere left to go, and marched in defeat to Khubilai's base at Kaiping, now openly called Shangdu, the upper capital. There, after an ominous silence, the brothers embraced, and Khubilai offered generously: 'Dear brother, in this strife and contention, were we in the right, or were you?' Arigh Boke sullenly replied that he had been in the right all along, but now that Khubilai had the upper hand, the situation had changed in his favour. It was merely the first of several embittered exchanges in Khubilai's presence, as the survivors of the family conflict sized each other up. A prince, Ajiqi, realized that a relative in Arigh Boke's entourage had been the slayer of his brother, and challenged him. In bold Mongol fashion, the killer replied that he had been following the orders of his then leader, Arigh Boke – now that Khubilai was unquestionably Khan, he would happily follow new orders and kill Ajiqi, too.

'This is not the time for such words,' cautioned Khubilai. 'There is violent anger in them.' With many princes on their feet and angry language already exchanged, it was left to another prince to remind the throng that the meeting was about a proclamation of peace, and not continued war. With the uneasy agreement to let bygones be bygones, the two rival factions settled down for a drunken evening.

The truce barely lasted into the next day. The following morning, Khubilai's lieutenants dragged Arigh Boke before Khubilai with his hands bound, and he was subjected to an inquisition. Arigh Boke boldly asserted that his followers had committed no crime, and that if anyone had been in the wrong it was he alone. Khubilai, however, noted that it was rather late to pretend that the civil war had been over a mere misunderstanding, and that even if it had been, that was no excuse for conflict. Khubilai recalled, for the benefit of those who might have forgotten, that in the days of the rule of their brother Mongke, 'the emirs of the time did not string a single bow against him, and there was no great revolt, only a little discord which they harboured in their hearts.'[14]

The defeated rebel leaders listened to him in silence, all except one, Tumen Noyan, who reminded his associates of their boasts during the glory days:

> Have your eloquent tongues become mute? That day when we set Arigh Boke upon the throne we promised each other that we should die in front of that throne. Today is that day of dying. Let us keep our word.[15]

Khubilai praised Noyan for his words, and wryly told him that his promise was sure to be kept. However, this was by no means the end of the trial of Arigh Boke. Khubilai's interrogation stretched on and on, and Arigh Boke's original shouldering of the responsibility soon collapsed into finger pointing and recriminations. Khubilai and the inquisitors seem to have been deliberately, gingerly, picking through the chain of command of the rebel princes, in an attempt to divide their relatives into categories of willing accomplices or loyal dupes. The former would pay with their lives; the latter would be forgiven for merely doing what they had thought was their duty to the false Khan.

Pointedly, although Khubilai could have ordered summary executions, he seems reluctant to have done so without the unanimous agreement of all the family members in his faction. Hence, the trial of Arigh Boke played out as a *kurultai* in reverse, with Khubilai's first act as unopposed Khan oddly transforming into a delegation of his powers to a family council. Eventually, Khubilai became so wary of the need for a consensus that he ordered an official *kurultai*, and waited for his powerful brothers and cousins to assemble and add legitimacy to his purges of the Mongol clans. Arigh Boke languished in confinement while the months turned into years, as Khubilai's distant brethren fobbed him off with excuses, both real and otherwise. In 1266, after the deaths of Hulagu, Berke and Alghu, the need to appease those high-ranking nobles was diminished. Brothers and cousins were one thing, but nephews and second cousins were lower in rank, and owed Khubilai respect as a matter of course. It is, perhaps, no coincidence that Arigh Boke died of unknown causes in 1266, while still awaiting a proper trial. He was still only in his forties, and poison remains a viable suspicion. Whatever killed Arigh Boke, it was a boon for Khubilai, who was finally able to accept the acclamation of the Mongol lords, and to rise to the rank of Great Khan.

However, one prominent noble was conspicuously absent. Prince Khaidu (1230–1301) was descended from two sons of Temujin – he was the grandson of Ogodei, and somehow also descended from Khubilai's uncle Chaghadai – and hence represented the dangerous potential to unite two houses. Considering Khaidu's double ancestry, Khubilai was only senior to him by a hair's breadth, and there were already murmurings that, should Khubilai die or prove 'worthless',

Khaidu would be a better candidate for his replacement than one of Khubilai's own sons. With a view to at least keeping things civil for the moment, Khubilai sent a polite invitation to his cousin:

> The other princes have all presented themselves here: why have you not come? It is my heart's desire that we should brighten our eyes with the sight of one another.[16]

Khaidu's response was innocent enough. He pleaded that the animals of his herd were half-starved, and needed considerable fattening up before he could start the slow journey to the east to pay homage. This excuse persisted throughout the 1260s, but concealed dangerous plotting that Khubilai would eventually have to confront. Neither his problems in Mongolia nor his problems in the south were anywhere near over.

5

A PLAGUE UPON THE THRONE

THE YANGTZE CAMPAIGN

At some point during this period, Khubilai and his favourite wife Chabi discovered a mutual love of Chinese history. Surrounded by Chinese ministers eager to cite precedents, one or both of them soon noticed that the same figures were recurring with great frequency. When Khubilai marvelled at the submission of the Koreans, and in doing so compared himself to the Tang emperor Taizong, he had not plucked the allusion out of thin air. Far from it; he and Chabi appear to have become great fans of the early Tang dynasty, and to have spent much time listening to stories of China's glory days.[1]

It is easy to see why. The Tang dynasty was forged in blood in the early seventh century, founded on the ruins of a short-lived predecessor. With strong ties to horse-riding clans, the family of the Duke of Tang rose up against their cousins and seized control of the empire. The 'founder' of the Tang dynasty was considered less instrumental in this than his young, dynamic son: the warrior remembered under the reign title

Taizong, who not only egged his father on in the succession dispute, but then contended against his own flesh and blood for the right to inherit it. In an infamous incident, the young Taizong murdered two brothers in a fight at the northern gate of the Chinese capital, leaving the throne open to him. He pursued wars against the Turks and Koreans, and presided over the greatest extent of Chinese imperial territory up to that time. He was a textbook figure for any would-be emperor to follow, widely regarded as the greatest Chinese emperor, and praised by many generations of scholars for his famous habit of listening to their advice. For these reasons, both Chabi and Khubilai appeared to adore him. Chabi, in particular, seems to have assumed not only that all Chinese rulers should behave like Taizong, but that his officials should behave like Taizong's officials. With that in mind, she once badgered Khubilai's advisers into standing up to him over an unpopular, pro-Mongol policy, reminding them that it was part of their job.

The couple's interest in Taizong, the first truly great emperor of China's greatest preceding dynasty, was sure to have been a major influence in their decision, apparently taken in mutual agreement, that the best way for Khubilai to rule China was to take on the institutions and practices not of a Mongol conqueror, but of a rightfully mandated Chinese emperor. The Great Khan Mongke might have been the ruler of the world, but if Khubilai wished to truly rule his Chinese section of it, he would have to go native in the most spectacular way, by becoming 'Chinese'.

In 1261, while Khubilai was still embroiled in the succession dispute with Arigh Boke, he received word of a new problem in northern China. Li Tan, an official in Shandong province who had previously paid lip service to the Mongols, had now been revealed as a fair-weather friend.

During Mongke and Khubilai's ill-fated attack on the Southern Song, Li Tan had been in their service as the leader of one of the smaller subsidiary armies. He was an unknown quantity, but he was married to the daughter of a Chinese turncoat whom Khubilai much admired, and hence had an easy path into military service. It had been his task to lead his force of Chinese soldiers down the coast from Shandong, in order to give the Southern Song yet another invasion to worry about. With Khubilai and the other Mongols drawing the main Southern Song defences away, Li Tan had found his progress along the coast largely unimpeded, and he had racked up great gains for himself. In 1260, when Khubilai had first aspired to the title of Great Khan, he had rewarded Li Tan for his previous successes by promoting him to military commissioner of the region. Although still technically an underling of a pacification commissioner, Li Tan became the vice-commander of an area the size of modern France, and his communiqués with Khubilai made him seem to be the ideal subject.

Soon afterwards, Li Tan sent word to Khubilai that Jia Sidao, his nemesis in the south, was preparing a counter-attack against his flank with 75,000 soldiers and an armada of 2,000 boats. He claimed to have extracted this information from captured Southern Song officers, and requested Khubilai's help.

Still preoccupied with Arigh Boke, Khubilai sent the best help he could – 300 solid silver ingots to pay for a refortification programme on the shore. He vetoed a request by Li Tan to renew the assault on the Southern Song, presumably on the assumption that when the time came to topple the dynasty, Khubilai wished to be seen as the man to do it. However, such action left Li Tan as the effective duke of a massive, wealthy region of China, the site of the nation's holiest mountain, with strong infrastructure and self-sufficient industries.

In 1261, Li Tan mounted a successful 'defence' of his borders at Lingzhou. The terminology was carefully chosen to make it appear as if he were obeying Khubilai's orders to the letter. In fact, he had marched out to 'meet' suspected Song invaders, and hence might equally be argued to have done exactly what Khubilai had told him not to do: invading Southern Song territory once more. Preoccupied with the war with Arigh Boke, Khubilai and his advisers misread Li Tan's victories against the Southern Song as the mark of a loyal subject, and sent further rewards. Understanding that Li Tan was busy holding the border, Khubilai did not even grumble when Li Tan's mandated tribute of horses for the fight against Arigh Boke failed to show up.

During the winter of 1261–2, Li Tan's son disappeared from Khubilai's court. The young man had been a hostage, held like others to ensure the continued loyalty of Khubilai's vassals. Suddenly he was nowhere to be found. The boy soon turned up in Shandong itself, where Li Tan's true colours were suddenly revealed. In a lightning strike in February 1262, Li Tan's Chinese soldiers turned with murderous fury on the skeleton crew of Mongol wardens and officials in Shandong. Li Tan broke into government granaries and handed out supplies to his people. To add insult to injury, he then turned over the border cities of Lianzhou and Haizhou to the Southern Song.

This not only drastically reversed the 'gains' he had previously claimed, but also placed new Southern Song strongholds far to the north at the edge of Shandong province, in walled, heavily defended cities – whose fortification Khubilai Khan had paid for with his own money.

Khubilai did not deal with Li Tan himself, but sent two of his more loyal turncoat Chinese generals to stamp out the unrest. The story was big enough news to attract the attention of Marco Polo:

> But the affair was a serious one, for the Barons were met by the rebel Liytan with all those whom he had collected from the province, mustering more than 100,000 horse and a large force of foot. Nevertheless in the battle Liytan and his party were utterly routed, and the two Barons whom the Emperor had sent won the victory.[2]

By spring 1262, Li Tan was on the run and losing support. By the summer, he was on his own; he was apprehended near a lake where he was attempting to drown himself. He was rescued by his Mongol pursuers, and then, in a rather dramatic flourish, condemned to death anyway. Polo wrote:

> When the news came to the Great Kaan, he was right well pleased, and ordered that all the chiefs who had rebelled, or excited others to rebel, should be put to a cruel death, but that those of lower rank should receive a pardon. And so it was done. The two Barons had all the leaders of the enterprise put to a cruel death, and all those of lower rank were pardoned. And thenceforward they conducted themselves with loyalty towards their lord.[3]

Refused permission to take his own life, Li Tan was a member of the enemy nobility, and subject to a Mongol superstition about shedding the blood of royalty. Consequently he was rolled up in a carpet (or thrown in a sack, sources differ) and then trampled to death by Mongol horsemen.

Suspecting that Li Tan could never have undertaken his rebellion without inside help, Khubilai soon found incriminating letters between the dead rebel and his father-in-law, Khubilai's trusted adviser Wang Wendong. Wang had been a valued member of Khubilai's cabinet, an architect of both the taxation and paper money systems that had helped bankroll the war with Arigh Boke. However, it seemed that he was a Song loyalist at heart, turning his service to Khubilai into an act of wily Chinese espionage, setting the Mongols against each other in order to leave the Chinese with a future advantage.

Khubilai was all the more shocked at Wang's betrayal. A rebel commander switching sides on the border was one thing, but it hardly compared with the discovery that one of his inner circle had harboured such a vendetta against him. After years of struggle against his own people, Khubilai was furious to discover that his adopted people, the Chinese, also despised him. Wang was executed along with his son in the wake of the Li Tan affair, but Khubilai arranged for his sentencing to be carried out by Chinese officials. This was Khubilai's way of reminding his subjects that the rebels had not only betrayed the Mongols, but the Chinese themselves – who deserved Mongol unifiers, rather than the hopeless, tail-end dregs of the Song dynasty.

Although it was a minor uprising in Chinese history, gone and forgotten within four months, and overshadowed by far more spectacular wars elsewhere in Khubilai's realm, the Li Tan affair would have wide-ranging consequences. In a sense, it marked the end of Khubilai's love affair with things Chinese. Betrayed by one of his most prominent Chinese advisers, Khubilai remained wary of Chinese officials ever after. If Khubilai could not trust the Chinese not to harbour regicidal urges, then he would have to dilute their influence, even in their own country. He would lean more on non-Chinese officials: not only Mongols, but men from faraway lands. The Gobi Desert and the Uighur realms of Central Asia had been loyal to the Mongols for much longer than north China, and Khubilai began to favour ministers from those regions. In Khubilai's disappointment over the Li Tan affair, we see the origins of a cosmopolitan empire, in which posts would be open in the most unexpected places for foreign candidates. For example, two decades later, when the Italian Marco Polo takes a civil service post in a Chinese city in Khubilai's service, he does so because he is one of these foreign officials, and he does so as part of a system deliberately designed to dilute the power and influence of the Chinese.

Khubilai's disappointment at the Li Tan affair can be seen in some of the policies implemented in the early days of his rule. Traitors were to be executed, and Khubilai offered a brief amnesty period for any Chinese doubters to work out which side they wanted to be on. After years stuck in the middle between the two societies, Khubilai's new system carefully amalgamated what he thought to be the best of both worlds.

Outside China, in the Mongol heartland and points further west, the Mongol princes were still in charge. Their fiefdoms were subject to periodic inspections by Khubilai's auditors, but otherwise they were often given relatively free rein, their administrations reduced in numbers to bring down expenses, and their loyalty a matter of Mongol duty towards a senior clansman: Khubilai Khan. Like his predecessors, Khubilai's best hope of maintaining order through this system was to ensure that all potential rebels were killed off before they could rise to a position of responsibility. The purges following the defeat of Arigh Boke appeared to have achieved this, although there were rumblings and rumours from the domain of Khaidu, the grandson of Ogodei.

Although Khubilai was welcomed and acclaimed as Great Khan, and nominally the ruler of all Asia, his reach into the west grew steadily weaker. In the realm of the Golden Horde (western Russia), the Ilkhanate (Persia) and the Chaghadai Khanate (the Taklamakan and what is now Xinjiang), powerful rulers were effectively left to their own devices, expressing cordial respect for their Great Khan, but unchallenged within their realms. They were, in essence, loyal to Khubilai – as long as he never put that loyalty to the test.

Instead, he counted on exploiting his position in the east, where institutions were already in place that would allow him to rule more directly. As had always been the plan all along, now that Khubilai was the Great Khan to the Mongols, he intended to also become the Emperor of all the Chinese.

In north China, Khubilai reduced the tax burden. He was able to achieve this, at least in part, by maintaining a government monopoly on salt and iron, effectively laying claim to the Chinese people's rightful possessions while they were still in the ground in raw form, and then selling them back to them. He also continued the circulation of paper money, which allowed the government to pay off all the debts it needed to, although Khubilai still seemed unaware of the likelihood of inflation. Khubilai's administrators within northern China were told to pander to some extent to the wishes of the Chinese population. After all, there was still the Southern Song to worry about, and Khubilai was determined to give the impression over the border that he was a legitimate, worthy and 'Chinese' successor to the throne of all China. He even allowed his ministers to debate the merits of reinstating the civil examination system, giving every indication that it was in the works, although it would never be reintroduced while Khubilai was alive.

His administration also tiptoed around the unpleasant reality that the Chinese greatly outnumbered the Mongols, by perhaps five to one in the north. In the realm of the Southern Song, which was home to another 50 million people, the Mongols would be diluted even further, so that if Khubilai conquered all of China, the Mongols would be outnumbered by perhaps twenty to one, and spread much more thinly. With that in mind, Khubilai could simply not afford to operate without the general support of his conquered peoples. It was not enough to attack them with terror and atrocity in the manner of Temujin – the comments on 'ruling from horseback' had never been better appreciated. But his aim, in part, was also to present a magnanimous face to the peoples of the Southern Song, to gradually introduce the idea that the Song had lost the Mandate of Heaven, and that it was he who could be their rightful new ruler. He was encouraged in this by his Confucian advisers, who cited maxims of Confucian statecraft about the power of a benevolent ruler to attract new subjects. Just as his uncle Ogodei Khan had been persuaded that a warrior could fleece his victims in a piecemeal fashion by harvesting tribute from them, Khubilai Khan was ready to take matters a step further, and to adopt the Confucian principle that the perfect state would not need to actively conquer new territory. Instead, peripheral nations would beg to be let in.

Khubilai's advisers avoided the other side of this coin, which was that comments from the work of Confucius about attracting new vassals were aimed largely at winning the hearts and minds of barbarians on the borderlands – in other words, the likes of the Mongols and their ancestors. Nor did they dwell on the fact that such leading by example was expected to take generations. Their dealings in both north and south China could be said to reflect a rather hopeful, doomed idealism, when compared to the brutal realism that Khubilai was sure to introduce if they kept him waiting too long.[4]

In 1260, an impatient Khubilai had sent his adviser Hao Jing as an envoy to the Southern Song to offer a peaceful resolution: the Southern Song should accept that Khubilai was the uncontested Son of Heaven. This would require, of course, the abdication of the Southern Song Emperor but would otherwise leave things much as they were. Southern Song lands could then be incorporated within the Mongol Empire, and the aristocracy of the Song rebranded as Khubilai's dukes and earls. There would, of course, be some supervision, and taxes would be redirected to a new home, but otherwise war would be averted. The ambassador arrived armed with ample precedents from Chinese history, when Chinese rulers (including earlier emperors of the Song) had bought off, rather than fought off, 'barbarian' threats – implying that this was really just another of those situations, the only real difference being that the barbarians would not be going away, but taking over.

Hao Jing's embassy made its case to Jia Sidao, the powerful minister who had already seen off a previous Mongol invasion. Hao added a testimonial of his own, Chinese to Chinese, to the effect that Khubilai was acting in the most Chinese manner imaginable. Hao pleaded that Khubilai was a ruler surrounded by Confucian advisers, and running a Chinese-style system. This Chinese side to Khubilai's character was the Southern Song's best hope of survival. If they resisted him, Khubilai would show his Mongol side, and descend upon the Southern Song in a merciless holocaust.

An indignant Jia Sidao ordered that the emissaries be detained in Hangzhou, although notably he did not rashly invite certain death by ordering their executions. Despite this obvious setback, Khubilai and his advisers continued their charm offensive over the following years. The immediate beneficiaries were Song dynasty merchants, who had been carrying out cross-border commerce on routes that predated the north–south split. Apprehended on the north side of the Yangtze and suspected of being spies or criminals, they were eventually freed, on the understanding that they were simply Chinese merchants trading goods with other Chinese merchants. Under Khubilai's rule, it was strongly implied, they would be free to cross the Yangtze whenever they wished, and hence in anticipation of that long-awaited day seventy-five were freed in 1261, forty more in 1262 and another fifty-seven in 1264.

The tense standoff on the border was a cause of concern for Khubilai. For every great gesture from his court, there was another misunderstanding or skirmish on the frontier. In 1264, he reprimanded some of his soldiers for executing two defecting Song generals – the troops saw only vulnerable former enemies, whereas Khubilai clearly wished to encourage such defections, and was furious that his own men had made the option less attractive to disillusioned Song officers.

Nevertheless, Khubilai should have expected tensions to run high on the border. Throughout the early 1260s there were repeated clashes at the Yangtze frontier, often on the wide waters of the river, where the Song navy offered strong resistance to the land-bound Mongols. Moreover, it was the Song who were unquestionably on the offensive, with the strength of Mongol defences tested by 'border raids' whose lowly title belied their true nature. Song border raids took months to plan and were often executed as major military operations.

Khubilai could not afford to wait. Despite taking on the trappings of Chinese civilization, the engine that drove his state still had a Mongol heart. He needed to keep expanding, and to keep winning, in order to have new wealth and lands to distribute, new slaves to put to work, and to keep the attention of his subjects focused outwards. Hence, the first great enterprise of Khubilai's new hybrid system was not the simple running of the state, but gearing up for the invasion of the south.

As abortive earlier efforts had already shown, Mongols were unsuited for life in the hot, disease-ridden south. It had, after all, been the climate that killed Mongke. Mongol cavalry was unstoppable on open plains, but greatly disadvantaged on mountains, in forests and wading through the waterlogged, swamp-like paddy fields that made up much of the southern Chinese land. Worst of all, Mongol horses achieved much of their success by requiring relatively low maintenance. In the steppes, they could often be simply left to graze, but in the heavily populated, rice-growing south, there simply were not enough meadows for a horde's worth of horses to graze on.

It did not help that the Song had ships. Hangzhou was a seaport, and the safest towns in Southern Song territory thrived as entrepôts for foreign goods. Shipbuilding was something that the Southern Song still did remarkably well, and that made the Yangtze frontier much harder for the Mongols to cross on a mere whim. Previous Mongol amphibian assaults had relied on impromptu measures or captured boats. Now, Khubilai was determined to have a mobile force that could transport its troops across the critical bodies of water that circled the north and east of the Song domain, and, more importantly, stop supplies from reaching the Song towns from the sea. With the Yangtze offering a countrywide barrier, thousands of troops to move and the Song heartland in possession of thousands of miles of unthreatened coastline, Khubilai needed a navy.

The seed of his new military outfit was obtained from the enemy in 1265, in the form of 146 ships captured from the Southern Song in a battle so far up the Yangtze river that it was practically on the borders of Sichuan. These ships, and others like them, formed the nucleus of the attack force employed against the city of Xiangyang in 1268 – the opening skirmish of Khubilai's grand scheme to bring the Southern Song down.

Xiangyang sat on the banks of the Han River, a tributary of the Yangtze and an important strategic position. Its inhabitants were plainly expecting trouble, and had expanded the width of the river, moving the water's edge some 200 metres 'inland'.

This proved to be a worthwhile scheme, as the Mongols arrived with a hundred trebuchets, whose range and effectiveness were greatly reduced by the widened river. Moreover, the inhabitants of Xiangyang had put up heavy nets along the walls, forcing the trebuchets to fire higher in order to hit the town beyond.

Khubilai's soldiers, led by both Chinese and Mongol generals, swiftly ringed Xiangyang with a network of forts, in anticipation of the inevitable counter-attacks by reinforcements from elsewhere in the Song territory. This double siege endured for several years, with the population of Xiangyang working through large supplies of provisions behind their walls, and the Mongols fighting off several relief efforts. There appear to have been times when Xiangyang's occupants were able to restock, escape and even return, which makes the Mongols' description of the town being securely enclosed for five years seem economical with the truth.

When it became clear in October 1268 that the Mongols were not only settling in for the long haul, but bringing ships to blockade Xiangyang's supply, the warriors of the city made a desperate breakout that failed with much loss of life. The first relief effort in 1269 failed to break through the Mongol blockade, which not only used ships, but also stone platforms sunk in the river's course, from which soldiers could open fire on ships as they closed in.[5]

Khubilai remained impatient. He had not expected Xiangyang to hold out for quite so long, and he soon sent another 20,000 troops, two *tumans*, to join the besiegers. A year later, he sent another 70,000 men, baffled at the continued success of the Chinese defenders.

Behind the scenes, Jia Sidao threw everything he had at propping up the defence of Xiangyang. It was not only a case of its undeniable strategic value: he had also assured his Emperor that the Mongols would not take it. Consequently, there were numerous rewards, accolades and promotions available to anyone who would run the gauntlet of Mongol attackers, smuggle in communications to the defenders, or otherwise volunteer for dangerous missions to keep the Mongols busy. In the meantime, he did everything he could to keep news of the siege from the Song Emperor. This careful manipulation was ruined by one of the Emperor's own concubines, who paid with her life when she blurted the news that the Mongols had not already retreated as Jia had claimed, but were still awaiting the fall of the town.

In 1272, a valiant effort by 2,000 Song men successfully smashed through the Mongol blockade on the Han River, and delivered much-needed supplies. However, their leader was captured in the process, and much of the vital supplies was lost en route. Moreover, the Song attack exploited a weakness in the Mongol defences that was swiftly patched up. Although the relief force was a great morale boost to the defenders, its very success led to the soldiers being trapped within the town along with the people they had been sent to supply. None of them were able to get out to inform the Song of the mission's success, ironically leading the Song to give up on sending any similar relief forces to the town.

Unaware that the Southern Song's will to resist was finally waning, an exasperated Khubilai called on new foreign assistance. He sent a message to his nephew Abaqa, son of the late Hulagu in Persia, asking for engineers skilled in siege warfare. In 1272, the long-awaited experts arrived. What happened next is a matter of some argument. The bare facts are simple enough – the siege engineers from Persia surveyed the scene in Xiangyang, and swiftly got to work building monstrously huge counter-weight trebuchets, or mangonels. These new weapons, taking months to complete, dwarfed the old trebuchets, and before long the Mongol besiegers had twenty of them, each able to sling a 300-lb rock more than 1,500 feet. Suddenly, the widened river was no defence, and the nets atop the walls were unable to stop any of the missiles.

The mangonels were put to work first against Xiangyang's nearby sister city of Fancheng, which fell soon after. The Mongols fell on the inhabitants, killing all 3,000 soldiers, and then turning on the non-combatants, women and children. In all, some 10,000 corpses were piled up in a massive mound, within sight of Xiangyang.

The engineers then dismantled their mangonels and reassembled them within range of Xiangyang itself, whose walls soon crumbled 'like sand' beyond the relentless bombardment.

The giant mangonels brought the siege of Xiangyang to a swift end, but who were their builders? Chinese sources call the weapons *Huihui pao*, or 'Muslim firearms' – suggesting some sort of explosive component, possibly flaming naptha or 'Greek fire'; Rashid al-Din, on the other hand, calls them *manjaniq ifranji*, or 'Frankish mangonels', and said that their builders had got their design after observing Crusaders at work in the distant Holy Land. It is generally assumed that the mangonels' *design* was Frankish (i.e. European), not their builders. Chinese sources name two Muslim builders, Ismail and Ala al-Din. Persian accounts name instead a man from Damascus, 'Talib the mangonel maker', with his three sons, Abu Bakr, Ibrahim and Mohammed.[6] In a dismal failure of credibility, the book of Marco Polo claims that the three engineers were Marco himself, his father and uncle, with a couple of unnamed European friends:

> The Great Khan had sent back word that take it they must, and find a way how. Then spoke up the two brothers and Messer Marco the son, and said; 'Great Prince, we have with us among our followers men who are able to construct mangonels which shall cast such great stones that the garrison will never be able to stand them, but will surrender . . .' And they had two men among their followers, a German and a Nestorian Christian, who were masters of that business, and these they directed to construct two or three mangonels, each of which cast stones of 300 lbs.[7]

This mendacious account has been a blot on Polo's record ever since. He was not even in China at the time of the fall of

Xiangyang, nor at any point in his life did he again demonstrate any aptitude for siege warfare. In Polo's defence, the pages of his book that describe the siege of Xiangyang are entirely out of character with the style of the rest of the text. Polo very rarely mentions himself in his writings, but the text levers him and his relatives into the siege of Xiangyang on four occasions in the space of less than a page. This alone is enough to suggest that the section of his text on Xiangyang is heavily corrupt, and not to be either trusted or blamed on him.

Xiangyang surrendered in March 1272, some five years after the siege began. Its collapse was a blow to the defences of the Southern Song, and to the reputation of Jia Sidao, who was then obliged to boost his public profile by volunteering to lead the next line of defence. Desperately casting around for sufficient funds, Jia tried to levy a new tax on Buddhist and Taoist monasteries, costing him the support of China's religious heartland.

In 1273, Khubilai took steps to consolidate the command of the forces attacking the Southern Song. He did so under the advice of his ailing childhood friend Shi Tianzi, now a commander of the expedition force, who was concerned about the inefficiency of resources and strategy brought about by the presence of so many different commanders. Accordingly, Khubilai appointed a supreme general, Bayan (1236–95), a veteran of the wars in Persia. Bayan was Khubilai's ablest commander in the field and an obvious choice, although Khubilai does not seem to have been aware of the implications of his appointment. According to a popular legend, a prophecy among the ruling family of the Southern Song held that they would reign supreme until 'a man with a hundred eyes would rob them of their kingdom'. Quite by coincidence, 'a Hundred Eyes' in Chinese is *bai-yan*.

This was news to all concerned. Bayan was a Turk, and his name came from an Arabic phrase, literally 'the Expositor' or 'Clarifier of Meaning'. Among the Chinese he wrote his name with characters that meant 'A Duke's Countenance'. The

'Hundred Eyes' pun soon grew with the telling, until, in later generations, legends arose that had the Chinese surrendering as soon as they heard of his approach.

Matters did not quite work out in that way in the real world. In fact, the Chinese resolutely resisted Bayan, and at first he appeared to have little interest in confronting them. Freed up from the long-running siege of Xiangyang, the bulk of his army marched along the side of the Yangtze, or drifted downstream in the newly acquired boats of the navy. Bayan's advance parties would ride up to each new town and demand its immediate surrender, adding a stern warning about the reputation of the Mongols – both for cordial treatment of the submissive, and brutal punishment of the disobedient. If the town refused, the advance guard would then depart, secure in the knowledge that overwhelming numbers of Mongol soldiers were close behind them, ready to lay siege to the town.

This dual approach made Bayan's downriver march remarkably rapid. Although pockets of his army dropped out to besiege towns along the route, the general aspect was one of constant progress. In January 1275 he ran into Jia Sidao's army close to the major metropolis of Yangzhou. The inexperienced Jia ordered his men straight into the path of Bayan's catapults, which rained destruction down upon the Southern Song defenders.

Jia survived the battle, but not the aftermath. Drummed out of office by annoyed courtiers, he was accused of appeasing the Mongols when he should have stood firm, and appeasing the Emperor when he should have spoken the truth about the situation. He also took the blame for putting the wrong sort of officer in charge of the military, although arguably his incentive scheme in Xiangyang had put a large number of very brave and committed men into the field. A national embarrassment, Jia was packed off to an obscure posting in the south-western province of Fujian, but died en route in suspicious circumstances, seemingly murdered by his Song-appointed bodyguards.

Bayan put a detachment of his army on to the siege of Yangzhou and continued with his race downstream, the capital of Hangzhou now within his sights. A warning arrived from Khubilai, warning Bayan not to commit atrocities or despoil the region he had taken. Luckily for all concerned, this was much easier for Bayan than for any other general, as the Mongols enjoyed an unhindered supply route along the length of the Yangtze. In short, Bayan would not need to take anything that did not belong to him, and the Mongol charm offensive was swiftly brought to bear on the surrendered towns. By the time Bayan was outside the gates of Hangzhou, many of the suppliers of provisions to the 'Mongol' army were newly defected merchants who had until recently been subjects of the Southern Song. Khubilai's mission of many years, to persuade the Chinese that he was not an invader but a better emperor, was paying off. He took his role of unifier so seriously that he was not above officially recruiting newly surrendered soldiers to his own cause. Rashid al-Din preserves an edict delivered in Khubilai's name to 'prisoners', a group likely to comprise freed inmates from Song jails, as well as captured soldiers in Mongol custody:

> You are all destined to die and be killed. For your heads' sake I have set you free and I will give you horses, arms and clothing and send you to the army. If you exert yourselves you will become emirs and men of standing.[8]

However, although Bayan's army was indeed swelled by many turncoats, a significant number of Southern Song loyalists refused to give in. The thirty-four-year-old Song Emperor had died, leaving the beleaguered empire in the hands of his four-year-old son. In a chaotic state, the reins of power now passed to the dual regency of the infant ruler's mother and grandmother – Empress Dowager Quan and Grand Empress Dowager Xie. The latter woman in particular would prove to be a thorn in the Mongols' side, since she not only proved eminently capable, but also charismatic. In a stinging decree of 1275, she repudiated all of Khubilai's carefully argued propaganda about his suitability to take over. In doing so, she not only scoffed at his credentials, but also noted that China had often endured barbarian invasions in the past. However, at no point in history, she said, had *all* of China succumbed to invaders. The Mandate of Heaven would never be handed over to a barbarian, no matter how many Chinese advisers surrounded him. The Grand Empress Dowager Xie proclaimed:

> The emperor has died and the successor is but an infant. [In spite of] my old age and decrepitude I reluctantly took charge of state affairs from behind the curtain . . . How infuriating are these ugly caitiffs who have trespassed the Yangtze River. Bypassing our barricades and reaching our hilltops, they seduced our recalcitrant subjects and violated the obedient. Since ancient times there has not yet been an age of total barbarian conquest. How has it come to this present state that deviates from the constants of Heaven and Earth? . . . Three hundred years of virtuous rule – surely that has made an impression on the people . . . Those worthy men with loyal livers and righteous galls, come forth and combat the forces that plague the throne and submit your skills.[9]

In fact, the Empress Dowager's claims were bordering on the facetious. On several occasions in the Chinese past, the throne had fallen to dynasties whose ancestors had been regarded, at least at first, as little better than barbarians. The first man to call himself Emperor of China, Qin Shihuangdi, had been from a semi-barbarous western state that had risen to prominence through its mastery of cavalry. Similarly, the short-lived Sui dynasty of the sixth century, and their cousins of the longer Tang dynasty were all closely tied to horse-riding clans.

While the Grand Empress Dowager split hairs, she also split heirs. She sent the infant emperors' two princely brothers off to relative safety in the south. She, however, remained in

Hangzhou, from where she sent an envoy in 1275 to tardily offer the payment of tribute. It was an ironic repetition of the situation with Jia Sidao years earlier (and miles upriver) – why would the Mongols agree to sell back that which they had already taken? Moreover, while Bayan was under orders to show mercy, he was ready to remind the Grand Empress Dowager that her regime had executed one envoy and detained another. Only an unconditional surrender would do.

As the end of the year approached, the Grand Empress Dowager capitulated, and sent the imperial seal to Bayan. It was, at least officially, a gesture of surrender, although Bayan did not discover until afterwards about the fugitive claimants already heading south. Nevertheless, the southern resistance could wait: for now, the capital of the Song was finally in Mongol hands, and Bayan was under stern instructions to make good on Khubilai's word that collaborators with the new regime would have cause to be thankful.

The infant emperor, still too young to really comprehend what was going on, was deprived of his imperial title and created a duke in Khubilai's realm. Eventually, he would be packed off to a monastery in Tibet, while his mother and grandmother were placed in genteel confinement in palaces in Beijing. The Song heartland was in Khubilai's hands, and the last of the Song dynasty were already on the run towards the south.

6

BEGINNING

THE YUAN DYNASTY

Khubilai did not wait for the news of the capture or deaths of the fugitive princes. In fact, he did not even wait for the fall of Hangzhou. In 1271, when Xiangyang was still under siege, Khubilai pre-empted the fall of the Southern Song by proclaiming the establishment of a new dynasty. In a gesture of respect to his forebears, he also retroactively conferred imperial status on Mongke, Ogodei, Guyuk and Temujin.

Khubilai was already the Great Khan of Mongolia and territories further west, but China required a different nomenclature, and within China, he intended to be known as the Emperor. Despite his old-fashioned aspirations, his choice of name deliberately broke with former Chinese dynasties. In the past, each imperial ruling house had usually taken its name from a surname or scrap of land – often being one and the same – denoting the birthplace of the founder. The Qin emperor, for example, had taken his name from the state of Qin, over which he had previously been king. The Han dynasty had derived its name from the same Han River over which Khubilai's forces had recently fought their prolonged siege of Xiangyang. The Tang dynasty took its name from the district of Tang, over which its founder had once been the presiding duke. If Khubilai were to name his dynasty in a similar style, he might perhaps have drawn a syllable from the name of his birthplace. Considering the Chinese pronunciation of Mongolia, we might have been speaking today of Khubilai's new 'Meng' dynasty, or perhaps the 'Xing' dynasty, after Xingzhou, where he had been appointed as lord in his youth.

However, each of these prospective names made it clear that the new dynasty came from outside China, encouraging precisely the anti-barbarian rhetoric that had characterized the proclamations of the Song Grand Empress Dowager. Khubilai was no stranger to protocols – he had, after all, just fought a long war with Arigh Boke over which of them had been truly acclaimed as Khan at a quorate *kurultai*. He was not about to remind the Chinese of his own foreign origins, and hence settled on a name that drew a firm line under previous history. This was Khubilai's 'Year Zero', an uncompromising statement that his subjects found themselves at the dawn of a new age. The dynasty was to be called 'Yuan': 'Beginning'.

The name was chosen by Khubilai's adviser Liu Bingzhong, not only for its awesome implication of a new era, but for the resonances it had to the ancient *Book of Changes*. Khubilai's pre-existing reign title, Zhongtong, already alluded to the *Book of Changes*; now he took it a step further, by approving 'Yuan' – a character sure to summon up images among his fortune-tellers of completeness, creation and unification. Buried in the etymology, there was also the concept of a great circle around the viewer, like the broad, infinite horizons visible to a man standing on the empty steppes. It was an ideal name for Khubilai's new regime, and was soon adopted countrywide.

Once Khubilai had proclaimed himself as the new Emperor, there was the matter of tributes. Decrees were sent out to all peripheral nations that had once paid tribute to the Song. The

Koreans, already much loved as Khubilai's first foreign supporters, soon came back with an enthusiastic statement of loyalty. King Wonjong had cause to be particularly pleased with Khubilai, since Mongol troops had recently entered his country to put down a tough rebellion. As a vassal king loyal to Khubilai, Wonjong was under attack from a powerful military faction, and had to rely on Mongol reinforcements to keep his throne. The rebels, known in Korean as the *Sambyeolcho* or the 'Three Patrols', were still preying on the Korean coasts, and, notably, were also seeking assistance from the distant island of Japan.

Khubilai himself sent his decree of enthronement to the Japanese as well, hoping to hear that they, too, would acknowledge that he was the Ruler of All Under Heaven. A similar document went out to the King of Annam – in both cases, the 'vassal kings' took their time in responding. In the meantime, while Khubilai's generals busied themselves in frontier wars, he devoted himself to his newest great project: a capital fit for a Chinese emperor.

In 1274, around the time of the fall of Hangzhou, a new source appears, from which we can draw observations of Khubilai's acts and empire. We have already encountered Marco Polo in earlier chapters, since some of his writings refer to events that happened before he reached China himself. However, for the next two decades, Marco Polo's writings refer directly to his own experiences of life in China.

Polo was in his early twenties when he reached China. He arrived in the company of his father, Niccolo, and his uncle, Maffeo, who were returning to the court of Khubilai after years away. The two elder Polos had visited Khubilai in the 1260s, where they had been mistaken, willingly or otherwise, for envoys of the Pope. Khubilai had sent them away with a letter for the Vatican, and a request that they return with some oil from the Holy Sepulchre in Jerusalem, and 100 of the best minds that Christendom could provide.

The Polos had been unlucky. They had returned to Europe to find that the Pope was dead, and that they faced a long wait for the election of his successor. They obtained their holy oil, and, by a stroke of luck, found that when a successor was eventually found, he turned out to be a personal acquaintance. That, however, was not enough to secure them 100 scholars, and they returned to Karakorum in a tiny entourage. Their monastic travelling companions deserted them partway, so that by the time they reached Khubilai's court, they had very little to offer.

So they bent the knee before him, and paid their respects to him, with all possible reverence. Then the Lord bade them stand up, and treated them with great honour, showing great pleasure at their coming, and asked many questions as to their welfare, and how they had sped. They replied that they had in verity sped well, seeing that they found the Kaan well and safe. Then they presented the credentials and letters which they had received from the Pope, which pleased him right well; and after that they produced the Oil from the Sepulchre, and at that also he was very glad, for he set great store thereby. And next, spying Marco, who was then a young gallant, he asked who was that in their company? 'Sire,' said his father, Niccolo, "tis my son and your liegeman.' 'Welcome is he too,' quoth the Emperor.[1]

One wonders, if the Polos had turned up at the head of 100 European scholars, whether the Mongol world would not have recognized it as the submission of Western Europe to them. Khubilai loved to surround himself with learned men, and would have surely put the Pope's men to work arguing at the great debates against the Nestorians, Muslims, Buddhists and Taoists. However, since the Polos had turned up all but empty-handed, Khubilai made the best of a bad situation. It is unclear how he treated Maffeo and Niccolo, but Marco was inducted into Khubilai's entourage, and spent many of the next twenty-four years working as one of Khubilai's officials, in a series of posts that remain a subject of some debate. Regardless, thanks to Polo we have a first-hand account of many events in

Khubilai's later reign, including notes on the appearance of Khubilai himself:

> The personal appearance of the Great Kaan, Lord of Lords, whose name is Cublay, is such as I shall now tell you. He is of a good stature, neither tall nor short, but of a middle height. He has a becoming amount of flesh, and is very shapely in all his limbs. His complexion is white and red, the eyes black and fine, the nose well formed and well set on.[2]

Some have taken Polo's description of the sixty-year-old Khubilai to be that of a wiry, dynamic leader, although it does not tally with the podgy figure depicted by Khubilai's court painter a decade later. Either Khubilai's old age saw gout and other disorders causing him to swell up to epic proportions, or perhaps Khubilai was already showing signs of this, but Polo was being kind in his description. Ultimately a lot depends on our reading of 'becoming amount of flesh' and 'shapely' – I personally suspect that Polo was already describing a man bearing the consequences of a life of good living. It would certainly be odd to assume that Khubilai was in good health in 1274 when only seven years earlier King Wonjong of Korea was asked to send him a tribute gift of supple fish skins – these were intended to make soft shoes for Khubilai's feet, already subject to painful swelling from the effects of gout.[3]

The Polos accompanied Khubilai soon after he left his summer residence at Shangdu and returned south to his imperial home. Called variously the Great City or the Khan's City by its residents, its modern name is Beijing, and it was built on the site of Zhongdu, the ruined capital of the Jurchens.

The construction of the city was an ongoing project for the rest of Khubilai's reign. Parts of it were completed with extreme rapidity, thanks to enslaved prisoners of war. Other parts only came into being after the initiation of the Yuan dynasty, such as the great sacrificial altars built in the year of Polo's arrival, so that Khubilai could carry out the ceremonies required of a true emperor. Another building completed in the 1270s was the observatory, an improvement on earlier dynasties' facilities for astrologers and astronomers, from which Khubilai's experts could watch the heavens and decide on appropriate auspicious days. Marco Polo was deeply impressed, both by the organization and by the competition between rival races to develop the most accurate almanac.

> They have a kind of astrolabe on which are inscribed the planetary signs, the hours and critical points of the whole year. And every year these Christian, Saracen, and Cathayan astrologers, each sect apart, investigate by means of this astrolabe the course and character of the whole year, according to the indications of each of its Moons, in order to discover by the natural course and disposition of the planets, and the other circumstances of the heavens, what shall be the nature of the weather, and what peculiarities shall be produced by each Moon of the year; as, for example, under which Moon there shall be thunderstorms and tempests, under which there shall be disease, murrain, wars, disorders, and treasons, and so on, according to the indications of each; but always adding that it lies with God to do less or more according to His pleasure.[4]

Polo claimed to have clambered to the top of one of the city gates, in order to get a better view of Khubilai's city. He left Beijing before it was completed, and never saw, for example, the extension to the Grand Canal that was only finished after he had begun his long journey back to Europe. Nevertheless, Polo's enthusiastic description of Khubilai's great project still retains his sense of awe and wonder.

> All the plots of ground on which the houses of the city are built are four-square and laid out with straight lines; all the courts and gardens of proportionate size . . . Each square plot is encompassed by handsome streets for traffic, and thus the whole city is arranged in squares just like a chess board . . . In the

middle of the city there is a great [bell] which is struck at night. And after it had struck three times, no one must go out of the city.[5]

Khubilai planned Beijing as the city to end all cities, not only as the capital of a domain that combined the Mongol steppes with the land of the Jurchens, but also as the capital of a reunited China. The clearest indication of this is his decision to ignore the ruins of the town that previously occupied the site, and to shift his planned layout of streets a way to the northeast. Although modern Beijing has grown to encompass the outline of its predecessor, in Khubilai's day the haunted ruins of Zhongdu sat forgotten on its outskirts.

The new location was intended to take advantage of two rivers that flowed through what had once been a royal park, swirling into two glittering lakes before continuing on their way. These rivers represented a much larger, more enduring supply of water, sufficient for the great metropolis that Khubilai intended, and designed to pre-empt hydrological problems that had made life in the old town less than perfect. A 30-kilometre channel was dug from a spring in the hills, augmenting the city's fresh water supply sufficiently to maintain a population in the hundreds of thousands. Khubilai even ordered the lakes to be expanded, putting slaves to work dredging and excavating the lakes, piling up the detritus to form the slopes of Coal Hill, still to be found just to the north of what is now the Forbidden City. Soon overgrown with attractive trees, Coal Hill formed a pleasing windbreak to the north, and also helped accentuate the feng shui required for an ideal site.

None of these considerations appear to have been appreciated by Marco Polo, who was not privy to Khubilai's architectural plans. Instead, Polo picked up the gossip from the taverns, which held that Khubilai's decisions were an attempt to hold off an awful curse. Over at the observatory, so the rumours went, the astrologers had identified a baleful prophecy, that anyone who attempted to rebuild the fallen city would be fated to suffer a rebellion from its inhabitants. Hence, Khubilai had found a cunning way around this problem: he was not *rebuilding* the city at all – he was building an entirely new one nearby. Khubilai's city included a walled enclosure set aside solely for his use – roughly equivalent to today's Forbidden City, The combination of the hill and the opportunity for onlookers to peek down from one of the eleven city gates has left us with several descriptions of the Khan's inner palace, albeit from a distance. Understandably, none of the Christian missionaries was allowed within a stone's throw; the *semuren*, like Marco Polo, never seem to have been able to appreciate the inner palace from close-up:

> Between the two walls of the enclosure are fine parks and beautiful trees bearing a variety of fruits. There are beasts also of sundry kinds, such as white stags and fallow deer, gazelles and roebucks, and fine squirrels . . . There extends a fine Lake, containing fish of different kind which the Emperor has caused to be put there, so that whenever he desires any he can have them at his pleasures. A river enters this lake and issues from it, but there is a grating of iron or brass put up so that the fish cannot escape in that way.[6]

A later observer, the Italian Friar Odoric, similarly noted that the Khan had a hunting ground set around the lakes, with water fowl in abundance, fish kept carefully from leaving their ponds, and all modern conveniences tantalizingly close at hand:

> In the city, the great emperor Khan has his principal seat, and his imperial palace, the walls of which palace are four miles in circuit. Near to his palace are many other palaces and houses of his nobles which belong to his court. Within the precincts of the imperial palace there is a most beautiful mount, set and replenished with trees, which is called the Green Mount, having

a most royal and sumptuous palace standing thereupon, in
which, for the most part, the great Khan resides.[7]

The most famous of the religious buildings in Khubilai's
golden age Beijing was the White Pagoda, a curious bell-shaped
structure that would have been the tallest building in the city
after it was completed in 1279. To the local Chinese, it was a
distinctly odd building, built to the design of a Nepalese
architect, and intended to impress the likes of Khubilai's
consort Chabi.

Although Khubilai is often cited in tourist accounts as the
builder of the White Pagoda, he should perhaps be better
remembered as a restorer. As the outlandish, un-Chinese design
already suggests, it was the product of another alien regime,
built by the profligate Liao emperor Shoulong in the eleventh
century in celebration of his succession. In something of a
dilapidated state after Beijing's fall to the Jurchens and then the
Mongols, the White Pagoda was restored to its former glory by
Khubilai Khan in 1272. Its prominent location, close to the
heart of Khubilai's empire, does rather suggest that Khubilai
was indeed a 'devout Buddhist'. At the very least, there does
not seem to have been any Christian or Muslim buildings of
similar scale in Khubilai's capital, which adds an intriguing
element to speculations about the true nature of his supposed
even-handedness towards all religions.[8]

He also seemed keen to play up to history. Khubilai
remained immensely proud of finally obtaining the submission
of Korea, and did not seem to be able to resist any chance to
mention that he had achieved what no Chinese emperor before
him had managed – the conquest of the notoriously defensible
mountain passes of Korea. But instead of openly bragging,
Khubilai chose to remind his subjects of the comparison
between him and Taizong, the emperor of the Tang dynasty
who had famously failed to conquer Korea. Hence, out in the
Western Hills, the hinterland to the north-west of Beijing
proper, a number of temples were to be found clustered around

the all-important freshwater resource, the Jade Spring. Khubilai ordered that one of them, a 600-year-old palace dating from the time of the first Tang emperor, be renamed the Monastery of the Manifestation of Filial Piety.[9]

Supposedly, criminals from southern China who had seen the error of their ways and taken monastic vows had founded the nearby Monastery of Clear Pools and Wild Mulberries during the latter days of the Song dynasty. In a curious turn of events, Khubilai's daughter, Princess Miaoyan, shaved her head and entered the temple as a nun, praying every day to the Goddess of Mercy. When she died, her remains were interred in the temple grounds, and a portrait of her hung in its Hall of Protectors of the Law for many centuries.[10]

Arguably, Khubilai's greatest achievement was the renovation of the Grand Canal, an overgrown, silted remnant of a forgotten age. During Khubilai's reign it was dredged, redug and replotted in stages, uniting distant Yangzhou and Hangzhou to the Yangtze River, and Yangzhou to the regions to the north. By the 1280s, when Marco Polo described it, the canal was still ten years from reaching Beijing proper, although he reported cargoes being unloaded from barges onto carts not far from the city. The Grand Canal endured as a symbol of Khubilai's benevolent rule because it emphasized his achievement in reuniting north and south China. As a vital conduit for trade and transport, it endured long after Khubilai and the Mongols were gone.

Far to the south, the operation against the last remnants of the Southern Song dynasty continued. Marco Polo commented that the last of the Song rulers 'never more did quit the isles of the sea to which he had fled, but died there,' which was only partly true.[11] The loyalists and the two young princes had taken to their ships, seeking help first in Fujian, a south-western province walled by the sea on one side and a forbidding mountain range on all the others.

There, with a nine-year-old boy as their nominal ruler, they waited in the port town of Fuzhou until it became clear that the Mongols had crossed the mountains and were only a few days' march away. Taking once more to their ships, the loyalists fled to Quanzhou, where they sought help from the powerful local figure Pu Shougeng. Pu was a 'merchant' who had achieved status in local government by dealing with pirate activity in the region – such postings, in many periods of Chinese history, tending to imply that the alleged pirate hunter was actually more of a poacher turned gamekeeper. Quanzhou was a great port with a large population from overseas; Pu himself was descended from Muslim immigrants, which perhaps explains his lack of interest in pandering to the Song.

By the time the Song fugitives reached Quanzhou, Pu was entertaining entreaties from both Khubilai and the Song. Both sides sought his approval and support, but the Song did so in a manner that Pu regarded as bossy and unrealistic. He thought it arrogant for members of a side that was clearly losing the war to order him around as if they still ruled the entirety of China. Pu made it clear to the Song loyalists that they did not even rule the city of Quanzhou, refusing to donate boats or supply to their fleet. He did, however, invite them to remain in Quanzhou as his guests, even as he sent word to the Mongols that he had Khubilai's enemies in his clutches.[12]

Suspecting that Pu was about to betray them, the Song loyalists went on the run again in 1277. Khubilai rewarded Pu for his support by appointing him military commander of the Fujian region, in which capacity Pu was still under attack from the Song loyalists who had previously sought his hospitality. Before long, however, the Song fleet was huddled in the far south of China near Canton, practically at the edge of the Chinese world. A terrible storm in early 1278 decimated the fleet, and nearly drowned the child emperor. He never quite recovered from the trauma, and reportedly died from its after-effects by May. The last pretender to the Song throne was the late emperor's younger brother, and the two sea captains who ruled in his name considered the unthinkable – leaving China behind.

Hoping to capitalize on the Chinese overseas community in the Indo-Chinese state of Champa (contiguous with modern-day south Vietnam), the regents sent envoys there to appeal for sanctuary, even as Mongol forces drew close to south China. Blockaded in a bay in the far south, the admiral Zhang Shijie ordered the last of the Song ships chained together – supposedly to stop anyone from deserting. As Song food and water supplies ran low, both sides made plans for a last-ditch assault.

Zhang tried to make his great breakout when he heard celebratory music drifting across the bay from the Mongol vessels. He assumed that his enemies were occupied with some kind of festival, but it was a trap. As Zhang drifted near, with extra troops hidden under tarpaulins on his decks, the Mongols sprang into action themselves.

Zhang Shijie realized that the battle was lost. Counter-manding his own orders, he cut a dozen ships free from the centre, hoping to flee. Zhang made it out, but the flagship carrying the child-emperor was badly damaged. Realising that they was about to be boarded, one of the child's chief ministers grabbed the boy in his arms and threw himself into the sea. Seeing the death of their ruler, many of the Song loyalists followed suit, leaving the sea littered with thousands of corpses.

Zhang Shijie turned his surviving ships for the south, claiming that he would find a relative of the Song ruling family in Champa and enthrone him as a new claimant. But Zhang sailed into a storm and was never heard from again, presumed drowned.

The death of the last pretender and the disappearance of his regents signified the true end of the Song resistance. With it came the Mongol occupation of the last two parts of the south that might be considered to be Song strongholds – Fujian and Canton. Khubilai's behaviour over these regions, as ever, was designed to accentuate the positive. It was, the argument went, counter-productive to think of the regime change as the fall of the Southern Song. Instead, surely it was far better to think of recent events as the final chapter in the reunification of China. For the first time in centuries, China was one complete political entity, under a ruler whose domains extended further to the west than ever before. There was not even a barbarian problem on the northern border, although the reason for this – that the barbarians were themselves in charge – was the major issue that Khubilai really did not want discussed.

In the aftermath, the changeover was remarkably smooth. Since often the same officials were in charge, and the same officers at work, the presence of a few Mongol supervisors usually did not make all that much difference to the local Chinese. There were certainly frictions at some levels – a significant number of officials refused to collaborate with the new regime, and quietly retired. They were not missed, and were soon replaced by appointees from Mongolia, Central Asia, north China or even, in the case of Marco Polo, locations even further away.

There would be other problems later on. The distant khans of the west, particularly the perpetually absent Khaidu, had yet to fully acknowledge Khubilai as their sovereign. There were still foreign overseers all over the empire, who were sure to take the blame for unpopular policies. Within a few years, southern China itself would be subjected to the same conscriptions and taxation as the rest of Khubilai's empire – but then again, there had been tax and conscription under the Southern Song as well. At least on paper, Khubilai's scheme appeared to be a success.

Nonetheless, we should not dismiss the awful impact of the new regime. Far from Khubilai's capital, there had been massive loss of life. Millions had died during the imposition of Mongol rule, in a war that had lasted for over sixty years. The buoyant economy was kept afloat by paper money, a currency backed by nothing but the stern promise of its imperial printer. Khubilai attained great things, becoming known as the builder of the Grand Canal and the architect of Beijing, although the true toil on those projects belonged to thousands of slave labourers, many of whom died in the process. There were curfews for years to come, and many homes had occupying soldiers billeted within them. Many southern towns lost a lot of their liveliness, not least because families kept their womenfolk carefully hidden from the prying eyes of the new rulers.

China was united, but it would take generations for the scars of its unification to heal. In the meantime, Khubilai had a new project for his subjects. Someone needed to teach Japan a lesson.

7

SAMURAI

THE FIRST MONGOL ARMADA

The great Mongol fleet's ill-fated invasion of Japan is often seen as a watershed in Khubilai's reign. It saw Khubilai acting not only as the Khan of the Mongols, but also as Emperor of China, working within expectations and traditions of court and diplomatic protocols. It also saw his beloved original vassals, the Koreans, experiencing the inevitable consequences of their rapid pledge of allegiance. Korea might have been the first nation to congratulate the new Khan on his appointment, but it was also the first to be subjected to his direct interference in local matters. King Wonjong of Korea, placed on the throne by Mongols, was now obliged to follow Mongol orders throughout the period where Khubilai plotted the invasion of Japan. With Wonjong's death in 1274, his son – Khubilai's son-in-law – ascended to the Korean throne with the title of King Chungnyeol, literally 'Loyal and Ardent'. As a reflection of their submission to the Mongols, successive Korean kings would keep the word 'Loyal' in their reign names for the next eighty years, and the invasion of Japan was the first true test of that devotion.

It was also, with hindsight, the moment when the Mongols' legendary invincibility was called into question for the first time – a sign that the tide of barbarian invasion had finally begun to ebb. The Mongols had experienced setbacks in the past, but had always, eventually, returned home with, at very least, the nominal submission of their enemies. Logistically, the Japanese invasion project was no smaller than the Mongol enterprises to take the empires of the Tangut, Jurchen or the Southern Song. However, historically, it became literally world famous. It is in Marco Polo's awestruck account of the plan to invade Japan that the island kingdom first enters European consciousness. When, 200 years later, Christopher Columbus waded ashore on a remote Caribbean island in search of 'Cipangu', he was merely the latest inheritor of Khubilai's propaganda, convinced that Japan was an island of untold wealth, there for the taking.[1]

Many Japanese accounts leap straight to the arrival of the first great Mongol fleet off the coast, and the heroic efforts by the samurai to hold them back.[2] However, Chinese and Korean annals present a very different story, and show the size of the Mongol threat steadily growing throughout the 1260s. The first approaches to Japan were little more than honeyed words and oblique threats, escalating in severity as years passed without a direct Japanese submission to Khubilai. The first signs of the Mongol invasion are rumours and tall tales from mainland visitors, the mere ghosts of direct contact, as careful Korean obfuscations kept the Mongols and the Japanese from making actual contact. Although history largely remembers the two great, apocalyptic battles in Hakata Bay and their almost supernatural ending, lesser accounts record a number of skirmishes long before the infamous days of reckoning. There were kidnappings and secret deals in the Korea Strait years before the Mongol armada officially set sail, and there was even a pre-emptive Japanese strike on the Korean coast, which saw part of the intended invasion fleet burned where it stood in the shipyards. Small parties of emissaries travelling aboard the ships of others, gradually transformed through the 1260s into an ambassador with his own honour guard and his own military escort: two ships, then a dozen, then hundreds. If we piece together the scattered references to 'Dwarf Pirates' or the 'Land of the Rising Sun' in mainland chronicles, we become witness to the inexorable gathering of a terrible storm. The question that remains for the modern historian to ponder is whether the Japanese or Mongols ever appreciated the terrible odds they *both* faced.

Khubilai's plans for Japan began, innocently enough, with the mention at his court that an obscure island in the east had occasionally offered tribute to previous dynasties. The matter was first brought up by Cho-I, a defrocked Korean Buddhist monk, who had become an interpreter at Khubilai's court. Cho-I revealed that Korea was merely a peninsula leading to another land, supposedly one with incredible wealth. Cho-I was not entirely to blame – Khubilai was sure to find out about Japan eventually, if not from Cho-I then from the Korean king, who had already alerted their new ruler to request that he do something about Japanese pirates preying on his coast. Thanks to Cho-I, however, Khubilai was to send an embassy to Japan in 1266, with a letter demanding that this newly discovered kingdom also submit to the Ruler of the World.

He also sent a letter to King Wonjong of Korea, ordering him to cooperate to the best of his abilities:

Recently your countryman, Cho-I, came to the Court and said to us: 'Japan is your neighbour and her institutions and administration are praiseworthy. Since the Han and Tang dynasties, moreover, she has sent envoys to our country.' We are therefore dispatching Hei-ti and others to visit Japan in order to establish amity. We desire Your Highness to show them the way to reach there, in order that they may enter the land and enlighten the people so that they will come and pay homage to us. The entire responsibility for the matter we wish Your Highness to take as your own. Do not make the risks and dangers of the stormy ocean a pretext for excusing yourself. Do not give lack of relationship with Japan as an explanation [for shunning this duty]. There is a chance [to be sure] that [Japan] may not be amenable to our demands and may force the embassy to return home. Therefore we are depending on your loyalty and devotion.[3]

Clearly, Khubilai or his advisers already knew that Japan cropped up occasionally as an irregular but cordial tributary in the annals of former dynasties. His letter lacks much of the military braggadocio of other Mongol communiqués. While there remains a remote chance that Khubilai was mincing his words, it would seem that his first approaches to the Japanese were genuinely friendly, 'remarkably courteous' in the words of one modern scholar.[4] We might speculate that with troubles elsewhere in his empire, and a large expanse of ocean separating him from Japan, he might have been easily fobbed off with a few pronouncements of alliance or allegiance.

The Koreans were understandably reluctant to get involved. They were no strangers to the Japanese, and fully aware that the more Khubilai knew about Japan, the more likely he would be to select Korea as the embarkation point for an invasion army. Korea was still reeling from the effects of its long war with the Mongols, and had no desire to become a staging point for another military endeavour. Indeed, true to form, the 'Mongol' invasion of Japan was sure to be carried out by proxies – apart from a handful of Mongol officers and foreign specialists, the 'Mongol' army was sure to largely comprise Korean conscripts. It is hence no surprise that the two Chinese ambassadors were given the runaround in Korea: they were taken to a remote island by their guides, and then persuaded that the weather was so bad that it was best for them to turn back. Having permitted his charges the merest glimpse of the island of Tsushima in the distance, King Wonjong then wrote back to Khubilai, claiming that the envoys had done the best they could, but 'when they saw the myriad leagues of ocean and the wind and waves raging sky high, they thought that the danger was such that it was not proper to let the embassy from Your Majesty's country proceed rashly and incur this risk.'[5]

Besides, protested King Wonjong, the people of Tsushima (not even Japan!) were 'obdurate and tough, with no sense of propriety or order'. He stopped short, but only barely, of suggesting to Khubilai that it would not be worth the trouble if the natives refused to cooperate. 'What then?' he asked, clearly hoping not to hear an unwelcome reply.

However, Khubilai did not believe this story for a moment. In 1267, he wrote an angry rebuke to King Wonjong, openly calling him a liar:

Your Highness's contrivance was flimsy indeed. Besides, Heaven is difficult to deceive, and humanity treasures sincerity. Your Highness has failed to keep your word a number of times. We recommend that you reflect well. As to the Japanese matter, we shall leave it entirely in your hands, and we desire your Highness to bide by our wishes and convey our message to Japan, resting only when the end is attained without mishap.[6]

Hence, the second mission to Japan, dispatched in 1268, successfully reached its destination, although its problems were only just beginning. Seemingly working under the assumption that Japan was a minor, all-but-forgotten vassal state of China, Khubilai addressed his decree to 'the king of a little country':

We make known to you hereby that according to the will of heaven, we have conquered the whole region of China, and even rebellious Korea has been forgiven, so that once more she is cherished under our great virtue. So we desire to remind you that Korea is now one of our eastern provinces, and that Japan is a mere appendage of Korea . . . But why do you neglect your duty of keeping a friendship with us? This is probably due to your ignorance of accomplished facts rather than to your wilfulness.[7]

There was more along the same lines, with Khubilai chiding the Japanese, patronizingly accepting their unoffered apologies, and sinisterly suggesting that everything would be better all round if relations remained friendly, hence not obligating him to go to war. Court officials in Japan sensed that Khubilai's letter spelt trouble, and drafted a carefully worded response that was sure to tie up diplomacy for another year without achieving anything. Like the Koreans, the Japanese were rather hoping that the problem posed by Khubilai would go away on its own. However, the reply was never even sent, as the court's careful diplomacies were vetoed by another figure. Japan was effectively run not by the Japanese Emperor, but by his nominal underling, the Shōgun. Nor would the letter have achieved much if presented to the Shōgun, since in the late thirteenth century, this post was also merely honorary, and was actually controlled in secret by an office of regents.

After these multiple levels of deferred responsibility, the letter ended up in the hands of the newly appointed shōgunal regent, a seventeen-year-old boy called Hōjō Tokimune, who ordered that the envoys should be sent back without any acknowledgement at all. Further embassies arrived from Khubilai Khan, and all were turned away. Korean members of one delegation attempted to impress upon the Japanese the likely consequences of continued arrogance in the face of Khubilai Khan, but it seems that the Japanese knew exactly what they were doing.

The emissaries pleaded that all evidence indicated that the Mongols would destroy the Japanese resistance, but it is easy to see why Hōjō Tokimune might have thought otherwise. The Mongols had, after all, taken twenty years to pacify Korea, and had yet to fully bring it under their control. Coded references to a 'Western Capital' in the chronicles of the time are to the relocation of the Korean court to Ganghwa Island, near modern Incheon. Ganghwa kept the Mongols at bay by simple virtue of its offshore location. It was within sight of the Korean coast, but presented enough logistical difficulties to keep the wayward Korean royals safe for many years. Even though Korea eventually fell under the Mongol influence, it is likely that the Japanese had an even greater faith in the defensive capabilities of the Korea Strait, which encompassed 120 miles of open sea between Japan and the mainland. Furthermore, although Khubilai may have hoped that the presence of Korean emissaries would have helped smooth diplomacy, his decision had the reverse effect. The Japanese had largely heard of Mongol prowess from mild-mannered Buddhist missionaries, whose assessments of the Mongol danger were scoffed at by confident samurai. Meanwhile, familiarity with the Koreans had bred a certain degree of contempt among the Japanese – instead of being impressed that the Mongol emissaries were accompanied by Korean vassals, the Japanese assumed that the Mongols were so weak that they needed Korean help.

Far from 'conquering' Korea and thereby achieving what Tang Taizong had not, Khubilai had merely meddled in its politics, backing a series of squabbles between disaffected noblemen and military leaders. Although he had secured the nominal vassalage of a new Korean king, it was plain to see that the Koreans were still being as obstructive as possible. The period 1270–3 found Wonjong's Korea undergoing a series of rebellions and reversals, as pro- and anti-Mongol factions struggled for control. The Japanese were even invited by one Korean faction to come to its aid, but sensibly stayed back.

Khubilai's subjects did everything they could to advise him against pushing too far. A Korean ambassador, well versed in classical accounts, told Khubilai that the Japanese were an arrogant, boastful race, infamous in Chinese chronicles for referring in communiqués to their own leader as 'the great emperor of the land of the Rising Sun', and addressing the Chinese Emperor as if they were equals. On frequent occasions throughout history, Chinese court diarists had ridiculed such presumption, and, the ambassador pleaded, never took it seriously. Instead, he suggested that Khubilai simply give up on the idea of attacking Japan, as claims regarding the island kingdom's wealth and status were greatly exaggerated, even by the Japanese themselves. Moreover, Khubilai should be aware that a seaborne assault was a difficult undertaking, and one best not attempted, for fear that bad weather and rough seas might reduce the prestige of the previously invincible Mongol hordes.[8] Khubilai was not swayed by these arguments, instead ordering the Korean ambassador to arrange for 'the construction of 1000 ships and [the supply of] 4000 bags of rice, together with a contingent of 40,000 troops'.

After literally years of prevarication, the ambassador hit him with the bitter truth:

> To build 1000 ships in a short time is never an easy task for Korea . . . But the difficulty is to cut them down for the timbers with her paucity of labourers, most of whom were lost in the continuous wars . . . For the same reason, to assemble such a large army is entirely beyond her power, particularly since the best have been killed in the frequent rebellions on the northern frontier, and those who remain are only the invalids or the decrepit who retain no longer their former energy.[9]

Khubilai's stern reply to such pleadings is worthy of his grandfather Temujin:

> How absurd! Is it not a law of Nature that while one is lost, another is born? Why could you not understand such simple reasoning? If your statement were true, mankind would have left the world.[10]

Khubilai's argument, outrageous in its pig-headedness, was that the Koreans had nothing to complain about because they still had women with whom they could breed a new generation of workers. In doing so, he recalled the swift turnover of

Mongol warriors, and the consequent immensity of their harems. Khubilai clearly had Temujin in mind, and soon began reminiscing about the vast atrocities committed by his grandfather against those who dared to oppose him.

Khubilai sent a third diplomatic mission, seventy men strong, in 1269, to determine whether the Japanese really were so foolhardy as to resist him. Unlike previous embassies, a high-ranking Tartar whom Khubilai trusted led this one, and hence made it through all the misdirection in Korea with little difficulty. However, the mission again only made it as far as Tsushima, the small island in the middle of the Korea Strait.

Tsushima has long been a key waypoint in the Korea Strait. Its ruling family, the Sō clan, had a surname that sounded suspiciously mainland in origin, even though they counted themselves as Japanese. The large Mongol ship surprised the local inhabitants, but does not seem to have scared them, as proved by the behaviour of the local lord Sō Sukekuni. A proud warrior in his early sixties, Sō appeared on the beach at the head of a band of his loyal samurai, commanding the Mongols to leave and refusing to let them come ashore. The envoy responded by invoking the name of Khubilai Khan, sure to strike fear into the heart of any reasonable man, but Sō merely shrugged and drew his sword.

It is implied in surviving accounts that the Mongols attempted to come ashore, and that Sō men not only fought them off, but pursued them until they were beyond the horizon. The sequence of events suggests that the initial band of samurai on the beach was soon augmented by unexpected seaborne reinforcements, causing the seventy-strong embassy members to doubt their chances, cut their losses and run. On the way home, they waylaid a Japanese fishing boat, kidnapped the two occupants, and eventually presented them to Khubilai as possible envoys to carry his message.

Bizarrely, Khubilai appears to have accepted this story, and after sternly telling the fishermen to inform their ruler that it was in everyone's best interests to be friends, he sent them back with two Korean emissaries a few months later. Avoiding Tsushima, this next mission put ashore at Dazaifu, a military base on the western tip of the island of Kyūshū, where its members were promptly locked up.

Yet another mission, the fourth, was led by the ageing Jurchen emissary Choyonpil, who commenced his journey in 1270 in search of news of his predecessors. By this time, Khubilai's patience was wearing thin, and he ordered the King of Korea to donate 6,000 ploughs, oxen and seeds to a rice-growing project designed to stockpile food for an invasion force. The ship-building exercise also continued, despite Korea's war-ravaged state. According to one Chinese chronicle:

> The carpenters and the other workers levied for the war were more than 30,500; in every quarter men and horses passed by in uninterrupted succession; all business was in confusion as the term was so short; everything went like the speedy blast of wind or the flash of lightning, and the whole world felt deep sorrow at this.[11]

Choyonpil saw for himself the deprivation and unrest in Korea as he made his way down the peninsula towards the coast. Undeterred, he put to sea in January 1271, with an honour guard of curious Koreans, twenty warships and 3,000 men. A Japanese official blustered that Chinese embassies had not bothered to travel further than Dazaifu in the past, and demanded to know why he would not simply hand over his credentials. Choyonpil, however, was much better at playing that game, and cited a precedent from the Sui dynasty, when upon the arrival of a Chinese ambassador in Japan, 'the ruler came out of the capital to extend welcome.'[12]

Eventually, the quarrelling officials found a compromise. Choyonpil kept his credentials, but handed over an exact duplicate to be ferried to Tokimune. It was found to contain a blunt ultimatum: Japan was to offer its official supplication to

Khubilai Khan within three months, or face his 'invincible army'.[13]

Discovering this, Choyonpil was unceremoniously ejected from Japan. Stealing an idea from his ambassadorial predecessors, he decided that it would be too dangerous to report such a response to Khubilai. Instead, he put his immediate military resources to work on the way home, stopping off at Tsushima, kidnapping a dozen locals, and then bringing them back to Beijing in the guise of a Japanese embassy. Under this pretext, they presented Khubilai with a time-wasting communiqué:

> We have been deceived by Korea, who has told us often that China would come to conquer Japan. How can we know that the Sovereign loves life and hates murder? His Majesty the Emperor has sent this emissary to give us a sealed message, but the ruler's capital is far, far away. We think we should, therefore, dispatch men to accompany the envoy home.[14]

Khubilai was not fooled by this either. Two of his trusted advisers agreed with him that the Japanese 'emissaries' were more likely to be spies sent to ascertain his strength. The story may at first seem bizarre, but perhaps we should consider the likely opinions of Khubilai's underlings. The Mongols alone were keen on battle, and even they were finding their ardour largely spent on conquest and its celebration. Scattered throughout the world as local rulers, swiftly fattening on fine food and wine, attended by legions of terror-struck serving girls, many of Khubilai's own kind were going native. Neither the Chinese nor the Koreans had any desire to fight a war against the Japanese, and even Khubilai himself would have presumably been easily mollified by a suitably contrite letter of submission from the 'ruler of Japan'. But with Japan's insubordination stretching from months into years, the issue was fast becoming a matter of honour and prestige, an insult that had to be avenged if the Mongols were to maintain their hold on the rest of their hard-won empire. However, an order to attack Japan was sure to ruin the lives and livelihoods of millions – conscript soldiers and farmers, as well as distant tax-payers, sailors, samurai and even lumber merchants. It would cripple Korea, still struggling to recover from its own wars, and was sure to cost the Chinese dearly. Moreover, this was the best-case scenario – if the Mongols somehow failed to defeat Japan, they would accomplish all of the above disasters, *and* also destabilize Khubilai's own hold on power. It was, in short, a war that nobody wanted except Khubilai, and even Choyonpil seems to have realized this. It is therefore not surprising that Choyonpil found himself able to secure the willing collaboration of so many of Khubilai's subjects, as well as representatives from Tsushima, itself sure to be right in the line of fire.[15]

Supervisors of agriculture were in place in Korea in 1271 to deliver oxen and farming tools, and inspectors assessed arable land for growing provisions in 1272. Khubilai originally intended Korean resources to be allocated to campaigns against local rebels or the continued pacification of the Southern Song, but as time wore on and the Japanese refused to acknowledge his rule, he reallocated resources to the invasion of Japan.[16]

The year 1273 was one of worrying portents. The Japanese and Koreans both reported a comet in February, while Chinese and Japanese chronicles reported a 'guest star' in the sky that same April, and again in October.[17] A 'fifth' embassy in Khubilai's records was a further deception, as Choyonpil returned to Japan, ostensibly to monitor Japanese compliance with Khubilai's demands. He returned, having surely observed the massive defence works under construction along the Japanese coasts, but neglected to mention them to Khubilai. Instead, he reported that matters were in hand, and that, besides, 'Japan is not a country worth having.' As far as Choyonpil could see, Japan possessed 'limitless valleys', and any attempt by Khubilai Khan to occupy it would merely fill those valleys with the corpses of Chinese and Koreans.[18]

Choyonpil's careful deception seems to have backfired – not among the Koreans, but among the Japanese themselves: the succession of meek embassies from across the water may have persuaded the Japanese that they had nothing to fear from the Mongols after all. This was certainly the impression left among a group of part-time pirates from Kyūshū, lured to the Korean island of Jeju by tales of its riches. Ironically, Jeju was 'rich' because it was being used as a stud farm – it was one of the places where Khubilai was rearing the next generation of warhorses, ready for his next conquests. Whoever these Japanese pirates were, they cowed the locals into submission, and departed with whatever they desired. As a result, the Koreans could not win. They were either willing collaborators of the emboldened Japanese, or they were timid procrastinators who had kept Japanese predations quiet until it was too late.

Either way, an attack by Japanese marauders on territory within Khubilai's kingdom was plainly no sign of either co-operation or submission. Soon afterwards, the same marauders attacked the Korean mainland, burning some twenty vessels under construction at a shipyard, and leaving with Mongol prisoners. The attacks of the Japanese pirates, whoever they were, spelled the end of years of obfuscation. The Koreans could cover up the deception no longer: the Japanese were in open defiance, and attacking the coast of Korea. It hardly mattered to Khubilai whether the pirates were acting inde-pendently or under the direct instruction of the ruler of Japan – the result was the same.

If the Japanese raiders had been hoping to capitalize on stories of unrest further to the north, they were to be disappointed. Any previous troubles in the north of Korea were now quelled, such that Khubilai was able to mobilize a proper army against his new Japanese enemies. Khubilai's daughter, Quduluq Kalmish, was betrothed to the son of King Wonjong, who would become King Chungnyeol of Korea in the year of their marriage, 1274.[19] Thereafter, dynastic marriages between Khubilai's dynasty and the ruling house of Korea, and the raising of Korean heirs in Beijing under Mongol tutelage, would lock the attitudes and aims of the Korean royal family firmly to those of Khubilai.

Jeju Island was swiftly taken back from its occupiers by a force of some 1,500 Mongol and Korean troops. Meanwhile, a much larger force began its slow mobilization from the Chinese border, down along the Korean peninsula, to an embarkation point near modern Pusan. In November 1274, pointedly after the end of harvest season, a force set out on the newest Mongol conquest. Some 300 large ships and another 400 smaller boats carried 15,000 Mongol, Chinese and Jurchen soldiers. The crews of the ships comprised another 7,000 or so, chiefly Koreans.

Their route was pre-determined. Sailing technology of the time, and limited knowledge of Japanese waters, ensured that the armada would essentially follow the same route as the embassies of the preceding decade. The island of Tsushima, at the mid-point of the Korea Strait, was the first piece of Japanese territory to come under attack, and presented a reasonable microcosm of what mainland Japan could expect.

Sō Sukekuni, the local lord who had repulsed the earlier attempted landing on Tsushima, soon realized that this time the Mongols meant business. As hundreds upon hundreds of Mongol ships entered the vast bay that cuts Tsushima almost in two, Sō sent an unarmed boat out to the lead vessel. However, the time for negotiations and time wasting was already past: as the boat neared the Mongol fleet, it came under fire from a cloud of arrows.

There was no parley. Instead, the Mongol army came ashore in a massed amphibious assault, a long frontline that was impossible for the local samurai to hold back. Samurai on Tsushima were used to a largely ritualized form of combat, almost like a blood-stained sport, in which champions from each army would challenge each other after reciting their martial resumés, building from single combat to larger mêlées and eventual massed skirmishes. For the samurai, a full-scale battle might take days to escalate, until such time as one side proclaimed itself the victor. Their emphasis on gentlemanly conduct hid another, more pressing matter – there had not been a full-scale war in Japan for decades, leaving many of the samurai with little more than a theoretical understanding of battle.

As was traditional for the Japanese, battle began not with actual combat, but with the exchange of humming-bulb arrows – blunt, whistling, screaming noisemakers used for signalling and scaring horses. Accordingly, a samurai launched a humming-bulb arrow in the air, which the Mongols watched in disdain, before replying with a volley of deadly, poisonous arrows. The samurai were unprepared for the Mongol onslaught, which delivered volleys of poisoned arrows and launched exploding catapult- or cannon-balls (it is not all that clear which). Samurai ripostes were deflected with shields made of metal. Single samurai approached the Mongol lines, calling out their lineage and demanding that the Mongols supply a worthy opponent. Instead, the Mongol lines charged the lone warriors en masse, enveloping them and cutting them down in overwhelming numbers. Realizing that conditions had changed, and that battle tactics were now returning to a format largely unseen in Japan for centuries, 100 samurai horsemen charged directly at the Mongol frontline. They were similarly cut down, by an efficient, trained war machine that was responding to signals from leaders observing the battle from a nearby cliff.

Although Sō's men rallied, they had already lost the shoreline by the time they began to press back against the invaders, allowing the landing forces to establish a larger beachhead, in turn allowing horsemen to wade ashore with their mounts. By sunset, pushed back into the pine forest that led down to the beach, the samurai were able to function in smaller groups, while the monolithic Mongol phalanx was broken up among the trees. In the fading light, scattered skirmishes rang out among the trees, including one notorious incident in a forest clearing, when an exhausted samurai was disturbed from a well-

earned rest by a hulking Mongol brute. The two men duelled in
the clearing, their shouts and clashing swords soon attracting an
audience from both opposing armies. Eventually, the plucky
samurai gained the upper hand, shearing off his opponent's
head, and brandishing it in gory victory at the watching
enemies. Men on both sides applauded, but soon resumed when
the victor taunted the Mongols with another challenge: was
there any other among the observers brave enough to face him
in single combat? A long silence followed while the invading
soldiers looked at each other. The response came in another
volley of the deadly poisoned arrows, three of which mortally
wounded the samurai.

While samurai numbers continued to dwindle in the face of
the continued assault, the Mongol force was so vast that it was
still disembarking soldiers even as the sun began to set. Any
gains on the Japanese side were soon negated by fresh
reinforcements. The day ended with a desperate, doomed
charge by the wounded Sō Sukekuni at the head of the tattered
remnants of his cavalry:

> The ear of heaven was deafened with the din of the Mongol
> drums, the earth shook at the tempest of war cries. Ah! Where
> is our forlorn hope that rode into the jaws of death? The shafts
> began to fall like raindrops of spring, and blood flowed till the
> field looked like a crimson sea. Where is the brave band of
> Sukekuni of Sō, in the smoke of the guns or the clouds of
> arrows? They were no more seen in the isle; all that came into
> sight again out of the smoke were a few masterless horses,
> returning and neighing for their empty camps.[20]

Sō's last stand left the Mongols' route ashore unimpeded. A
new glow lit up the night as the town caught fire, and the
attacking troops massacred the survivors. The ladies in Sō's
mansion mostly committed suicide before the attackers could
break in, but the womenfolk of the rest of the town were not so
lucky, and were captured alive.

The fall of Tsushima is not part of most Japanese narratives of the Mongol armada. It is often a mere line or two in passing as the fleet crosses the strait, largely because the Japanese had so much more documentation and so many witnesses to the main assault. We might also observe that the entire programme of Japanese defences centred around holding the shoreline at Hakata Bay on Kyūshū – in other words, the inhabitants of Tsushima and Iki were abandoned to their fates. What survivors there were of the holocaust on Tsushima only told their stories long after the events, and were not part of the military aristocracy that tended to record such tales. Curiously, a Korean report of the same events lacks all of the heroism and bravado, and simply notes: 'the dwarves surrendered once, but rallied once again.' There is no mention of surrender, even as a ruse, in any Japanese account.[21]

It is implied that the inhabitants of Iki, the next island on the Mongol's route, had some presentiment of what happened on Tsushima, although it is not clear how – fisherman fleeing ahead of the fleet, perhaps. As little more than a remote fishing port, Iki was sorely lacking in samurai, particularly since the bulk of the region's warriors were already assembled on Kyūshū itself for the main defence. Consequently, the sack of Iki was a repeat of the events on Tsushima, with an additional atrocity.

The defenders on Iki first saw the Mongol ships bearing the spoils of war from Tsushima – naked womenfolk, dead or dying, nailed to the prows of the approaching vessels like ghoulish figureheads. This atrocity is no Japanese propaganda, but faithfully reported in the Yuan dynasty's own annals: 'When they captured women, they pierced the centre of their palms with wires and tired them to the sides of the ships.'[22]

Captured ladies of Tsushima also formed a human shield during the first landing, as the Mongol troops pushed a wall of wailing women ahead of them. Many of these prisoners begged the defenders on Iki to kill them where they stood – the only way of getting through the frontline of the Mongol phalanx.

The defenders on Iki were even less prepared than those on Tsushima. The local lord had only a handful of actual warriors under his command. The rest were literally peasants with pitchforks, lacking the most basic armour and hence even more vulnerable to the Mongols' poisoned arrows. Soon pushed back into Iki's 'castle' – little more than a walled mansion – the defenders settled in for a siege, in the vain hope that the main army at Hakata Bay would get word of their predicament and come to the rescue.

The Mongol assault renewed the following dawn – the defenders able to hold out for a mere day while fatigue took its toll on the invaders' side – wearing down the irreplaceable defenders on one of the gates, and allowing a body of enemy men inside to wreak havoc. While men and women fought a holding action in the mansion grounds, the lord's daughter was tasked with running for the Japanese mainland to warn the defenders at Hakata Bay. However, her small boat came within range of a Mongol ship as she fled, and she and her steersman perished under a hail of arrows.

Four days later, the Mongol armada reached Hakata Bay itself, the largest anchorage in southern Japan, and the natural choice for any invasion fleet. This was understood by the Japanese, who had fortified the surrounding miles of coastline – or rather, re-fortified old coastal defences that had been extant for many centuries, ever since the threat of an invasion from Korea in ancient times.

The Mongol ships had grisly trophies at their prows, where the bodies of captured women had been left to rot. The defenders were also subjected to an aural assault; they were unprepared for the Mongol war drums, which maddened many of the samurai horses and made them difficult to control. Crucially, however, at Hakata Bay, there was at least a sea wall that the defenders could hold. Albeit still outnumbered by the Mongol troops, the samurai at Hakata were better able to manage their resources.

The samurai Takezaki Suenaga left a long account of his participation in the defence of Hakata Bay, prepared years later as part of his application for material rewards. If Takezaki is a typical defender – and there is no reason to doubt it – then the samurai were spoiling for a fight. Takezaki's report, diligently naming his fellow combatants, counting their victories where relevant and also where they were wounded, has him disobeying a direct order to hold back and wait for reinforcements. Instead, he charges into battle, past several fellow warriors who are already carrying enemy heads. His horse stumbles in the mud on the shoreline, and is then hit, seemingly by the blast from a catapult-launched explosive. Takezaki struggles to his feet, his life saved by the timely available of another horseman, which distracts the Mongols who would otherwise have slain him where he stood.

Japanese casualties on the first day have been estimated as high as 30 per cent – although the presence of the sea wall would have left the Mongols with little indication of just how large a fraction of the defenders had been accounted for. One lucky shot from a young bowman managed to strike a 'Mongol general' (actually a Korean in Khubilai's service) in the chest, causing one of the force's main leaders to be carried away, wounded, to his ship.

While the Japanese huddled, demoralized and dejected, behind their walls that night, they were unaware of the impression that they had left on the Mongol generals. Uncomprehending of the damage that had been inflicted on their enemies, the leaders of the Mongol forces were not confident enough in their achievements to sanction holding the beachhead. Fearing that the Japanese were planning a night assault, they clambered back in their ships, which were stronger and more defensible positions than the long stretch of soggy sand at Hakata Bay. They may have been encouraged in this decision by the November weather, which was already wretched, and by the secret knowledge, unavailable to their enemies, that the assaults on Tsushima, Iki and Hakata had severely depleted the Mongol supplies of arrows.

In reports of the leaders' shipboard conference, we revisit the tensions between the races involved. Sources cannot even agree who favoured which tactic. Hol-Ton, the Mongol leader, seems to have pushed for hostilities to continue into the night, pressing for a continued Mongol assault, regardless of the hour. Against such a predictable, gung-ho strategy, the Korean general Hong Dagu offers a more cautious approach: 'Our troops are entirely fatigued . . . and it is of the first importance to give them a good rest tonight in the ships and to supply them with new weapons.' Moreover, as no stranger to the Japanese, Hong was sure that even if the exhausted Mongols somehow got through the sea wall, the road to the main city of Dazaifu was sure to be riddled with ambushes and traps, best approached in daylight. Liu Huxiang, still nursing a serious arrow wound, was in no state to argue, and meekly concurred with his fellow Korean.[23]

It was an interesting standoff. Hol-Ton was the nominal superior, but in no way equipped to order around the foreign soldiers. Whereas the Japanese saw only 'Mongol' attackers, the reality of the 'Three-Winged Army' was that the limited Mongol numbers could not function without the support of their supposed vassals. Hol-Ton's exasperated response may have lost a little in translation: 'Alas! You are becoming old. The smart Japanese will surely come tonight to make a counter-attack.'

Hol-Ton was more right than he knew. Even as he tried to bully his nominal underlings into a renewed assault, the samurai were preparing their retaliation before the moon rose and ruined the evening. Some 300 tiny boats, few capable of holding more than a dozen men, were drifting in the night sea towards the massed Mongol fleet.

They towed other boats, piled high with tinder, and managed to get within arrow range of the massed Mongol fleet before anyone spotted them. Even then, it appears to have been the Japanese who made the first move – according to some versions, the Mongols did not realize they were under attack until enthusiastic Japanese archers not only shot a watchman, but cheered. As the crews of the vessels stumbled to their feet in surprise, the Japanese lit their fireboats and pushed them towards the Mongol vessels. Soon, the Chinese drummers were beating out the alarm, and marines aboard the vessels were firing arrows blindly into the night. Ironically, the most obvious targets were the fireships themselves, which glowed brightly on the swelling sea, and attracted many Mongol arrows while the samurai lurked in the shadows.

Several of the fireships made contact, tongues of flames climbing up the rigging and ropes of the Mongol ships. Ironically, the fire spread particularly swiftly on those ships whose holds had been kept as dry as possible to preserve gunpowder. The gunpowder itself ignited, and the Mongol fleet began to burn.

Not all the fire was coming from the ships. Samurai were seen leaping aboard Mongol vessels with lamps and torches, taking the fire and the fight right to the enemy. As the night battle wore on, the sea became noticeably rougher, and rain began pelting down. Onshore, in the ruins of Hakata town, but also on the ships themselves, the rain staunched some of the fires, turning them into a choking pall of smoke, only adding to the stealth capabilities of the Japanese and the confusion of the invaders.

When the sea became too rough for the attack boats, the samurai ran for shore. Realizing that the bad weather was turning into a terrible storm, the Mongols ran in the opposite direction, attempting to move their fleet away from the huge swells of the inshore waters, and out into deeper channels where they could better ride out the rough seas.

The move was not enough: by the time the Mongol fleet was heading out to sea, the storm was already much too powerful. No waters would be deep enough to ride it out – Japan was hit by an awful typhoon, and the only place to shelter from it would be somewhere on dry land. Stuck out at sea, the Mongol ships were smashed into each other, became waterlogged and were capsized by the powerful waves.

By the following morning, the beach at Hakata was a forest of driftwood, lost supplies and slicks from smashed storage pots. The entire Mongol fleet had disappeared, with the ships still afloat taking advantage of an unseasonally strong easterly wind to run back for Korea. They left behind hundreds of wrecked vessels, and a handful of bedraggled shipwreck victims. As the elated samurai approached, the half-drowned men on the beach ran to find swords or don fragments of their armour, but they could offer no resistance against the Japanese. Khubilai's much-feared fleet had been defeated, most impressively, by the weather.[24]

Yet again, it seems that each side took away a different sense of its accomplishment. In Japan, the samurai celebrated their daring defence of their coastline, while the rest of the country scrambled to take part of the credit. Several priests and court diarists even suggested that the storm was heaven-sent, a 'divine wind' or *kamikaze*, sent to protect Japan in her hour of need. The Mongol invaders, it seemed, had been repulsed by the combined military and spiritual might of the people of Japan, and stories about the invasion grew ever taller with the telling. It was a very different story back in China, where Khubilai was given a matter-of-fact report that the Japanese resistance had been stronger than expected, and informed that he would need a larger invasion force. The account of the 'divine wind' entered in the Chinese records was significantly briefer and prosaic: 'That night there was a great storm and our fighting craft were dashed against the rocks and destroyed in great numbers. [Hol-Ton's] forces thereupon went away under cover of darkness.'[25]

It remains possible that the hearts of the Koreans and Chinese were still not in the fight, and that a call for a significantly larger force was yet another bluff. In one sense, it could be read as a reiteration of Choyonpil's claim that Japan was simply not worth taking, as it would require an enterprise of great expense. Reading between the lines, the first Mongol armada may also have been intended purely as a reconnaissance force, or an economy invasion fleet that had hoped to rely on the Mongols' fierce reputation to cow the Japanese into submission without committing too many resources. Regardless of the true intentions behind the armada (and it is likely that not even Khubilai's own ministers would have been able to entirely agree), Khubilai continued his attempts to bring the Japanese under his authority.

8

THE MISCELLANEOUS ALIENS

KHUBILAI'S COSMOPOLITAN EMPIRE

There was every reason to suspect that Khubilai would be a distant, absent ruler, leaving much of the running of the state to his Chinese ministers and their Mongol supervisors. By all accounts, he was often in Beijing only for the three months around New Year, soon heading off to his 'summer capital' in Shangdu, which he loved for its milder climate. However, Marco Polo implied that Khubilai took an active, dynamic interest in the way his state was run, and some Chinese documents of his life bear that assumption out. One has him adopting yet another idea from his beloved Tang dynasty, and instituting a suggestion box:

> Those who present memorials to make proposals may present them with the envelopes sealed. If the proposals cannot be adopted, there will be no punishment. But if the proposals are useful, the Court will liberally promote and reward the persons in order to encourage the loyal and sincere ones.[1]

Marco Polo's reports of a Khubilai who fostered debate, who was open to new ideas, and who seems to have sought consultations with the smartest men in his realm, does not appear to have been limited merely to religious debates. Tibetans, Uighurs and other Central Asian Muslims held high positions in his empire, and mostly appeared to do so on the basis of merit. How long they remained in that position would depend on how 'Chinese' Khubilai allowed his state to become.

Khubilai retained his aversion to the reinstatement of the Confucian civil service examinations, thereby keeping the Chinese government open to foreigners, including Mongols and the Uighurs he regarded as most trustworthy. He reclassified the population into four groups, with Mongols at the top, and foreigners (*semuren*) next. Then came the people of north China, which lumped together both the ethnic Chinese and the former ruling class of Jurchens. The people of southern China, still only recently conquered, came last in the hierarchy. This division split government approaches to the *Hanren* (literally: Chinese) in the north and the *Nanren* (literally: Southerners).

Despite Khubilai's boasts of unifying China, the south remained under a form of martial law. Moreover, many generations under separate regimes had caused a minor but still appreciable element of drift between the two cultures. It is notable that Marco Polo, when writing of China, should consistently treat it as if it were still two separate countries – 'Cathay' in the north (derived from Khitai, the land of the Jurchens), and 'Manzi' in the south (likely derived from his mishearing of something like Nanshi: the 'southern sector'). The two lowest classes, the Chinese, were excluded from many government positions, putting non-Chinese on the fast track for promotions. This was designed to favour men from Central Asia, on the assumption that the realms of the Xixia and the Uighurs had been conquered a generation earlier, and the peoples of those countries were fully assimilated into the Mongol world.

The definition of *semuren* is problematic. If we insist on a neutral, blunt translation of the original Chinese, we find ourselves with 'persons of the various categories'. And yet, in poetic Chinese, the same term can mean 'people with coloured eyes' – perhaps a reference to the melting pot of foreign advisers who flocked to the Yuan dynasty's occupation administration. Morris Rossabi, in his own account of the realm of Khubilai Khan, prefers 'miscellaneous aliens'.[2]

Khubilai abolished several arms of the Chinese administration, dividing the country into provinces under secretariats. Each province had a general governor, often a Chinese, who reported to pacification commissioners, who were usually Mongol or *semuren*. Governors were usually forced to share their rank with a *darughachi*, a Mongol-appointed cadre. The specification that the *darughachi* and governor were equals remains an interesting aspect of Khubilai's unification scheme. In local matters, we can easily see that there might be occasions where a native governor might have a better appreciation of how to deal with a problem than his arbitrarily appointed watchdog. By leaving it to the two of them to fight it out, or appeal with evidence to a pacification commissioner in times of deadlock, Khubilai ensured that many issues were settled in a means likely to meet with local approval, or at least comprehension.

As one might expect for an occupation system haphazardly hammered over a partially dismantled earlier regime, Khubilai's system was riddled with redundancies and excesses. The further one travelled from Beijing, the greater the absence of clear command. Purviews of many commissions, governors and provinces often overlapped, causing long delays in decision-making. Chinese governors, who could be whipped, fined or executed for numerous vaguely defined signs of corruption, were hence often obliged to defer to their *darughachi* anyway, for fear of otherwise raising suspicion.

In matters of law, Khubilai usually followed the Mongols' own code of conduct, the *Yasa*, which had been purportedly written down by Temujin himself. Since no copies survive, and it was only for the eyes of the ruling class, adhering to these unwritten rules was difficult for the populace. We might even prefer to translate the word, as in modern Mongolian, as something more like 'custom' than 'law'. Regardless of what the *Yasa* really meant to the Mongols, surviving fragments of it often come across as little more than harsh battlefield justice, with death as the punishment for almost everything, and precise classification of crimes infuriatingly absent. Men could be killed for disobedience, for adultery, for corruption, for 'sorcery', but it seems that definition was left largely in the hands of one's superior. Some scholars have countered that the *Yasa* seemed remarkably kinder than the pre-existing Chinese codes, but such an argument is not assessing comparable practices. Certainly, in the course of the *History of the Yuan*, there are only 135 crimes mentioned as being capital offences, as opposed to the 963 in the legal code of the Southern Song. However, we should remember that those are only those crimes *mentioned* in the *History of the Yuan*. As argued by George Lane in his *Daily Life in the Mongol Empire*,

> the Yuan rulers had a reputation for leniency, a fact that has often been overlooked by both Chinese and foreign historians unwilling to dispel the myth of the barbarian interlopers and the picture of uncouth marauding hooligans trampling Chinese culture and sophistication underfoot.[3]

Nevertheless, those apparently lenient rulers were the same Mongols who had massacred entire towns, and caused the deaths of millions during their rise to power.

If this argument seems self-defeating, Lane offers his own path through the odd contradictions. Just as Khubilai's forebears saw the benefit of taxation over war, Khubilai himself seems to have come to comprehend the economic benefits of slavery over execution. Many of the sentences of death issued during Khubilai's reign were commuted at the last moment to what we might call life imprisonment with hard labour. Khubilai himself provided a persuasive explanation in 1287, when he pardoned 190 men on the verge of execution: 'Prisoners are not a mere flock of sheep. How can they be executed? It is proper that they instead be enslaved and assigned to pan gold with a sieve.'[4] In 1291, three years before Khubilai's death, his ministers would come up with a better legal code, incorporating Chinese models and definitions.

Khubilai also oversaw the institution of powerful economic measures designed to get the depopulated north China back on its feet. As early as 1262, he was issuing edicts that forbade nomads from grazing their flocks on north Chinese farmland – no wonder his rivals accused him of going native. In 1270, he ordered the organization of peasant communities at a sub-county level – what we might best describe using the archaic agricultural term 'hundreds'. Khubilai's scheme combined nearby villages into collectives of perhaps fifty households. A local headman would be the nominal head of agricultural operations within these areas, and would be empowered to draft the help of his fellow villagers in projects for the general benefit of the community – particularly the sinking of wells, the clearing of waste ground and the planting of new orchards. These local headmen were also expected to set up a local school, to arrange for grain storage as insurance against famine and to report any unrest to higher authorities. Khubilai thereby hoped to delegate the day-to-day running of the Chinese state into small groups of only a few hundred people, each encouraged to remain essentially self-sufficient. Moreover, these new collectives were responsible for their own tax, and would pay it directly to the central government. Only once the tax was collected would Khubilai redistribute half of it to the local lord of the manor.

As a young man Khubilai had enjoyed a free rein over his fiefdom and, we might recall, ran it into the ground through neglect. As Emperor he made it much harder for the next generation to make the same mistakes. A young Khubilai, were he transported to the older Khubilai's realm, would have been able to keep a watchful eye on a handful of reports from village headmen. Nor would this hypothetical leader have been able to delegate tax collection to untrustworthy minions. He would have only seen his personal fortune grow once the tax money had been to the capital and the Emperor took his cut.

While many remembered the Mongols only as marauders, Khubilai's attitude towards non-farmers seemed rooted in his childhood experiences in Karakorum. Artisans and craftsmen were not disregarded by Mongols; far from it, as the writings of William of Rubruck repeatedly showed, artisans and craftsmen were greatly valued. Old-time Mongols were often proud of their own self-sufficiency, but it is telling that so many of the 'slaves' and hostages in attendance at the court of Khubilai and his predecessors were men who could make the items that Mongols could not make for themselves. Mongol crafts do not appear to have extended far beyond blacksmithing and a little wood- and leather-work. Khubilai's reforms placed a high value on foreign artisanship, offering tax breaks for silk manu-facturers struggling to restart the harvesting in their mulberry groves, but also offering them exemption from certain tax obligations, and from corvée labour. He was similarly generous towards other skilled professions, particularly doctors. Muslim practitioners – at the time, arguably the most skilled physicians in the world – were highly prized in Khubilai's empire, particularly as the golden age of Khubilai's reign, following the fall of the Song, also coincided with the decline of Khubilai's personal health in his sixties and seventies.

Communications in Khubilai's empire were speeded up through the use of his famous post-stations. During his reign, China had 1,400 stations on main thoroughfares, each either built at, or soon becoming the nexus of, a cluster of inns, taverns, hotels, grain silos and stables. A post-rider between major cities would ideally be able to cover up to 250 miles in a day, charging down wide roads built by slave labourers, and protected from thieves by the symbol of the Khan. The post-riders achieved such speeds by working their horses in sprints, not trots. An animal could be ridden as fast as possible between two post-stations, and then exchanged for another at each stop. The riders, of course, could also work in stages – it was only the mailbag that needed to run the whole length of a particular course. Such a system radically increased the speed by which Khubilai could communicate with his officials elsewhere in the empire. As a welcome side effect, slower transport could use the same routes, and take advantage of the same facilities. 'The thing is on a scale so wonderful and costly,' wrote Marco Polo, 'that it is hard to bring oneself to describe it.'[5]

Under Khubilai's reign, exotic items from distant corners of the empire were suddenly introduced into the Chinese world. Khubilai's court could dine on Tibetan curries; effervescent sherbet arrived from Persia as a panacean tonic; and rhubarb from the Gansu corridor was used as a laxative – Marco Polo took some dried rhubarb home with him, and it appears as one of the items in his will. China was swiftly integrated into trade routes to Central Asia, south-east Asia and the Middle East, largely benefiting the Muslim middlemen who led goods west on camel caravans, or transported them by sea from the Fujian and Canton ports. Foreign merchants were welcome in Khubilai's China, so long as they abided by the most crucial of Khubilai's economic rules:

Furthermore all merchants arriving from India or other countries, and bringing with them gold or silver or gems and pearls, are prohibited from selling to any one but the Emperor. He has twelve experts chosen for this business, men of shrewdness and experience in such affairs; these appraise the articles, and the Emperor then pays a liberal price for them in those pieces of paper.[6]

Khubilai pushed similar schemes throughout his empire, encouraging his subjects everywhere to give up their old coins and jewels in favour of the paper money, which was worth whatever Khubilai said it was worth. The shaky valuation of paper money was already all too clear to the Chinese, many of whom discovered that paper notes issued by Guyuk and Mongke were now deemed valueless by their successor. The idea of paper money was so bizarre that Marco Polo wrote about it at length, although he was not the first to mention that China used paper currency, nor was Khubilai the first to use it. Nonetheless, Khubilai's 'paper' money, made from the tough bark of mulberry trees, was treated with the utmost respect. Its use as legal tender was enforced by capital law – refusing to accept it could lead to a merchant's death. Forgery was also an offence met with execution. Subjects did their best to handle their money as well as possible, because notes that were too badly damaged to use could only be swapped at Khubilai's bank for fresh banknotes on payment of a 3 per cent transaction fee.

The admiring Polo wrote:

> Now you have heard the ways and means whereby the Great Kaan may have, and in fact *has*, more treasure than all the Kings in the World; and you know all about it and the reason why.[7]

However, the use of paper money was clearly open to abuse. In the aftermath of the fall of the Song, and still reeling from the impact of the unsuccessful invasion of Japan, Khubilai authorized the printing of large amounts of extra money in 1276.

Khubilai's grandest scheme, perhaps even more ambitious than the Grand Canal, was to unify his empire under a single language. He put his long-standing Tibetan adviser on the project, ordering the 'Phags-pa Lama to come up with a script that could function all over the empire, which could be used among the Mongols, the Chinese, the Tanguts and the Uighurs.

By 1269, the 'Phags-pa Lama had come up with a phonetic script that read from top to bottom, and was based to some extent on the script of his own native Tibetan. This phonetic system was soon used in many Mongol documents, seals and passes, and was taught all over the empire, although it never really caught on, as it was not even an artificial language, merely an artificial script. It was useless in foreign affairs, since countries not under the Mongol dominion were not obliged to learn it. Among the Mongols themselves, it was enthusiastically adopted in teaching them Chinese, as a gloss to teach them how to pronounce the characters, but it could never compete with the languages already in use in Khubilai's realm.

If it had worked, Khubilai's unified script could have changed Asia in unprecedented ways. It would have both unified disparate races with a shared culture, while simultaneously cutting many off from their own cultural roots. As previous experiments in new scripts have shown – in the China of the First Emperor, in seventeenth-century Vietnam, in twentieth-century Turkey – one of the long-term effects of a new writing system is that it rears a generation unable to read anything written before it. This in itself can be useful for a regime that wants to rewrite history and suppress debate, but Khubilai's scheme was doomed to failure from the very outset.

In part, this was because he seemed to be looking in the wrong place. Khubilai's time already had three languages that, between them, united all Eurasia. Merely changing the way they were spelt was not going to help anyone. Chinese already functioned as a lingua franca throughout East Asia – when Khubilai wrote letters to Japan, Vietnam and Champa, his envoys took those messages in Chinese, since even if the natives did not pronounce the ideograms in the same way as the Chinese, their educated ministers would usually understand the meaning. Japan was 'Riben' to the Chinese, 'Yatbun' to the southerners, 'Nhatban' to the Annamese and 'Nippon' to its own residents, but in all cases it was written in Chinese with the same characters: 日本 – 'Rising Sun'. Similarly, in Central Asia and Persia, one could not be an educated Muslim without being able to read Arabic. In points further west, although it really did not concern Khubilai by this stage, all educated men read Latin. As a result, the script of the 'Phags-pa Lama lasted only as long as Mongol dominion in a particular area.

At least part of Khubilai's efforts at unification – be it political, scriptorial or economic – was aimed at reducing the chances of further unrest. The Li Tan affair still smarted, and he took full advantage of China's concentrated, sedentary population to institute a surveillance system that would never have worked on the steppes. Marco Polo's descriptions of life in Chinese cities are of curfews and regulations, of troops quartered in homes and of womenfolk carefully sequestered from the occupation forces – Polo's complaints about Chinese women seem largely borne out of frustration that he never gets to meet any, except, that is, for the prostitutes in the red light district. This tallies with broader claims that the Yuan dynasty saw a resurgence in sexual conservatism, as the newly conquered Chinese sought to keep their daughters away from the eyes of Mongol soldiers.[8]

As the emperor, Khubilai was also discreetly regarded as the high priest of the Chinese state religion. He accepted this role, making seasonal sacrifices as was an emperor's duty, without officially declaring that any other religion in his realm was out of bounds, because as long as Khubilai refused to claim there was one 'true' religion, no single group of believers could gain the upper hand. It seems that Khubilai hoped that this would prevent any abuses such as those he had seen between the Buddhists and the Taoists earlier in his life.

Marco Polo relates an incident where Khubilai diplomatically hedged his bets among contending missionaries:

Learning that this was one of our principal feasts [Khubilai Khan] sent for all the Christians, and desired them to bring him the book containing the four Gospels. After treating the book to repeated applications of incense with great ceremony, he kissed it devoutly and desired all his barons and lords there present to do the same. This usage he regularly observes on the principal feasts of the Saracens, Jews and idolaters. Being asked why he did so, he replied: 'There are four prophets who are worshipped and to whom all the world does reverence. The

Christians say that their God was Jesus Christ, the Saracens Mahomet, the Jews Moses, and the idolaters Sakyamuni Burkhan [Buddha], who was the first to be represented as a God in the form of an idol. And I do honour and reverence to all four, so that I may be sure of doing it to him who is greatest in heaven and truest; and to him I pray for aid.'[9]

Although Khubilai claimed to rule a unified China, he faced simmering unrest in his homeland, and would continue to do so for the rest of his life. Far to the west, Ogodei's grandson Khaidu had yet to come and pledge allegiance. By the late 1260s, it had become obvious that he had no intention of ever coming to do so, and was setting himself up as the ruler of a large tract of land in Central Asia contiguous with 'Chinese Turkestan', modern Xinjiang.

News of this was carefully suppressed for as long as possible, as it was sure to cause (and eventually *did* cause) countrywide panic. One of the few obvious benefits, for the Chinese, of submitting to the Mongols was the understanding that with Khubilai in charge, there would no longer be a 'border problem' as technically there were no more borders. Hence the continued defiance of Khaidu, occasionally flowering into open conflict, remained a constant reminder to Khubilai that while he might have won China, in Mongolia there were still vestiges of his rivalry with members of his own family.

To make matters worse, Khaidu appeared to have gained the friendship, or at least guarded neutrality, of the Chaghadai Khanate and the Golden Horde on his own western flank, and was prepared to resist any attempts by Khubilai to bring him to heel. What form this resistance took is often difficult to determine. We know that in 1271 Khubilai took the peculiar step of appointing his son Prince Nomukhan, to a pacification office in the west. Nomukhan, as a younger son, was destined for a military life, but in endowing him with responsibilities for quelling the region, Khubilai was admitting that there was something going on there that needed to be quelled.

Even then, there was no great battle in the desert to set matters straight. Khaidu's opposition remained passive-aggressive. He and his horsemen were rarely to be found – always one step ahead of Nomukhan, never quite insulting him enough to justify a fight, never quite paying him enough homage to ensure that there was no question of disloyalty. Meanwhile, Nomukhan's assault on Khaidu took a similarly stealthy form. He moved to Khotan, in the heart of Khaidu's territory, and busied himself taking a census. When push came to shove, the matter of who was loyal or disloyal in the region came down to who collected taxes: Khaidu could sulk all he wanted, but if the locals were still paying tax to Beijing, it was unlikely to bother Khubilai too much.

By 1276, the desert intrigues had taken an unexpected turn. Many Mongol princelings under Nomukhan's command seem to have defected to Khaidu's side. Far from Beijing, they were more susceptible to Khaidu's thesis: that the sons of Tolui should never have been permitted to lord it over the other descendants of Temujin. Nomukhan was kidnapped with two of his associates and held under house (or rather, tent) arrest for almost ten years. The great general Bayan headed west to bring Nomukhan back, but like the man he now sought, found it impossible to even find Khaidu in the desert wastes.

As later rulers discovered to their cost, Chinese Turkestan is a difficult state to govern. The largely Muslim population owed a closer allegiance to the Middle East than the Far East. The conditions were harsh; the land area was immense. For year upon year, the 'war' between Khaidu and Khubilai amounted to little more than men stumbling around from oasis to oasis, occasionally fighting a skirmish or proclaiming a particular interest, but without any decisive battle.

Khaidu was a ghostly apparition – a figure at the periphery of Khubilai's world that never left him alone. He would pick and poke at Khubilai's defences for the rest of Khubilai's life, occasionally seizing territory outside his fiefdom, occasionally retreating into the steppes. He darted towards Karakorum itself, as if hoping to convene a rebel *kurultai*. He meddled in Tibetan affairs in an attempt to foster anti-Mongol feeling in the monasteries; he put out feelers to disaffected princelings on the other side of China, in the hope that together they might rise up against the sons of Tolui. Khaidu would even outlive Khubilai by a few years, but never quite got enough support to mount a true challenge. Had Khubilai and Khaidu been duelling over nothing more than Mongolia, perhaps Khaidu would have had the upper hand. Ironically, the very Mongol-based feud that Khaidu perpetrated served to drive Khubilai further towards a Chinese perspective. Without China, Khubilai might not have had the support he needed to shrug Khaidu off.

Marco Polo found the whole thing baffling, and described the endless conflict as if it were properly arranged battles (as some of the skirmishes undoubtedly were):

> The battle lasted so long that it was one of the hardest the Tartars ever fought. Either side strove hard to bring the matter to a point and rout the enemy, but to no avail.[10]

Polo was far more interested, though, in stories circulating about Khaidu's daughter, a towering Amazon whose name he recorded as Aiyaruk ('Bright Moon').

> Her father often desired to give her in marriage, but she would none of it. She vowed she would never marry till she found a man who could vanquish her in every trial; him she would wed and none else. And when her father saw how resolute she was, he gave a formal consent . . . that she should marry whom she wanted and when she wanted. The lady was so tall and muscular, so stout and shapely withal, that she was almost like a giantess.[11]

Khaidu had set himself up as the protector of old-time Mongol values, in opposition to Khubilai the Sinophile. It was hence only to be expected that Khaidu's daughter was set up in local legend as some sort of woman warrior, who boasted that she would only marry a man who could beat her at wrestling, and that anyone who failed in this would have to pay her 100 horses.

Aiyaruk supposedly successfully fought off 1,000 challengers over the course of the 1270s. Perhaps a little worried that his daughter might be getting long in the tooth, Khaidu is even reported as suggesting that she should try to let the next one win, but she refused, and won another hundred horses for the family herd. With a tacit admission that nobody was going to be good enough for her, she gave up on men entirely and accompanied Khaidu on his endless war against Khubilai's warriors.

> And ye must know that after this her father never went on a campaign but she went with him. And gladly he took her, for not a knight in all his train played such feats of arms as she did. Sometimes she would quit her father's side, and make a dash at the host of the enemy, and seize some man thereout, as deftly as a hawk pounces on a bird, and carry him to her father; and this she did many a time.[12]

Remarkably, most scholars suspect that there is an element of truth in the story of Aiyaruk, not least because while Polo in China is hearing of her exploits, his contemporary Rashid al-Din in Persia is writing down the same story, with the same names. Rashid, however, injects a disapproving note, that 'people suspected there was some kind of relationship between [Khaidu] and his daughter.'[13]

The story would grow with the telling, particularly in Persia, where legends arose about a king of 'Turan' (Persian: Central Asia), whose beautiful daughter insisted that any suitor should overcome a series of trials in order to win her hand in marriage. The story flourished in several variants as *The Daughter of Turan* – in Persian, 'Turan-dokht'.

It is perhaps most familiar to the Western reader in a libretto by Giuseppe Adami and Renato Simoni, first performed in 1926, shortly after the death of the composer of the accompanying music, Giacomo Puccini:

> This is the law: Turandot the Pure
> Will be the bride of the man of royal blood
> Who shall solve the riddles which she shall set.
> But if he fail in this test
> He must submit his proud head to the sword![14]

Puccini's *Turandot* is a world away from Khaidu's real-life resistance in western China. It retains garbled concepts of China and Tartary, and mixes elements of Mongol and Chinese culture. Nevertheless, it is fascinating to see a strand of true history informing a strand of modern history. Khaidu would eventually die in 1301, from wounds received in a failed strike at Karakorum itself – but his daughter, or a phantom of her, would spring to life on the opera stage in Milan six centuries later.

9

DRAGONS IN THE WATER

THE SECOND MONGOL ARMADA

In spring 1275, Khubilai sent a new embassy to Japan with a 'sealed message'. It was sealed because of its literal value – it was made of gold – and its explosive contents, for it conferred upon its recipient the title of 'King of Japan'. At other periods in Japanese history, such an offer might have been regarded as something of an honour, but it was met with disdain and anger when it reached Tokimune. Japan did not have a king – Japan had an emperor, and it did not require Khubilai Khan to confer such ranks upon him anyway. The men of the embassy were permitted to advance from the landing point at Dazaifu all the way to a place called the Dragon's Mouth, near Tokimune's headquarters at Kamakura. Tokimune was aghast at the suggestion that Khubilai was the 'great emperor', and that he had the power to confer a kingly title upon him. Ridiculing Khubilai as the 'highwayman of the world,' he turned on the shocked ambassadors:

Listen, Mongol. Whosoever threatens a peaceful nation or tribe with the object of confiscating its resources, and wherever he goes works a wanton destruction, leaving the innocent folk in misery, is without any doubt a robber . . . Since Temujin arose . . . till Khubilai's day, not a single day has been spent in peaceful rule, but the east and west have been terrorized by his brutal acts.[1]

The ambassadors begged to differ, pleading that Khubilai surely had the Mandate of Heaven, otherwise he would not have been permitted to unify the world to the extent that he had. With that in mind, one envoy tentatively suggested, Japan was rather out of touch, like 'a plant isolated from the sunshine'. He also offered an intriguing explanation for the invasion attempt of 1274, claiming that it was not an invasion, but a punitive expedition against Japanese criminals:

As to [Khubilai's] expedition to your western district, it was to my great regret, simply a chastisement of some wicked freebooters of that region, who had been afflicting the Korean coast; but it was never aimed at your country.[2]

It was here, unwisely, that the envoys proceeded to take out the golden statuette that bore the notice from Khubilai that Tokimune was henceforth proclaimed king. In answer, the samurai threw it to the ground in disgust, with the words: 'A curse be on Khubilai, who attempts the sacred throne of our empire!'

Soon afterwards, the envoys were executed, amid rumours that 'Mongol spies' had been apprehended in other parts of Japan. Such sightings seem incredibly doubtful, but must have exacerbated a general sense of paranoia in Japan. We know that there was at least one case of 'Mongols', shipwrecked far from the battles of 1274, who had transformed into a nest of bandits, terrorizing the local community with raids on food and resources for seven months, before they were summarily dealt with by vengeful samurai. Other stories, however, have the whiff of hysteria. It is difficult to believe, for example, the claim in Japanese records that a 'Mongol spy' was apprehended in Sendai, a far northern town. Considering that Mongol, Chinese and Korean comprehension of Japanese waters was so vague as to require them to attack repeatedly at Hakata, it seems unlikely indeed that an agent would have managed to make it all the way to Sendai. It seems more likely that anti-Mongol paranoia was gripping the Japanese nation, and that a number of local scores were being settled in the name of patriotism.

Tokimune had other local difficulties, about which Khubilai was sure to be unaware. The Buddhist leader Nichiren, a fervent opponent of the Zen sect favoured by the samurai, enjoyed considerable grass-roots support, and had frequently suggested that the Mongol invasions were a punishment decreed by Heaven in answer to corruption in Japan. His fulminations, in the wake of the 1274 invasion, had gained the aura of prophecy. At first exiled, then taken to the Dragon's Mouth for execution, Nichiren was saved at the last moment when, according to legend, his would-be executioner was struck by lightning.[3]

Nichiren's sect was part of a general sense among Japanese Buddhists that the end of the world was nigh. It was widely believed in medieval Japan that humanity was living in the 'latter days of the Law', a time when Buddha's teachings would falter and evil would slowly gain ground. Tokimune's decision to resist the Mongols should be considered in the light of all these pressures, as the act of an over-confident, inexperienced leader, acting in an era when many believed that doomsday was approaching. The Japanese resistance may have even been an act of calculated suicide – a determination by the younger samurai to fight a hopeless battle simply because it was the right thing to do. One account summarized the attitude in melancholy, vainglorious terms: 'The panther dies, but his skin retains its beauty; man is mortal, but his fame and reputation are immortal.'[4]

The Japanese, surely, would have known the likely penalty for executing a Mongol envoy. Moreover, Tokimune would have done so knowing, or at least hearing rumours to the effect, that the Southern Song dynasty had finally fallen, and that Khubilai Khan was the master of all China. He was even reminded of this in a letter sent from an unidentified Song official, which simply said: 'The Song dynasty has met its downfall at the hands of the Mongols. There is a chance that this danger may come to Japan, and we have therefore taken the risk of informing you.'⁵ To put it another way, the military might of the Southern Song was no longer directed at resisting the Mongols: it was now assimilated within Khubilai's realm, and was just about to be turned against the Japanese.

In 1278, with the Koreans already preparing a new fleet of their own, Khubilai ordered the foundation of the East Coast Office of Reconciliation – a military commission tasked with requisitioning, stocking and dispatching a new armada. However, the commission was based in Yangzhou, hundreds of miles to the south, connected to the Yangtze River by a canal. Such a decision shows Khubilai's resolve to involve conquered Song China in his scheme to attack Japan, as well as his determination to put a far greater number of his subjects to work on the project. Whereas the previous armada had largely used resources and manpower from Korea and the old Jurchen areas, now Khubilai insisted that the Song Chinese would also play their part.

We are quite fortunate, then, that one of the *semuren* officers in distant Yangzhou was one Marco Polo, who appears to have been one of the cogs in the great wheels of Khubilai's war effort, put in an administrative position in the city sometime after it fell to the Mongols. Polo's sojourn in China included a period spent working in an unspecified role in Yangzhou, where he reported 15,000 ships assembled on the river,

> all belonging to the Great Khan and available to carry his armies to the isles of the sea; for I must tell you that the sea is a mere day's journey from this place. Each transport ship has a crew of

twenty and carries about fifteen horses with the riders and provisions.[6]

It is through the writings of Marco Polo that knowledge of Japan first entered Western consciousness, although the information he had about the islands he called 'Cipangu' was entirely filtered through the requirements of Khubilai's war machine. Polo faithfully reported, for example, that Japan was 1,500 miles away from Khubilai's realm, ten times the actual distance across the Korea Strait. In claiming so, he appears to have been calculating the distance from where he worked in Yangzhou, and not from the state's closest borders.

Since Marco Polo never went to Japan, and only repeated what he heard, and what he heard was likely to have been from fellow servants of the Mongol occupying power, he seems to have been caught up in a forgotten propaganda offensive. There is no talk, in Polo's book, of Japan being the 'little kingdom' that Khubilai once patronized in his communiqués. Instead, it appears to have taken on a legendary status, as some sort of El Dorado – with 'endless quantities' of gold and 'pearls in abundance', tantalizingly out of reach just over the horizon, and seemingly couched in terms designed to whip up the Chinese conscripts into some semblance of military fervour:

> I will tell you a wonderful thing about the palace of that lord of that island. You must know that he has a great palace that is entirely roofed with fine gold, just as our churches are roofed with lead, insomuch as it would scarcely be possible to estimate its value. Moreover, all the pavement of the palace, and the floors of its chambers are entirely of gold, in plates like slabs of stone, a good two fingers thick; and the windows are also of gold, so that altogether the richness of this palace is past all bounds and all belief.[7]

In 1280, the news finally reached Khubilai that Tokimune had executed his ambassadors. His underlings, including a

newly eager King of Korea, immediately began requesting to
be given the honour of leading a punitive mission, but were
advised by Khubilai that it was time to wait. It seems that he
was determined that this time the much larger second armada
would chastise Japan once and for all. He chose as leaders Hol-
Ton and Hong Dagu again, charged with organizing a repeat
of their earlier assault, leapfrogging from Korea, via Tsushima
and Iki to an attack on Hakata Bay once more. However, this
time there would be a second fleet, led by the Mongol general
Arakhan, setting out from the mouth of the Yangtze, crossing
the dangerously open waters of the East China Sea, to
rendezvous with the first fleet somewhere near Iki Island. It
was hoped that the 'Chinese' fleet would be able to solve some
of the supply problems that appear to have troubled the
Mongols in their earlier invasion.

Even at this point, the Mongols appear to have been confused about the nature of their enemy. In 1281, at a conference
with Khubilai and Arakhan, one of the generals, Fang Wenhu,
asked to be given 2,000 extra horses, and a squad of Muslim
siege engineers specializing in explosives. However, Khubilai's
reply, recorded in the annals, was that 'in naval combat there
would be no opportunity to use them.'[8]

In a presentiment of trouble, Khubilai was also recorded
waving off his commanders with a strangely conciliatory
message, reminding them that a land is of less worth if its
occupants have all been slain, and imploring his commanders to
stick together:

> Another matter about which we are considerably concerned is
> the danger you might fall into discord among yourselves. In case
> the Japanese come to discuss matters, we desire you all to be of
> one mind, planning together and answering as though out of
> one mouth.[9]

'Discord' is a difficult term to translate here. Khubilai may
have simply meant that two fleets, leaving from ports

hundreds of miles apart, were sure to arrive at different times and find themselves communicating (and fighting) with different representatives of the Japanese state. However, after the disagreements between the Korean and Mongol generals during the previous invasion, Khubilai may have feared similar frictions among his multiracial force. Hol-Ton's army included 'criminals whose death sentences had been commuted', alongside regular Korean conscripts. Fan Wenhu was a surrendered general of the Song dynasty, leading a body of largely Chinese troops, loyal to him. Arakhan, meanwhile, was a younger figure in his late forties, a Mongol general who seems to have lacked much of the natural charisma of his non-Mongol officers. Relations between Arakhan and Fan Wenhu seem to have been particularly frosty, and were widely enough known at the time to make their way into Marco Polo's writings: 'You must know that there was much ill-will between these two barons, so that one would do nothing to help the other.'[10]

With such a presentiment of disaster, the two fleets got underway in June 1281. The Chinese fleet left port first, while its Korean colleagues waited an allotted number of days before also setting out, in the hope that such staggered departures would allow them to reach Japan at the same time. The Chinese fleet was to attempt a landing and occupation on the island of Hirado, while the Korean counterpart would land further to the west at Iki.

That, at least, was the original plan, but either the Chinese fleet took longer than expected, or the Koreans jumped the gun. Hol-Ton, Hong Dagu and their boats left Korea early, swooping down on Tsushima much as they done in their earlier attack. Realizing that Tsushima was merely a waypoint for an invasion of the mainland, many of the locals did not fight, but instead fled to caves in the nearby hillsides. There, they might have been able to hide and wait out the Mongol raids, were it not for the cries of their children, which gave them away, leading to a new massacre.

A far stronger resistance awaited on the island of Iki, where two samurai commanders were waiting with forces estimated in Chinese chronicles at 'many tens of thousands'. They were routed by Mongol explosives, but it is not clear from extant accounts whether the 'defeat' of the Japanese was sufficient to leave Iki in Mongol hands. Regardless of whether Iki belonged to the Mongols, the bulk of the fleet continued westwards.

Fully aware that Hakata Bay and the road to Dazaifu were heavily fortified and laden with enemy soldiers, Hong Dagu appears to have made an abortive attempt to land a little further west along the coast, at Shiga Island. But Hakata Bay was the port of choice in the region *because* there were no comparable anchorages. Hong Dagu and a number of his men tried to wade ashore, but were swiftly repulsed by Japanese defenders, with Hong himself narrowly avoiding capture.[11]

An unspecified disease appears to have broken out on the Mongol ships, probably as a result of the men crammed together in close quarters for over a week. According to Chinese annals, this disease alone killed 3,000 soldiers.

Still avoiding Hakata Bay, and determined to find another place to land, Hol-Ton ordered the Mongol fleet lashed together into a massive, circular, floating fortress off the coast of Munakata, even further to the west. The Mongols made periodic raids all along the coast, but were repulsed at every juncture by the samurai.

Weeks wore on, with still no sign of the second fleet. Unknown to Hol-Ton and the others, commander Arakhan had been taken ill (in some sources, had actually died), and his underlings had been forced to wait for his replacement. The replacement in question, the Mongol general Atahai, arrived in port to discover that his underlings had given up waiting and set sail anyway.

Quite by accident, the 'Chinese' fleet now genuinely had a Chinese commander in the form of Fan Wenhu, who arrived late in Hirado. Seemingly encountering little resistance, he left a group of his men to fortify the island and continued down the coast towards Shiga, where he found the earlier arrivals in their floating fortress, bickering about the best plan of action.

Kim Banggyeong, a veteran of many Korean wars, set down the position in logistical terms:

> In accordance with the order given, three months' provisions were brought here. A month's provisions are still left. It will not be too late, therefore, if we wait for the arrival of the southern forces, and resume the attack in concert.[12]

Kim went on the record with this assessment after a month of skirmishes – suggesting that the phantom month's worth of missing provisions must have been sunk or captured by the Japanese. Pointedly, none of his fellow commanders were prepared to go on the record with their own thoughts – none dared suggest a withdrawal, though considering that it would take them at least a week to get home, supplies were dwindling dangerously close to the point of no return.

Fan Wenhu's reinforcements finally arrived in mid-July, leading the Mongol forces to try a succession of further sallies. The best that the Mongol forces managed was the seizure of a small island in Hakata Bay, where they were able to quarter some of their horses. Otherwise, the Mongol forces had trouble pushing ashore any closer than the high-water mark. The defensive walls gave the Japanese the upper hand, while the invaders continued to be troubled by supply issues.

As before, the Japanese were ever ready to take the fight to their enemy. With the invaders largely confined offshore, the samurai were seen literally fighting each other to win places in the small attack boats that harried the Mongol fleet each and every day.[13]

Takezaki Suenaga, veteran of the first invasion, was at the forefront of the brawlers, and hatched a devious scheme to use against the enemy. While many of his fellow samurai failed to distinguish between the races of the invaders, Takezaki realized that many of the ships were crewed by Chinese and Koreans, who lacked any motivation to fight on behalf of their Mongol masters. With that in mind, Takezaki came up with a cruel plan of luring them into apparent capture with a grappling hook, and then killing them anyway:

> I don't think [the invaders] will fight with abandon, fearing not for their life, until we board their enemy ships, take a 'bear claw' and capture them alive. They will prefer capture to death, for they want to return to their foreign lands. Once we have them hooked, stab them by impaling them where there is a join in their armour.[14]

Another samurai, Kono-Michiari, was so eager for battle that he legendarily pitched his tent on the wrong side of the defensive wall, in full view of the enemy. On one occasion, he witnessed a heron pick up a fallen arrow and drop it onto one of the largest ships, and interpreted this occurrence as a 'message from the gods' that he should lead a suicidal assault on the Mongol flagship.

This enterprise was so obviously insane that none of the captains on the outlying clusters of Mongol boats thought that Kono-Michiari could be attacking. Instead, they assumed he was approaching the Mongol leaders to surrender, and hence stood blithely back to watch his two attack-boats manoeuvre through their lines. It was only when Kono-Michiari was close to the flagship and chopped down his own mast to make a boarding ramp that the Mongols realized they were once more under attack. Kono-Michiari led a daring assault into the heart of the ship, finding, as had Takezaki before him, that many of the 'Mongols' were all too ready to surrender. Twice wounded, and losing an uncle to an enemy arrow, Kono-Michiari lingered onboard long enough to defeat a hulking marine in single combat, set fire to the vessel, and retreated – he even appears to have dashed off a celebratory poem on the way back to shore.[15]

Morale was at an all-time low for the sailors in the Mongol fleet, besieged by fanatical defenders, forced to spend weeks at sea in sight of a hostile land, decimated by disease and constantly hounded by samurai raiding parties. Unfamiliar with coastal waters, steersmen were constantly jumpy about the 'shadows of hills in the water', a poetic term for treacherous shallows. There were complaints among the crews about the 'smell of sulphur' (probably paranoia about shipboard arson), and superstitious reports of 'dragons in the water'.

Fresh samurai were constantly arriving to replenish the defenders on the shore. Arrows and swords were replenished daily. Even the priesthood was mobilized, praying all the while for some sort of divine aid. In late August, their prayers were answered, with what the Chinese annals would describe as a 'furious hurricane' and what the Japanese would infamously call a *kamikaze*:

> And it came to pass that there arose a north wind, which blew with great fury and caused great damage to the coasts of that island, for its harbours were few. It blew so hard that the Great Kaan's fleet could not stand against it. And when the chiefs saw that, they came to the conclusion that if the ships remained where they were, the whole navy would perish.[16]

There is no reason to doubt the Chinese sources. Modern marine archaeologists have even found evidence of the terrible ruin unleashed by this second 'divine wind', right where medieval accounts said it would be, off the coast of the southern Japanese island of Takashima. The wreckage of sturdy, purpose-built warships, but not designed to withstand unearthly storm conditions, lies scattered about the seabed. A modern-day scholar has estimated the power of the storm that would have been required to smash apart one of the stronger ships:

> It would have broken apart in a storm with winds gusting to approximately 124 miles per hour – a storm powerful enough to be rated as a 'catastrophic typhoon' by the Japanese Meteorological Association. That's enough wind, on the

Saffir Simpson Hurricane Scale, to form a Category 3 'major typhoon' capable of generating storm surges of 9 to 12 feet.[17]

In 1994, Japanese archaeologists excavated the seabed near the place where the Mongol ships were supposed to have been anchored offshore, lashed together in their odd marine fortress. Beneath centuries of silt, they found dozens of anchors, their cables all broken, all tellingly pointing towards the shoreline, as if all the ships had been lifted in one terrible wave and hurled towards the rocks.

Modern research has also afforded us an intriguing view of something that the defenders never noticed and the invaders never mentioned. What few planks and boards survive from the actual invasion fleet are a world removed from the towering, floating castles of popular lore. True, the flagships of Khubilai's invasion fleet were probably massive, purpose-built battleships, as large as thirteenth-century Chinese marine technology would permit. But the other wrecks are noticeably smaller; many of them lack keels suitable for seaborne travel. Perhaps we should return to Marco Polo's astonished account of the fleet assembling on the river, and ask ourselves if his great fleet did not comprise a fatal number of *river* boats.

The Yangtze is a wide river, easy to mistake for a sea at its broadest point. River boats on the Yangtze would be impressive enough to Mongol assessors to perhaps escape close scrutiny. With funds squeezed and a local population keen to get the mission over and done with, had Khubilai's officials sent a fleet across the sea that was never designed for open water? If they had, then it is no wonder that so many of the vessels would fall prey to a storm.

Revisionist historians of the 'divine wind' now have actual pieces of the fleet to look at, although archaeologist Randall Sasaki has cautioned his colleagues that the enterprise is 'analogous to reconstructing 4000 different jigsaw puzzles with only 1% of the pieces remaining and no templates'.[18] Even so, there are telling scraps of evidence to be gleaned from the wreckage found scattered across the seabed. Surviving nails are rich in sulphur, suggesting that they were fired in a hurry, using lower quality iron. The quality of pottery shards, thought to have once been used for food or oil storage, is surprisingly slapdash. We can look at their workmanship and ask ourselves if officials, such as Marco Polo, might not have cut corners, creamed off funds and otherwise made the Mongol invasion resources look good only on paper.

Some of the wreckage displays conspicuous signs of bad workmanship. Other parts appear to have been hammered together from pieces of older ships. There are inspection seals, giving the names of Mongol officials, suggesting that even before the armada set sail, there were enough doubts about its seaworthiness for a call on official sanction. Most of the nails are long gone, but they have rusted away to reveal the holes where they were hammered in, and some are to be found in clusters, as if shipbuilders have hastily bodged the planks roughly into place. Many of the anchors recovered near Takashima are in two pieces – a cheaper, faster means of manufacture than the one-piece, carved stone anchors habitually carried by Chinese ships. However, such a design is also more apt to break apart: so many of Khubilai's mariners were trusting in an anchor design that was weaker than the one they were used to.

That is not all. One reason for the 'jigsaw puzzle' element of the armada wreckage is that, in the words of Randall Sasaki, 'more than 80% of the timber fragments are less than 50 cm long.'[19] There may be a perfectly mundane explanation for this – the many centuries of turbulence and waves have crushed the wooden beams into smithereens. However, it is also possible that they were smashed into pieces *before* they hit the seabed. Could it be that the armada vessels, chained together in calm seas, ground against each other with the increased friction of the storm, destroying each other on the surface before sinking?

The question of the fate of the Mongol armada is an ongoing investigation, but there is already enough evidence to suggest that the 'divine wind' had many mundane assistants. Bad, hurried construction, vessels unsuitable for the sea, weak anchors and brittle nails may have all played their part in the downfall of Khubilai's great fleet. Sasaki is prepared to go even further, proposing a working hypothesis that 'ill-preparation may have been the real cause for the failure of invasion.'[20] The storm still happened, and there would still have been casualties among the Mongols, but as research continues on the marine archaeology of the Takashima wreckage, the possibility remains that it was shipbuilders and finance controllers in distant Yangzhou, not the weather in Japan, that devastated Khubilai's fleet.

Many of the invaders survived the storm. Up to 37,000 of the sailors and soldiers scrambled ashore at Takashima, a small island just to the north of Hirado, where a bedraggled Fan Wenhu discovered that, although much of his fleet had gone, his underling Zhang Xi had wisely kept his own ships neatly spaced off the shore of Hirado, and had hence managed to ride out the storm. Consequently there were enough ships to get a large number of the men home, and this is what Fan Wenhu argued for. Zhang Xi begged to differ:

> A great majority of the troops are drowned but those who have escaped are all strong men. Let us take advantage of their spirit, which knows no retreat, and, depending on our enemies for provisions, try once more a daring assault.[21]

Zhang Xi, it should be noted, had probably not seen any action for a month – if he was quartered in Hirado, he would have spent the intervening weeks waiting expectantly for the landing forces to report the securing of a beachhead at Hakata or a point further west. Thus, he may have lacked any direct experience of the kind of resistance that the landing forces had faced. With several casualties among the leading officers and Hol-Ton still missing in action, Fan Wenhu pulled rank, saying that he was the man who would be held responsible in Beijing, and he was not about to hand over strategic planning to an underling. Disgusted, Zhang Xi took seventy horses off a surviving transport ship and handed it over to Fan Wenhu. Fan sailed back towards Korea in the requisitioned vessel, leaving Zhang Xi to his fate, combing the beaches for supplies for a doomed counter-attack.

It is this impasse, not the previously mentioned tensions between the generals, that appears to have informed Marco Polo's account of rivalry between the 'barons'. His own reporting of the Japanese disaster tallies closely enough with the Chinese annals, noting that the fleeing ships reached a small island (i.e. Takashima) some four miles from the Japanese coast:

> ... on which they were driven ashore in spite of all they could do, and a great part of the fleet was wrecked and a great multitude of the force perished, so that there escaped only some 30,000 men, who took refuge on this island. These held themselves for dead men, for they were without food, and knew not what to do, and they were in great despair when they saw that such of the ships as had escaped the storm were making full sail for their own country, without the slightest sign of turning back to help them. And this was because of the bitter hatred of the two barons in command of the force; for the baron who escaped never showed the slightest desire to return to his colleague, who was left upon the island in the way that you have heard.[22]

Polo's version is remarkably accurate. Khubilai's own chronicles, the *History of the Yuan*, describe events in much the same way, noting that by the time Fan Wenhu reached safety he had already a concocted a story of his own, which suggested the storm struck much earlier in the campaign, and that he had been troubled by numerous desertions by generals he knew to be safely dead and hence unable to defend themselves. Unfortunately for him, he was not the only man to make it back alive.

A sailor called Yu Chang also made it back to Korea, having somehow escaped his Japanese captors. He, too, said that the fleet had been wrecked by a great storm, but added that the highest-ranking generals and admirals had commandeered one of the last serviceable vessels and fled, abandoning thousands of their men to their fate. Zhang Xi, in this version of the tale, was not a 'general' at all, but a humble 'chief of a hundred', a mere captain, elected as the new leader by the deserted men. This luckless junior officer put his men to work cutting down trees on Takashima, hoping thereby to construct enough boats – not to make a new assault, but to follow his superiors home in defeat. It was during this exercise that the Japanese arrived in overwhelming numbers, killing many of the survivors. Only the Chinese and Korean conscripts were permitted to live on as slaves, the narrator somehow later escaping.

Many other stragglers drifted back to Korea over the months that followed, largely confirming the troopers' version of events, and not that of their leaders. Fan Wenhu and his accomplices were indicted for dereliction of duty, and the heroic Zhang Xi was given a posthumous decoration.

Back in Beijing, Khubilai immediately ordered a third expedition. However, the news of the cataclysm soon began to spread. When a government censor in the Yangtze River area dared to suggest that yet another attack was a bad idea, the putative third invasion attempt of Japan was put off, ostensibly to allow the Chinese and Korean people some time to recover from the tax burden and bereavement incurred by the earlier failures. Even while postponing the invasion, Chinese rhetoric attempted to salvage some honour at the expense of the Japanese. One southern Chinese communiqué to Khubilai noted: 'The dwarves should be punished and never overlooked, but rate them not too lightly. We do not dread a venomous viper the less because it is so small and weak.'[23]

In 1283, Khubilai ordered an invasion again, appointing the Mongol general Atahai to arrange a new attack. Requisitioning some 670 ships, and preparing armour and supplies, Atahai had got as far as staging military exercises off the coast of Korea before his expedition was again cancelled. The reason, this time, was that Khubilai was no longer the unquestioned ruler of China. His feud with the distant Central Asian Khan Khaidu had led to dissent among the people, and what appear to have been riots and revolts. Rather than push the Chinese into another foreign war, Khubilai devoted his efforts to maintaining peace in his own realm, and shelved the invasion scheme yet again.

In 1284, he sent a Buddhist monk as an envoy to sound out the Japanese once more, but, perhaps mercifully for many thousands of potential casualties, the man was murdered by the ship's crew taking him to Japan. Khubilai's embassy thus never had the chance to fail, nor was he repudiated by the Japanese, and the criminal crew took the blame for what might have otherwise started another war. Although Khubilai occasionally brought up the subject of Japan, the matter was quietly allowed to drop in 1286. Throughout the Mongol dynasty, Korean administration maintained an office for the subjugation of Japan, but it never saw its purpose fulfilled.[24]

10

THE ACCURSED DOCTRINES

POLITICAL INTRIGUES AND RELIGIOUS PERSECUTIONS

The later years of Khubilai's rule are distinguished, at least in the official record, by a series of scandals and vendettas. While many of the problems that beset him were valid and crucial, the hysterical portents of disaster, particularly in the *History of the Yuan*, often overlook some of the achievements of Khubilai's late-period administration.

In Yunnan for example, where he had won one of his earliest victories, Khubilai had put a Muslim governor in charge. It would appear that in the former kingdom of Dali, Khubilai had none of the qualms about Muslims that he had in areas nearer to Khaidu's realm. In fact, with Yunnan as a vital sector on the road to both Annam and Mian (Burma), its governor needed to be entirely loyal to Khubilai's policies, and Saiyid Ajall Shams al-Din (d.1279) behaved impeccably in this regard. Like many governors in Khubilai's realm, Saiyid was a *semuren*, in charge of Chinese and Mongol troops, but also leading yet another ethnic group – the local Dali people being a different race from the Han Chinese. And yet, Saiyid seems to have turned Yunnan into a model province.

The ideal of a fair-minded, lawful state, with a multi-ethnic administration, seems ably represented by Saiyid's tenure in Yunnan. In the early days of his reign, some Chinese/Mongol soldiers were caught assaulting some locals. Saiyid brooked no excuse and had the men executed, teaching a valuable lesson to both the local people and his own soldiers. He seems to have incurred the respect not only of his subjects, but also of the Muslim traders in the region. Saiyid's 'golden age' was accompanied with public works that transformed the Yunnan region for centuries to come – water-conservation projects, irrigation schemes and construction of terraces, which remained in use until recent times. He also adopted a gentle attitude towards fiscal change, permitting the locals to continue to use their pre-existing monetary system based on cowrie shells. It certainly did no harm, and the use of the former regime's currency in occupied Yunnan saved it from some of the worst problems of the paper money inflation that was ruining the empire's economy elsewhere.

Most notably of all, Saiyid built two mosques, a Confucian temple and schools, and a Buddhist monastery. He left Chinese traditions intact, and did not interfere with local superstitions or beliefs. When he died, his five sons continued to hold high office in Yunnan and two other provinces – it was a textbook case of what Khubilai intended for his empire. Moreover, Saiyid was a perfect product of the Mongol system – he had been raised among the Mongols because his grandfather had surrendered to them during the fall of Bukhara in 1225. His family had hence embraced the Mongol expansion, been transformed by it, and become instrumental in its furtherance.

Saiyid was, however, the exception rather than the rule. Despite the benevolent state of affairs in Yunnan, Khubilai did not see its success story repeated in many other parts of his realm, where religious and political intrigues were tearing many of his institutions apart.

Things took a turn for the worse in the 1280s. Certainly, in terms of the stories that have survived to the present day, the decade found him surrounded by embittered conflicts over religious belief, with his carefully cultivated neutrality subjected to constant battering, with appeals for intercession in disputes that he wanted no part of. Despite Khubilai's hope that his adjudication between Buddhists and Taoists had stopped further antagonism, the rival religions were literally attacking each other again. A fire at a Buddhist temple in Beijing in 1280 was later found to be arson committed by Taoists. Mongol investigators uncovered the conspirators, executed one, mutilated another and sent six more into exile. Emboldened by such a show of force against the Taoists, factions within the Buddhist community came forward to ask that other Taoist crimes be taken into consideration. To Khubilai's great indignation, the inflammatory Taoist texts that he had banned in 1258 were now revealed to have been in circulation throughout his realm. Far from being taken out off the Taoist curriculum, the *Book of Barbarian Conversions* was still a popular part of it, and appeared to have fostered an entire new generation of Buddhist–Taoist confrontation.

Khubilai's response was drastic. He ordered for the offending Taoist scriptures to be hunted down and burned. Moreover, realizing that this decree had been carried out at least once already to no great long-term effect, he ordered that the means of reproducing multiple copies of the scroll should be destroyed. The carved wooden printing blocks, the true engines of dissemination of the Taoist heresies, were smashed to pieces.

Khubilai's exasperated intent was to preserve 'true' Taoism. He still revered the ancient sage Laozi's *Book of the Path and the Power*, but strongly objected to the many fortune-tellers, diviners and conjurors that were selling trinkets, charms and doubtful prophecies under the guise of being Taoist priests. Marco Polo even claimed to have visited one – an old woman of the 'Idolaters' who told him where he could find his lost ring:

> If anyone has lost anything, either because he has been robbed or because he does not know where he left it . . . he will go . . . to the old woman, so that she may inquire of these idols about the missing object. She will then instruct him to offer incense to the idols. After this she will question them about the lost object, and they will reply as the case may be. Then she will say to the loser: 'Look in such-and-such a place and you will find it.'[1]

Impressive though this might have been for Polo, it had little to do with Taoism. Although Khubilai's purge of such heresies pointedly preserved copies and printing blocks of the *Book of the Path and the Power*, it was sure to be misinterpreted – particularly among the lower-rent, uneducated 'hedge wizards' who thought of themselves as Taoists without having any real instruction in the religion's history or literature. Far from regarding Khubilai as a friend of 'true' Taoism, many self-identified Taoists regarded his latest reaction as a form of persecution. This belief became even more widespread when it was revealed that 'Taoists' were being forced to become Buddhists, and that Buddhist overseers (who else?) had been appointed to trouble-spots to make sure that the newly chastised 'Taoists' had reformed their criminal ways.

In fact, some of Khubilai's supposedly anti-Taoist enforcers were actual Taoists, as the emperor made a deliberate effort to involve true Taoists in the removal of the charlatans. In the case of the burned books and smashed printing blocks, the decision over which were true scriptures and which were forgeries had been left in the hands of the highest-ranking Taoist in China, whom Khubilai had deliberately appointed to avoid any accusations that he was not acting in the best interests of the Taoists themselves.

As if the Buddhist–Taoist conflict was not causing enough trouble, Khubilai also became increasingly hostile towards the Muslims in his realm. In the early 1280s, a group of Muslim merchants from the Lake Baikal region attended one of Khubilai's banquets. In the very Mongol spirit of hospitality,

Khubilai offered them meat from his own table, only for the visitors to refuse it because it was not *halal*. This was a public embarrassment for Khubilai, and soon led to the order that all animals in his realm should be slaughtered in the prescribed Mongol manner – the 'hunter' (or butcher), should bind it, cut it open and pull out its heart.

It is surprising that this issue had not come up before. Mongol butchers, presumably to avoid waste, preferred to keep the blood inside their meat. As one observer noted:

> They make a slit with a knife between two ribs, through which their put their hand and squeeze the heart till the creature expires; by this method all the blood remains in the carcass.[2]

Such an idea was entirely at odds with the Muslim provisions for *dhabihah* or ritual slaughter, which called for an animal to be drained of its blood. This does not seem to have bothered anyone until the fateful banquet, where the Muslim guests were seen to publicly trample on the stern Mongol rules of hospitality:

> [Khubilai] was offended and commanded: 'Henceforth Muslims and People of the Book shall not slaughter sheep, but shall split open the breast and side in the Mongol fashion. And whoever slaughters sheep [in the forbidden manner] shall be slaughtered likewise, and his wife, children, house and property given to the informer.'[3]

Specifically, animals were not to be slaughtered by cutting their throats – guaranteed to cause trouble in the Muslim and Jewish sectors of the population. It seems like a curiously petty law to introduce, but we might suspect that even if Khubilai were unaware of its implications, other factions within his government must have been fully aware of the trouble it would cause. A similar ban on circumcision was equally sure to alienate Jews and many Muslims.

The *halal* scandal was a calculated act of provocation, and the likely culprit was Jesus the Christian (Isa Tarsa Kelemechi, or Aixie to the Chinese), an influential Nestorian within the Mongol administration. Jesus the Christian could also be blamed for the epilogue to this story, which saw general concerns about rebellious elements twisted to new ends. The proclamation offered irresistible incentives to servants to inform on their masters for any rebellious behaviour, real or imagined. The decree was seemingly made by officials who already knew well enough that devout Muslims were sure to be slaughtering their livestock in a *halal* manner in the privacy of their own homes – relying, in essence, on the assumption that the new law was a temporary anomaly, best dealt with in terms of 'don't ask, don't tell'. In pointedly soliciting such disloyalty, Khubilai's administration was guaranteed to precipitate a new crisis. Hundreds of disgruntled servants and neighbours soon informed on their Muslim associates and their supposed 'law-breaking' activities. In a truly ludicrous, manufactured scandal, Khubilai's ministers were hence able to report a vast upsurge in Muslim criminality in his realm.

In a propagandist masterstroke, Jesus the Christian then mentioned to Khubilai Khan that the holy book of the Muslims called for the deaths of anyone who worshipped more than one god:

> But when the sacred months are passed away, kill the idolaters wherever ye may find them; and take them, and besiege them, and lie in wait for them in every place of observation. (Quran IX: 5)

Chapter nine of the Quran remains a controversial passage, regularly cited even today in arguments over *jihad* and Islamist extremism. It was certainly the wrong thing to point out to a despot with mounting paranoia – particularly when it was translated to him, as Jesus the Christian appears to have ensured, as an open call for the death of anyone who refuses to declare for any particular god. With Khubilai having diligently encouraged a syncretist policy for decades, it is easy to see how he might be persuaded that the Quran contained a secret message calling for his assassination.

Marco Polo, who had no love for 'the accursed doctrine of the Saracens', takes evident glee in recounting the story, particularly when Khubilai summons a leading imam to his court to explain.[4] The luckless imam, either through a translation error or an overwhelming lack of tact, replied that Khubilai was quite safe, as 'the time had not yet come, and we do not have the means.'

'I at least have the means,' replied Khubilai curtly, initiating proceedings for the execution of the imam.[5]

With great haste, another imam was found who could put a more friendly spin on the offending passage. Hamid al-Din, of Sarmakand, was brought to Khubilai's court and breezily pointed Khubilai to the clauses that could be seen to identify him as a friend of the Muslims, and they as loyal subjects of his. We can only speculate what passages they may have been, but a likely candidate is Quran IX: 6: 'Then while they stand by you, stand ye by them; verily, God loves those who fear.'

The deadly inquisition came to a halt, but clearly reflected a general state of resentment among the factions at Khubilai's court. Amid rising tensions, Khubilai lost his greatest stabilizing influence in 1281 with the death of his favourite consort, Chabi. An ageing Khubilai began to feel, justifiably or otherwise, that forces were at work in his empire that conspired to undermine his legacy. In fact, he may have contributed to that sense himself, by starting to rely on Chabi's replacement, Nambi, to convey messages between him and his courtiers – Nambi may have begun issuing proclamations in the increasingly reclusive Khubilai's name without his knowledge. Meanwhile, Chabi's death also appears to have removed a limiting influence from a previously unmentioned faction – the officials and royals who had accreted around her son, and Khubilai's heir apparent, Zhenjin.

Zhenjin had had the best possible education one could expect. He had been tutored from an early age by Confucian scholars, and was at the heart of the politics and politicking of the early Yuan dynasty. He enjoyed the personal attention of the prominent Tibetan Buddhist, the 'Phags-pa Lama, who is said to have written his didactic work *What One Should Know* for the benefit of the young prince. When Zhenjin was aged twenty, in 1263, Khubilai had made him the Prince of Yan, appointing him at the nominal governor of the Beijing region, where the new capital was already taking shape. Ten years later, when Zhenjin was thirty and his father pushing sixty, Khubilai officially announced that Zhenjin was his successor. Not for Khubilai the vague, foggy deathbed mumblings of Temujin or Ogodei; true to his Chinese tendencies, he specifically named a successor, so that his empire was sure to be in good hands after he was gone.

While the nomination of Zhenjin at least made matters clear, it put Zhenjin in the frustrating position of many a royal heir, forced to wait on the sidelines during the twilight years of his predecessor. In this capacity, it is unsurprising that he may have been lured into some of the intrigues surrounding Khubilai's later administration, particularly if Zhenjin were attached to a faction with its own views on the future of the Yuan state.

Matters came to a head in the sudden scandal of the Ahmad Fanakati case around 1282. The tale is presented, by both Marco Polo and Rashid al-Din, as a riveting political whodunit, in which a seemingly simple crime soon spirals way beyond the expectations of the investigators, with implicating evidence against men in high places that is impossible to ignore.[6]

Ahmad was an official of high rank within Khubilai's organization, described by Polo in terms befitting a grand vizier:

This person disposed of all governments and offices, and passed sentence on all malefactors, wrote Marco, and whenever he desired to have anyone whom he hated put to death, whether with justice or without it, he would go to the Emperor and say: 'Such a one deserves death, for he has done this or that against your imperial dignity.' Then the Lord [Khubilai] would say 'Do as you think right,' and so he would have the man forthwith executed.[7]

It was hence a matter of some scandal when Ahmad was found murdered, and suspicion increased when his murderers were first suspected of being Mongols, and then revealed as Chinese *disguised* as Mongols. Ahmad had gone to meet what he thought were Mongols, though neither he nor his surviving underlings were able to discern their precise identity, as they were dazzled by the strangers' torchlight. Ahmad was grabbed and beheaded, though an archer immediately shot the actual murderer. However, Khubilai's investigator, a man called Kogatai, refused to accept such a neat denouement, and delved deeper into the events surrounding the murder.

Marco Polo was ready to believe the next layer of the unfolding story, which was that Ahmad had got what he deserved:

And you should know that all the [Chinese] detested the Great Khan's rule because he set over them governors who were Tartars, or still more frequently Saracens, and these they could not endure, for they were treated by them just like slaves.[8]

Polo's claims are somewhat exaggerated, and do not wholly reflect realities of the time, although they certainly played to his own prejudices. In fact, there was only one Muslim 'governor' and that was the moderate Saiyid whom Khubilai had appointed as the lord of Yunnan. However, the embers of the earlier *halal* scandal were still smouldering in some parts of the empire, and had led to a general fall in the numbers of Muslims in Khubilai's realm. In fact, taking such data to a logical conclusion, those Muslims left in China by that point were far more likely to be moderates or at the very least pragmatic.

Nonetheless, Polo's own account taps into an apparent source of enduring resentment towards Muslims, in particular for being representatives of the foreign order that had conquered China. Men 'with beards' it seemed – and that meant all *semuren*, but in particular the Muslims – were held responsible for all modern ills, in a hate campaign that would surely eventually progress beyond the agents of the conquerors to the conquerors themselves.

As the investigations proceeded, the ever more outlandish explanations inspired wildly differing reactions. Polo, playing up to a Christian readership, is ever ready to believe that Ahmad the Muslim finance official was venal and corrupt, and even cast evil spells over Khubilai. The *History of the Yuan*, written by the Chinese, similarly pillories him as one of the 'three villainous ministers'. But Rashid al-Din, writing in a Persia under the rule of an Islamic Mongol dynasty, stresses that Ahmad performed his duty 'with honour' for twenty-five years, but was brought down by a long-running feud with a Buddhist called Gao. The two men had been at each other's throats for nine long years, and Gao – the murderer who was so conveniently killed at the scene of the crime – had even made a previous attempt on Ahmad's life, but had been pardoned after performing useful service at the siege of Xiangyang.[9]

Ahmad had been a competent, indeed an able, tax official. He had established government monopolies in several lucrative areas of commerce, including the production of copper tools, gold, silver, tea and liquor, all of which drastically increased revenue for Khubilai. Admittedly, Ahmad had also overprinted paper money and contributed to inflation, and had found plum government posts for two of his adult sons, despite protests from Chinese officials who thought themselves better qualified.

Polo's account of Ahmad's downfall makes extraordinarily lurid accusations about sexual corruption, suggesting that Ahmad demanded sexual favours from, in one case, the same man's mother, daughter and wife. It all seems oddly dramatic, and does not tally with the actual accusations levelled against

Ahmad once he was conveniently dead. Supposedly, Ahmad's true downfall was posthumous, when Khubilai's officials 'found' a gemstone at his house that had been earmarked for use in Khubilai's crown. Once again, the accusations are suspicious – if Ahmad really were embezzling from Khubilai, would he really have taken something so unique, and left it somewhere so obvious? Regardless, the 'evidence' now assembled against Ahmad was sufficient for Khubilai to order the desecration of his corpse. Ahmad's body was exhumed, exposed in the marketplace, his head crushed beneath cartwheels, and finally torn apart by Khubilai's dogs. Ahmad's death and dishonour were swiftly followed by the dismantling of much of his legacy – several of his sons were killed, his property was confiscated, and, tellingly, many men whom he had appointed were removed from office. To a cynical twenty-first-century reader, it surely looks more likely that enemies among the Chinese and Tibetans might have been manoeuvring against a perceived threat from a pro-Muslim faction. Certainly, both Polo and the Chinese annals played up the fact that Islam had both brought the alleged conspirators together, and empowered them to defy Khubilai's laws:

> These circumstances called the Khan's attentions to the accursed doctrines of the Saracens, which excuse every crime, and even murder itself when committed [against those] who are not of their religion. And seeing that this doctrine had led the accursed Ahmad and his sons to act as they did without any sense of guilt, the Khan was led to . . . the greatest disgust and abomination for it. So he summoned the Saracens and prohibited their doing many things that their religion enjoined.[10]

Anti-Muslim feeling in China persisted until 1287, and saw a continued drop in the number of Muslims prepared to enter the region. But the removal of Ahmad merely freed other factions to fight each other over control of the reins of power. What remains unmentioned in all these intrigues are the true participants. These archers and swordsmen, plaintiffs and victims, now known only to us through the records of their downfall, are all mere pawns. Surely, each of these factions had coalesced around a high-ranking figure; the tawdry revelations that are left to us conceal something much deeper and unspoken – likely to have been a genuine battle over the souls of the Mongol rulers.

Khubilai, long believed to have been leaning towards Tibetan Buddhism, still remained steadfastly undeclared in terms of his preferred religion. However, the theoretical debates over which he had presided for many years were now breaking out into open warfare among his officials. Soon China would have a new emperor, and with that new ruler would come an opportunity to make solid gains on religious ground. Zhenjin, Khubilai's heir, had Buddhist leanings like his father, but other religions were available. The influential 'Phags-pa Lama had died in 1280, reducing the hold of Tibetan Buddhism on the centre of the empire. The power of Nestorian Christianity was waning; Catholic Christianity had lost its chance long ago, arguably on the day that Maffeo and Niccolo Polo returned from the west with nothing but a vial of oil and some travel stories. Abaqa Khan, the ruler of Persia, was an unknown religious quantity, but had a Nestorian mother and had recently taken an Eastern Orthodox wife, an illegitimate daughter of the Byzantine Emperor, who had arrived as a petrified bride, accompanied by an Eastern Orthodox patriarch. But elsewhere, Islam was gaining ground. It was surely a characteristic of many of Zhenjin's enemies at court, and already exerted a powerful influence on other members of Khubilai's family – most notably his grandson Prince Ananda, who had been raised by Muslim foster parents, was deeply respectful of the Islamic faith and commanded an army of 150,000 men in the Tangut regions of Central Asia. Ananda, who would eventually convert to Islam along with his entire army, was dangerously close to the realm of Khaidu, who famously enjoyed a great deal of Muslim support.

Meanwhile, a different sort of upheaval was linked directly to Khubilai. After the death of the 'Phags-pa Lama, Khubilai appointed the lama's thirteen-year-old nephew Dharmapalaraksita as his replacement. It was clearly intended as a gesture of trust and respect, but was regarded by many Tibetans as an insult because the boy-administrator – effectively the new viceroy of Tibet – had hardly seen the land that he now called home. Dharmapalaraksita had been raised in Beijing and was thoroughly assimilated – a fact that made him such an attractive appointment for the Mongols, and such an unattractive one to his own people, who rightly regarded him as a Mongol stooge.

Since Tibetan Buddhism was not a single, monolithic sect with a single leader, a faction was sure to arise that challenged Dharmapalaraksita's authority. Sure enough, there was unrest and protest at the rival 'Bri-gung Monastery, which soon attracted assistance, or at least rumours of assistance, from Khubilai's rival khans to the west. Unwilling to provide the khans with an excuse to interfere within his own borders, Khubilai sent in the troops, for a tough five-year campaign that saw the'Bri-gung sect wiped out and 10,000 dead in Tibet.

For those who would prefer not to see religious conspiracies everywhere, there is also a simpler explanation. Basic finances, the downfall of many a dynasty, were of constant concern in Khubilai's empire during the 1280s – particularly after decades of Mongol expansion had ground to a crawl. After the fall of the Southern Song, Khubilai lacked a great new frontier for conquest to which he could point his disaffected soldiers. The propaganda over Japan's riches was powerful but unfulfilled; Annam was proving difficult to bring to heel; and the realms west of Mongolia were part of Khubilai's empire in name only.

This left the ageing Khubilai presiding over a territory that was, at least for the foreseeable future, trapped within its own borders. There were reconstruction projects to oversee, and infrastructure issues to address, with a generation of prisoner-of-war slave labourers dying off and not being replaced. Could any official, of any religion, no matter how competent, ever expect to succeed? The scenario was tested soon enough, with the appointment of Ahmad Fanakati's replacement as finance minister. In the wake of the Ahmad incident, his post was split and the job fell to two people: Antong, an unimpeachable Mongol of good family, and a Chinese official, Lu Shizhong, who was destined to be remembered as yet another 'villainous minister'.

With his predecessor still lying in pieces in a ditch outside the palace, Lu was put to work reforming Khubilai's revenue stream. He suggested a series of well-argued schemes for increasing government assets, which soon landed him in trouble with a whole new group of enemies. Lu's proposals included simple tax increases on import duty at the southern ports, as well as on the levy collected from salt merchants. He also identified a loophole in the liquor laws, which was that while the government's monopoly allowed it to levy a cut of all alcohol sales, some groups were able to get around this. The owners of large estates, for example, with their own vineyards, slaves and presses, could produce large quantities of homemade wine, which entirely escaped the government's notice.

So, Lu managed to anger the merchant population (largely Chinese and Muslims), and a large number of wealthy landowners, which included all racial groups in Khubilai's empire. He also managed to annoy the Mongols themselves, who were presumably also implicated in their traditional homebrew manufacture of *koumiss* from fermented mare's milk. He managed to make even more enemies for himself by pointing out that although the Mongols constituted a ruling class, many of them were 'idle'. In a deft combination of traditional values and job creation, he suggested that they be put to work as herdsmen on government-owned cattle and sheep stations, and allowed to keep 20 per cent of the proceeds. On one level, this was an excellent means of utilizing both human and animal resources in the provision of meat, leather and dairy products for Khubilai's military. To those directly affected, however, it felt like one of the conquered Chinese was instigating a subtle counter-attack. A generation after the Mongols imposed taxes on the Chinese, the Chinese were now arguably imposing taxes on the Mongols. And moreover, they were calling the Mongols lazy, demanding that they do an honest day's work, and then confiscating 80 per cent of their profits. Pointedly, the best that Lu could actually do in the face of such opposition was simply to print more money, which was part of the problem in the first place.

Eventually, Lu made an enemy of the same key player that Ahmad presumably had – he incurred the wrath of Khubilai's heir apparent Zhenjin. As soon as Zhenjin let it be known, however obliquely, that he disapproved of some of Lu's policies, an anti-Lu faction gained critical support. It was only a matter of weeks before someone accused Lu of embezzlement on shaky, yet somehow acceptable, evidence – he was thrown out of office and executed shortly afterwards.

The origins of the third and final 'villainous minister' mentioned in the *History of the Yuan* are unclear. He is variously called Sengge, Sangko or Sangha in competing sources, and could have been either Uighur or Tibetan. He was certainly a foreigner, and made an early living as an interpreter in the entourage of the 'Phags-pa Lama, and then as a *semuren* administrator. With the death of the 'Phags-pa Lama, Sangha rose to a high position in the office for Tibetan/Buddhist affairs, in which capacity he had travelled to Tibet to put down the 'Bri-gung revolt in 1280.

Sangha was hence a long-time associate of Khubilai, and a poster-boy for the *semuren* system. But the office for Tibetan affairs was largely a closed shop, confined mainly to Tibetans and Mongols. For whatever reason – snobbery, lack of experience, inability to speak the language, an unspoken mistrust of the newly conquered Chinese – it attracted no Chinese staffers, and hence Sangha was left to get on with his job. In the late 1280s, in recognition of his sterling service, he was promoted out of the Tibetan office and into a high-ranking, dangerous position within Khubilai's Chinese administration.

It was assuredly a poisoned chalice. Sangha would have been all too aware of the fates of his two predecessors, the dismembered Muslim Ahmad, and the unfortunate Chinese Lu. He may not have been aware of the enemies that they had made, especially the crown prince Zhenjin and a powerful minister, Antong – both Mongols, both seemingly resentful of the power that non-Mongols continued to enjoy within Khubilai's administration.

Antong, in particular, was openly hostile to Sangha. Sangha dutifully tried to propose schemes and models that might alleviate the financial issues facing China, but found himself blocked at every turn. It was no wonder that he, like Lu and Ahmad before him, was soon faced with a desperate dilemma – raise taxes on a number of essential items, or print more money and hope for the best. The former option was sure to invite accusations that he was merely feathering his own nest, the latter troubled nobody among the Mongols, but would only lead to further inflation.

One cannot help but be reminded of the warning from history issued to a much younger Khubilai, many decades before: 'One can conquer the world on horseback, but one cannot govern from horseback.' The tone of reporting of the 1280s suggests that his great experiment in unification had gone as far as it could, but now the Muslims, Tibetans and Chinese were at each other's throats, while those among the dwindling Mongol ruling class only played at politics, but were all too prepared to answer with violence if pushed too far.

Admittedly, this is precisely what the Chinese authors of the *History of the Yuan* intended; drawing the reader to the conclusion that the Mongols and their cronies are unsuited to govern China. Once a barbarian, always a barbarian – Khubilai's system was failing because Chinese civilization was *too* complicated, *too* sophisticated, *too* civilized for mere foreigners to run with any degree of competence. Lu Shizhong had also failed, but that only helped prove the point – not even the Chinese could run China when foreigners were in charge, opening civil positions to all and sundry, and then attacking anyone who tried to keep the state on an even keel.

Simple attrition was also taking its toll: the same period saw the deaths and retirement of many of the old guard of Confucian advisers. With Khubilai still refusing to reinstate the Confucian examination system, Chinese scholars were witnessing the swift erosion of their numbers, with the only available replacements being uncouth *semuren* or untrained Chinese who had grown up under Khubilai's rule.

The Chinese record railed against Sangha's deliberate appointments of cronies into powerful positions, and noted several rivals whose executions or suicides he appeared to engineer. Accusations against him, however, did not merely issue from Chinese quarters: the chronicles of the ruling house of Korea, the *Goryeo-sa*, also accuse him of corruption, claiming that he insisted on being sent fresh young Korean virgins to warm his bed. Nor did he get any sympathy from the Muslim chroniclers – Rashid al-Din, writing a decade later, had no compunction in calling him a corrupt and light-fingered official.

Reading between the lines, Sangha made most of his enemies by association with Yang Lianzhenjia, a Buddhist monk he appointed as one of his underlings. Yang's oddly multi-syllabic name implies that he, too was a Tibetan; as a *semuren* official in occupied Song China, Yang soon made a multitude of enemies, sowing troubles that Sangha was sure to reap. Once again, the controversy arose from a potent mix of religion and politics, and the melting-pot confrontations of Khubilai's 'unified' realm. Under the auspices of the office of Tibetan/Buddhist affairs, Yang was sent to southern China on what was supposedly a humanitarian mission: to restore dilapidated Buddhist temples.

Hangzhou in the mid-1280s was still a thriving town, but parts of it were run-down. Marco Polo recalls that the Song emperor's old palace, for example, was largely in ruins, apart from an occupation authority office in some of the main buildings:

As it is occupied by the King appointed by the Great Kaan, the first pavilions are still maintained as they used to be, but the apartments of the ladies are all gone to ruin and can only just be traced. So also the wall that enclosed the groves and gardens is fallen down, and neither trees nor animals are there any longer.[11]

The temples were in a similar degree of disrepair, not only from the chaotic times of the fall of the Southern Song, but from the prolonged period of make-do and jury-rigging during which Hangzhou had been used by the Song as a 'temporary capital'. When Yang arrived with his restoration programme, the first steps appeared generally benign. Reports arrived back at Sangha's office, and were entered in the Yuan court record, that between 1285 and 1287 Yang had donated funds for the restoration of some thirty temples in the area. However, this simple information obscured a very different story. Whereas the head office in Beijing was liable to assume that Yang was walking into a derelict temple precinct, shaking his head sadly and asking what needed to be done, many people in Hangzhou saw it differently. More often than not, Yang was not so much restoring a building as he was restoring its *use*: seizing Confucian temples and Taoist monasteries that had been used in that function for years, sometimes decades, and handing them over to rival sects. In some cases, there would be nobody left in a local community who remembered that their local temple had once been Buddhist, or that it had been repurposed during the dark, desperate days when so many Song loyalists fled to the south. But in many cases, Yang was absolutely correct. In one incident, he angered local Confucians by restoring the Glorious Dragon temple to its former Buddhist use. This was particularly irritating for the locals, because, for as long as most of them could remember, it had utilized as the Heaven and Earth altar for the Southern Song rulers in their 'temporary capital'. It was seen as disrespectful to ride roughshod over what many saw as Southern Song 'tradition', albeit only a tradition of relatively recent times.

However, that was nothing compared to what else Yang had in store for the Southern Song. His restoration programme was largely self-funding, deriving its finances from confiscations of property that had once belonged to the Southern Song and their loyal subjects. In some cases, opposition involved more complaining about the countrywide scheme to convert precious metal assets to paper money. In others, Yang was openly accused of daylight robbery, stripping richly appointed Confucian and Taoist sites of their valuables, and then using the newly acquired wealth to pay for Buddhist remodelling. Most notoriously, Yang plundered the tombs of the Song imperial family.

If 'plundering' is a problematic term, so too is 'restoration'. Chinese observers were horrified when Yang's men arrived at the sacred tomb of the Ningzong Emperor, thirteenth ruler of the Song dynasty, who had died in 1224. The seals were broken, the grave goods plundered, and numerous outbuildings demolished. Yang then built a new Buddhist temple on the site, and had the temerity to name it 'Taining': 'place of safe tranquillity'. That, at least, was how it appeared to the Chinese, many of whom were descended from refugees, and hence did not know their 'local' history as well as Yang himself. He pointed out that a Buddhist place of worship, the Taining Temple, had been on the site long before the arrival of the Southern Song, who had abruptly torn it down to make space for Ningzong's mausoleum. If they were so enthusiastic about preserving local heritage, perhaps they should look back a little further than 1224![12]

Needless to say, Yang was already regarded among the Chinese as a high-handed meddler. It is easy to see why the survivors of the Southern Song were appalled at the treatment meted out to their legacy. Meanwhile, local farmers and artisans were similarly affronted, when land that had been in their family for a couple of generations was suddenly revealed to be temple property, repossessed, and handed over to Buddhists, who then added insult to injury by benefiting from the new tax-free status of the 'religious' land. Yang was accused of taking bribes to register the original occupants as 'temple tenants', thereby conferring the same exemption on them, and allowing them to remain on the land where they lived. This supposed crime is mentioned in the Chinese sources as if nobody had ever thought of it before, whereas tax avoidance through tenancy on supposed temple land had been a feature of the Chinese system since the coming of the Buddhists six centuries earlier.

Yang's restoration programme, despite what may have been in the nation's best interests, was causing serious ructions in Hangzhou. Witnesses at the tomb of a more recent Song monarch reported Yang's men not only tearing the place down, but dragging out the late emperor's body, hanging it from a tree for three days, hacking off its head, and then shoving the pathetic, skeletal remains into a pile of animal remains. The story is shocking, and may even be true – though some doubt the whole escapade, and suspect that the whole thing was dreamed up after Yang's death to blacken his name.[13]

In Yang's defence, he was arguably the inheritor of a tradition in his native Tibet that took Buddhist concepts of reincarnation and spirituality to their logical conclusion. While religions elsewhere largely buried or cremated their dead, the Tibetans lived in an environment with little spare earth, and often far above the treeline, so that even timber was in short supply. Accordingly, the Tibetan tradition embraced the Buddhist notion of the body as a mere vessel for the soul – when an individual died, his empty vessel was so much dead meat, and as such was often subjected to 'sky burial', or in Tibetan, *bya gtor*: 'alms for the birds'. A corpse would be literally scattered on a mountaintop as a feast for the vultures, and human remains would often be recycled in priestly society in macabre forms – skulls as teapots, or necklaces of vertebrae.

Yang might have been tactless or uncaring about the reaction of the Chinese; or indeed he might conceivably have been deliberately desecrating the tombs of the Song emperors, but we should remember that, to many of Yang's order, there was no desecration to be committed. At the time of his own death, he fully expected his body to be torn apart by vultures, his bones scattered among the mountains. To a Tibetan Buddhist, this was no better or worse than being riddled with worms in the ground or committed to ashes atop a pile of burning wood. In the meantime, the bodies of the Song emperors were in the way of vital institutional renewal in the south. If Yang's behaviour appeared arrogant or thoughtless, we should also remember that he was a high-ranking official in an occupation regime, whose founders still retained the power of life and death over the former Song subjects.

Yang was certainly settling scores in Hangzhou with the Taoists and the Confucians. Perhaps we even have him to blame for the lack of evidence of any Nestorian churches in Hangzhou in the thirteenth century. But here, again, we see the essential dilemma at the heart of Khubilai's melting-pot culture: the cultures were not melting at all – they were clashing, as traditions born of cold mountaintops were thrust in the face of agrarian Chinese. A ruler who had spent his life choosing no single religion, now reigned over a realm of many religions, each sure that its traditions, its heritage, its priesthood would somehow rise to prominence over all the others.

With news drifting northwards of terrible deeds in Hangzhou, of corruption and desecration, Yang's boss Sangha lost his purchase on power. It was a Muslim nemesis that brought Sangha's downfall – an official called Mubarak Shah, who secretly accused the vizier of hoarding precious gifts from Tajik tributaries. Mubarak was so sure of his claims, and enjoyed such support from the centre of power, that he enlisted Khubilai himself in the entrapment scheme. Khubilai Khan hence found himself running a distraction operation, keeping Sangha busy at court while Mubarak raided the vizier's home. When Mubarak arrived with the evidence, a donkey-load of pearls and jewels, an enraged Khubilai exchanged harsh words with Sangha before ordering his mouth 'stuffed with filth'.

Khubilai later executed Sangha and his alleged Tajik accomplices; he repeatedly struck another of their associates, Baha al-Din, before ordering him locked in a cangue restraint and thrown down a well, although he was eventually recovered and pardoned.[14]

There were various explanations for the awful series of appointments and putsches at the top – Buddhists fighting Taoists, Christians fighting Muslims, Chinese fighting *semuren* – but it all reflected badly on the man who was supposed to unite them, Khubilai. The continuing war in the west with Khaidu had made Khubilai particularly suspicious of Muslims. In 1287, the doomed vizier Sangha had pleaded with Khubilai to reverse some of his anti-Muslim policies, which had been damaging enough to put most devout Muslims off even travelling to Khubilai's realm. This in turn had seriously reduced tax revenue, particularly in trade. Marco Polo himself wondered at the 50 per cent tariff paid on goods arriving by sea in Quanzhou; but with Muslim sailors staying away, the revenue accrued was dropping steadily and only compounding the problems.[15]

Another problem dogged Khubilai in the later years of his realm. Several of his sons pre-deceased him, including Prince Zhenjin in 1285. Zhenjin had been groomed for the succession for many years, and had represented the great hope of Khubilai's advisers, as well as a rallying point for many court factions. He was the 'Golden' boy, his name a reference to the departed Jurchens, and to the bright hopes of the Mongol imperial family. Marco Polo assuredly got this wrong, thinking instead that Zhenjin's name was somehow derivative of his great-grandfather Temujin's title: *Genghis*. Regardless of his error, Polo wrote that: 'as the Eldest Son of the Kaan, [he] was to have reigned after his father's death; but, as it came to pass, he died.'[16]

Zhenjin's son Temur was the new presumptive heir, regarded as an imperfect candidate even by Khubilai himself. Rashid al-Din reports that Temur was already a heavy drinker. Khubilai, who was increasingly keen on booze himself in old age, made several attempts to reduce Temur's addiction, but failed.

> Temur . . . was extremely fond of wine. However much [Khubilai] rebuked him, it was of no avail. He even on three occasions beat him with a stick, and he set several guards over him to prevent him drinking wine.[17]

Despite Khubilai's attempt at tough love, Temur had an enabler called Radi, a high-functioning fellow alcoholic from Bukhara, who was always ready to encourage him in his drinking binges, and to frame elaborate excuses and arguments on the morning after. When Khubilai's guards eventually embargoed all alcohol around Temur, it was Radi who concocted an ingenious scheme worthy of the boozing khans of old, bribing the bath attendants to fill their cistern with wine instead of water, so that when Temur ran a bath, he was able to drink the evidence. When Khubilai found out about this new trick, he had Radi forcibly removed from Temur's presence, and quietly killed off on his way to a remote exile. It did not, however, bode well for the new heir apparent, who was already complaining in his twenties of terrible pain in his feet – the first sign of gout.

Temur would be just one of the disappointments that characterized Khubilai's last years, as the man who had conquered China was himself conquered by old age.

11

DEATH TO THE MONGOLS

THE ANNAMESE RESISTANCE

The surviving accounts of the Mongol armada have made it world-famous. Marco Polo's writings brought Japan itself to the attention of the western world, and the Japanese people's own mythologizing has contributed towards its powerful, iconic place in the history of the Mongols. However, Japan was by no means the first time that the Mongols had suffered setbacks. Even if we ignore several convenient retreats to attend *kurultais*, there were numerous occasions when the supposedly invincible Mongols met with unexpected defeat. In most cases, these embarrassments were glossed over in hindsight, as the arrival of a later, more powerful force turned the tables and rendered the Mongols victorious. The Japanese victory is largely regarded as unique because the Mongols never quite made it back for a third invasion, turning Japan's resistance into the high watermark – the moment when the Mongol expansion began to stumble and collapse.

However, this is overly simplistic. The Mongols were experiencing considerable difficulties elsewhere. Moreover, the Japanese had invisible assistance in the form of another long-running resistance movement in the deep south, where the rulers of Annam (modern North Vietnam) held out against the Mongols. This generation-long war is often overlooked in accounts of Khubilai's reign, because it genuinely stretches throughout his active life. Its earliest events began when Khubilai was still a junior princeling, commanding an army on behalf of his brother Mongke. Its last acts were not played out until after Khubilai was dead. It stretches over such a long period that it tends to be broken up and smeared across several chapters in accounts of Khubilai – a paragraph here when discussing the foundation of the empire, a paragraph there when mentioning Khubilai's mid-reign foreign relations, a paragraph elsewhere when summing up his legacy. If we take the Annamese resistance as a subject in its own right, though, we soon see that the Japanese struggle was far from unique, and that signs of the decay of Mongol vigour were apparent long before the fateful day of the *kamikaze*.

The first encounters with Annam came during Khubilai's campaign against Dali. As part of the mopping-up operations in 1258, Khubilai sent Uryangkhadai south to ascertain the strength of the Annamese. As a sign of the communications barrier he faced, the Annamese mistook Uryangkhadai for the Chinese Emperor himself.[1]

Uryangkhadai's emissaries found themselves dealing with the wily, dynamic Thai Tong (1218–77), first ruler of the Annamese Tran dynasty. Thai Tong ignored the Mongol order to submit, and refused to permit Uryangkhadai's envoys to leave. Consequently, Uryangkhadai did as would have been expected of any Mongol leader – he pushed his army into Annamese territory and advanced along the Red River towards the city that is now known as Hanoi. Thai Tong was forced to quit his capital and flee east of the Red River, while the Mongols poured into Hanoi, rescuing their envoys and razing the city to the ground.[2]

However, the local climate was in Thai Tong's favour. When he mounted a counter-attack against occupied Hanoi, he found the Mongol army decimated by disease and the heat. The Mongols were soon put to flight, dogged constantly by guerrilla attacks, and withdrawing with such speed from Annam that local slang ridiculed them as the 'Buddhist Warriors' – so eager to flee that they did not even stop to plunder any of the settlements they passed.[3]

Thai Tong's soldiers only stopped pursuing the Mongols once they were back over the border in Yunnan, but the Annamese leader clearly had been rattled by the attack. In the interests of avoiding a rematch, he sent an embassy to Mongke Khan, offering to send a tributary mission every three years. Hence, while Uryangkhadai and Khubilai were doubtless aware of the troubles they had experienced in the deep south, their overlord would have only received word from the borderlands that his armies had been successful.

Thai Tong then abdicated. Despite remaining the power behind the Annamese throne as a 'retired emperor' until his death in 1277, he left the official running of the state to his eighteen-year-old son Thanh Tong (1240–90). If this was calculated to deflect Mongol attentions, it worked. By the time the news reached the north, Mongke was dead or dying, and Khubilai was locked in the power struggle over his succession. These factors bought Annam several years of respite. By the time Khubilai sent an envoy of his own to congratulate the new ruler on his accession, the Annamese were already dickering over previous promises.

Khubilai's first emissary presented the Annamese with a demand for a representative sample of the best skilled workers that the nation had to offer – in effect, a new contribution to the college of dignitaries, holy men and thinkers with which Khubilai loved to surround himself. He expected Thanh Tong to supply scholars, doctors, astronomers, geomancers and other skilled workers, in addition to more material goods such as rhinoceros horns, ivory, tortoiseshells and gemstones. But

Khubilai Khan also had his eye on other matters. With the nominal submission of Annam, he had effectively encircled the last stronghold of the Southern Song, and probably expected to be able to call on the Annamese for military aid to attack the Song resistance from behind. Khubilai also sent a *darughachi* – a viceroy whose job would be to oversee the transition of Annam from independent state to fully integrated Mongol vassal.[4]

By 1266, with Khubilai's plans to push against the Southern Song underway, Thanh Tong began building up his own troops, ostensibly to help with the Mongol war effort, but actually for his own use. Thanh Tong sent a new envoy to Khubilai in the same year, asking if perhaps Khubilai could reconsider some of the terms agreed in haste by his 'retired' father. Khubilai responded with the standard list of Mongol demands for vassal behaviour:

> The ruler [of Annam] must attend Khubilai personally in Beijing.
> He must send his children or brothers as hostages.
> He must carry out a census of his population.
> He must allow the conscription of his subjects for Mongol wars.
> He must pay taxes.
> He must permit the presence of the supervisors.

Although Khubilai's position could not be clearer, Thanh Tong still delayed, perhaps aware that Khubilai himself had seen conditions in the south as a younger man, and might appreciate the benefits of diplomacy over open conflict. However, in 1271, Khubilai lost patience and bluntly ordered Thanh Tong to come to Beijing, in fulfilment of the first condition. Once again, Thanh Tong postponed, pleading that he was too ill to travel.

Khubilai's next approach to the Annamese was beautifully subtle. He sent a mission of scholars far to the south, and asked Thanh Tong for his help in locating an ancient archaeological artefact. In fact, the scholars were searching for a legendary

bronze pillar, said to have been erected in the Annam region by
the ancient Chinese hero Ma Yuan, sometime around AD 43.
This was no innocent academic enquiry, it was a gentle
reminder to the ruler of Annam that Chinese forces had
conquered the region in the past, and *could readily do so again*.
Two could play at that game, though: Thanh Tong offered all
possible aid to the investigators, but eventually sent them home
with the message that the pillar was impossible to find because
it had been erected many centuries ago, in the distant past,
when times were very different.[5]

In 1275, perhaps emboldened by the news of the Japanese
debacle, Thanh Tong presented an act of open defiance, sending
an envoy to Beijing to inform Khubilai that Annam required
no Chinese supervisors. Whatever Thanh Tong's reasons for
pushing his luck, he was sufficiently cowed by 1278 to abdicate
in favour of his own son Nhan Tong (1258–1308), who swiftly
changed the name of his era to 'Introducing Fees'. On the
surface, at least, it would appear that the difficult ruler had been
ousted, and replaced by a more amenable substitute. In fact, as
in the case of his own late father, Thanh Tong was now simply
ruling behind the throne.

This would have become abundantly clear to Khubilai's next
appointee, who arrived soon afterwards in Annam to supervise
the handover of power. He appears to have busied himself
informing the new ruler of Khubilai's plans to organize an
invasion of Champa, the coastal region to the south of Annam:
roughly equivalent to what is now South Vietnam. Attempts
by Khubilai's envoys to drum up support and material for the
putative invasion, however, were regarded by the Annamese as
'extortion and corruption'. The envoy soon left to return to
Khubilai's court, and strongly encouraged Nhan Tong to
accompany him. The young ruler refused, claiming that he was
sure he would not be able to bear the foreign climate. Instead,
he sent an embassy that included his uncle, Di Ai. The envoy
appears to have agreed to this because he knew what Khubilai's
reaction was sure to be. As one might expect, Khubilai angrily

appointed Di Ai as the new ruler of Annam, creating his two travelling companions as the new prime minister and field marshal. As he had done in Korea, he had lost patience with the incumbent ruler, and preferred to back a new, more pliable candidate with a little military aid.

The mission was a failure, though – the pretender was backed by a pitiful amount of troops, a mere 1,000, largely because the bulk of Mongol military strength was still massed in Korea ready for an attack on Japan. Khubilai's representative lost an eye to a lucky arrow shot, and fled back to China. The pretender and his accomplices were captured and stripped of their noble ranks, thereby ending Khubilai's attempt at regime change, and leaving Nhan Tong all the more confident.

As the envoy had explained to Nhan Tong, Khubilai's next military operation was aimed at Champa. Considering that Champa was also the stated destination of Zhang Shijie, the fugitive admiral of the Southern Song fleet in 1279, we might presume that the historical record has carefully deleted the rise of a new Song pretender somewhere in the region. If Zhang Shijie or some of his crews reached Champa, or even were rumoured to have done so, it is not difficult to see why Khubilai might have wanted to establish that Champa was under Mongol control.

A marine assault led by Sogetu, the Mongol governor of Canton, had failed in 1282, largely because he only had a fleet of 100 ships, while most other shipping had been diverted to the ill-fated attack on Japan. Therefore, this time Sogetu recommended to Khubilai that instead of sailing to Champa, the invading army should simply walk there, through Annam. This was, to be sure, the ultimate test of Annamese loyalty.

At a hastily convened conference in Annam, the ruler and his subjects voted reluctantly for an armed resistance. He selected Tran Hung Dao (1228–1300) as the leader of his army. Hung Dao was already a legendary figure among the Annamese. A cousin of sorts of the ruler, he was an ardent student of Sun Tzu's *Art of War*, and the best leader that the

Annamese could hope for, particularly as news drifted in that
Khubilai Khan's own son, Toghan, was leading the invading
army, estimates of whose strength rose as high as 500,000 men.

Tran Hung Dao's address to the Annamese soldiers on the
eve of the battle with the Mongols remains a stirring historical
document. True to the rhetorical tradition of his time, he began
with a series of arcane ancient parallels (not shown here), but
suddenly discards them with a homespun appeal to the hearts
of his men:

> You and I were born in a period of troubles and have grown up
> at a time when the Fatherland is in danger. We have seen the
> enemy ambassadors haughtily travelling over our roads and
> wagging their owlish tongues to insult the Court. Despicable as
> dogs and goats, they boldly humiliate our high officials.
> Supported by the Mongol emperor, they incessantly demand
> the payment of pearls, silks, gold and silver. Our wealth is
> limited but their cupidity is infinite. To yield to their exactions
> would be to feed their insatiable appetites and would set a
> dangerous precedent for the future.
>
> In the face of these dangers to the Fatherland, I fail to eat
> during the day and to sleep at night. Tears roll down my cheeks
> and my heart bleeds as if it were being cut to shreds. I tremble
> with anger because I cannot eat our enemy's flesh, lie down in
> his skin, chew up his liver and drink his blood. I would gladly
> surrender my life a thousand times on the field of battle if I
> could do these things . . .
>
> And now, you remain calm when your emperor is
> humiliated; you remain indifferent when your country is
> threatened! You, officers, are forced to serve the barbarians and
> you feel no shame! You hear the music played for their
> ambassadors and you do not leap up in anger. No, you amuse
> yourselves at the cockfights, in gambling, in the possession of
> your gardens and rice fields, and in the tranquillity of family
> life. The exploitation of your personal affairs makes you forget
> your duties to the State; the distractions of the fields and of the

hunt make you neglect military exercises; you are seduced by liquor and music. If the enemy comes, will your cocks' spurs be able to pierce his armour? Will the ruses you use in your games of chance be of use in repulsing him? Will the love of your wives and children be of any use in the Army? Your money would neither suffice to buy the enemy's death, your alcohol to besot him, nor your music to deafen him . . .

If you refuse to fight the Mongols in order to wash away the national shame, if you do not train your soldiers to drive out these barbarians, it would be to surrender to them. If that is what you want, your names will be dishonoured forever. And when the enemy has finally been defeated, how will you be able to hold your head high between Heaven and Earth?[6]

While a Mongol fleet headed straight for Champa, Prince Toghan halted at the border between China and Annam, and officially requested permission to pass through Annamese territory on his way. Nhan Tong denied that any useful route existed between Annam and Champa. Toghan's reply, sent via what appears to have been a Muslim envoy, was crystal clear:

You should have no fear, because our only intent is to borrow your territory . . . So you had better open the gate for my troops, and wherever they arrive, supply them with food. You will be lavishly rewarded after [Champa has] been destroyed. But if you resist my troops, I will not pardon you, but will ravage your country, and there will be no time for repentance.[7]

It was an empty threat – the Annamese intended to ravage their own country. Hanoi was back in Mongol hands by July 1285, already abandoned by its defenders. Tran Hung Dao led the Annamese troops against the Mongols in a series of battles, while the Annamese people fled south behind him. As they retreated, they laid waste to their own villages, burned their own crops, and poisoned their own wells, luring the Mongols ever further into territory that offered no means of support for many hungry mouths.

All the while, the Annamese risked a terrible fate, retreating southwards in the very real risk that they would run into the northward advance of Sogetu's army from Champa. However, Sogetu found the resistance in Champa stronger than he had expected, and did not materialize in the Annamese rear to stop their retreat.

Even at this late stage, the Mongols were prepared to offer a compromise. Capturing the Marquis Bao-Nghia, a member of the Annamese nobility, Toghan offered him the chance to end all the troubles. If he were to merely acknowledge the suzerainty of Khubilai Khan in the far north, the southern lands would lose all their troubles, and the marquis would be promoted to prince. The Marquis' response brooked no argument: 'Better to be a Devil in the South than a Prince in the North!' For speaking so to Khubilai's son, he was beheaded, but entered Annamese annals as a national hero.[8]

Not every Annamese subject was as fiercely loyal as Marquis Bao-Nghia. The ruler's own younger brother, Tran Ich Tac, swiftly surrendered to the Mongols, and was, at least nominally, created as the new ruler of Annam by the invaders. Toghan's forces also had enough sway among the locals to enlist the aid of collaborators. These included spies who informed the Mongols that the fugitive 'royal boat' was actually a decoy, and that the ruler of Annam and his family were travelling in a less ostentatious vessel.

The jungles and rice paddies of Annam proved predictably unsuitable for Mongol military tactics, and indeed for the tactics of the Chinese. With the invaders flagging in the summer heat, Hung Dao launched his counter-offensive, deliberately picking coastal areas where the Mongols' horses would get bogged down in the soft mud. Hung Dao also took the battle to the forces limping north from Champa, in a concerted effort to capture their leaders alive. In this he failed – one leader died in the battle, while another escaped to Hanoi, and thence by

boat back into Chinese waters. However, Hung Dao successfully captured 30,000 enemy soldiers, and was able to present
his ruler with the head of an enemy general.

Hung Dao now turned his attentions to Toghan's force,
deliberately cutting off its escape route. Prince Toghan
smuggled himself out by hiding in a bronze cylinder, dragged
through hails of Annamese arrows by his retreating soldiers.
The pretender Tran Ich Tac fled with him to China, but was
immortalized ever after for his cowardice in poems and
scurrilous songs in his native Annam as 'the woman Tran'.

Back in Beijing, the story of the Mongol assault on Champa
took on a very different perspective. Champa is one of the tiny
handful of places in Marco Polo's writings that he directly
asserts he has visited, sometime between the years 1275 and
1288. Accordingly, the reader is apt to infer that Marco knows
his subject when he writes briefly about Champa, and claims
that the Mongol invasion was a resounding success:

> It happened in the year of Christ 1278 that the Great Kaan sent
> a Baron of his called Sagatu with a great force of horse and foot
> against this King of Chamba, and this Baron opened the war on
> a great scale against the King and his country. Now the King
> (whose name was Accambale) was a very aged man, nor had he
> such a force as the Baron had. And when he saw what havoc the
> Baron was making with his kingdom he was grieved to the
> heart. So he bade messengers get ready and dispatched them to
> the Great Kaan. And they said to the Kaan: 'Our Lord the King
> of Chamba salutes you as his liege-lord, and would have you to
> know that he is stricken in years and long hath held his realm in
> peace. And now he sends you word by us that he Is willing to
> be your liegeman, and will send you every year a tribute of as
> many elephants as you please. And he prays you in all gentleness
> and humility that you would send word to your Baron to desist
> from harrying his kingdom and to quit his territories. These
> shall henceforth be at your absolute disposal, and the King shall
> hold them of you.' When the Great Kaan had heard the King's

ambassage he was moved with pity, and sent word to that Baron of his to quit that kingdom with his army, and to carry his arms to the conquest of some other country; and as soon as this command reached them they obeyed it. Thus it was then that this King became vassal of the Great Kaan, and paid him every year a tribute of 20 of the greatest and finest elephants that were to be found in the country.[9]

We should note the obvious sign of Polo's characteristic hyperbole. Despite lines of communication stretching for thousands of miles, Khubilai is somehow able to give his gracious and immediate assent to the pleadings of King 'Accambale' – most likely a corruption of Indravarman. It seems more likely that Polo has drastically compressed the sequence of events, running the diplomatic aftermath of embassies and treaties into the dramatic reportage of the war itself. He also avoids mentioning one of the great ironies of Khubilai's campaign – that the Mongol invasion achieved what years of local politics had failed to do, uniting the warring peoples of Annam and Champa against a common enemy.[10]

Regardless of the spin put on the southern campaign by later writers, Khubilai was annoyed enough at its failure that he had to be dissuaded from executing the leaders. An invasion fleet already under construction for use against Japan seems to have been repurposed and redirected southwards towards Annam during the years 1285–7. With a force of 300,000 men, the vengeful Prince Toghan was back in charge, entering Annamese territory alongside a massive fleet of warships and supply ships, and marching, largely unopposed, as far as the Red River.

The fanatical resistance of the Annamese, many of whom had tattooed themselves with the words 'Death to the Mongols', was once again wisely channelled by Tran Hung Dao into fighting on his own terms. Rather than face the invaders in open battle, against overwhelming odds estimated at two to one, Hung Dao returned to his guerrilla campaign, planning his *coup de grâce* with a flourish of classical knowledge. The

Mongols turned inland from Hanoi, which they were unable to take, crucially separating themselves from their attendant fleet. There, the Annamese scored one of their first victories, with Hung Dao's behaviour after the battle amply demonstrating the difference between him and the Mongols. The invaders, particularly the Muslim general Omar, continued the Mongol policy of atrocities as insurance against resistance – reserving the very worst of their punishments for anyone caught with a 'Death to the Mongols' tattoo. Rather than slaughter his own prisoners, Hung Dao set them free to report on the disaster to Prince Toghan, hoping thereby to scare the Mongols even more.

Occupying an island near Haiphong as a defensible position, Prince Toghan sent his underling Omar, with 500 ships, to requisition supplies from the Annamese mainland. It is telling that the chain of command appears to have comprised a Mongol and a Muslim. A classically educated Chinese leader might have noted the worrying precedent, that the Mongol supply fleet was using the same Bach Dang River route that had seen a crushing defeat of Chinese invaders by Annamese locals in AD 938. The incident was anything but obscure – it had, at the time, been the watershed moment that destroyed the power of the Chinese in Annam. It was, arguably, the most important battle that the Chinese sources were likely to recall in the region, and it was hence all the more ironic that Hung Dao not only lay in wait at the same location, but even employed the same tactics as his illustrious predecessor.

Out in Halong Bay, dotted with 1,000 tiny islands, Hung Dao had secreted groups of his men armed with sturdy, iron-tipped wooden stakes. Once the Mongol fleet had passed on its way upstream, the men rushed out into the water at low tide, and rammed the stakes securely into the riverbed, pointing either straight up or upstream. They thus formed a serrated, zigzagging barrier of sharp spikes, entirely blocking the river, and creating a dangerous barrier against any large vessel heading back down towards the sea.

Hung Dao, so the legend goes, thrust his sword into the ground so he could whisk up and knot his hair, the better to gaze upon his handiwork – the site of this iconic moment is now a temple. Hung Dao's men swarmed out of the forest and into the river, forcing the invaders to head downstream, where the local resistance seemed lightest. Light Annamese decoy boats, sitting lightly on the surface, scraped easily over the stakes, while the heavier, larger Mongol ships impaled themselves directly on the points. Some were damaged enough to sink; others took on water; still more were stuck, helpless before a renewed onslaught of Annamese fire-rafts. It was only then, as the Mongol fleet listed, sunk or burned before them, that Hung Dao led the actual physical assault, shouting at his eager troops: 'If we do not destroy the Yuan in this battle, we will not return to this river!'[11]

It was a rout for the Mongol invaders. Hung Dao successfully captured several of the leaders, while the rest of the men were butchered in the water. In the aftermath, the King of Annam ordered three days of feasting, while news drifted in of the dogged pursuit of Prince Toghan's fleeing troops, as they made a desperate dash for safety through the thick, forbidding Annamese jungle. It was another embarrassing defeat for the Mongols, and one that was sure to lead Khubilai to order yet another reprisal. It would, of course, also split Khubilai's attentions and budgets yet again between the equally recalcitrant border regions of Japan and Annam.

In late 1288, in a bizarre reversal, the Annamese ruler sent a new envoy to Beijing, offering the tribute that Khubilai had long demanded. He had, he noted, several Mongol generals in captivity, but would happily return them, although one of them had already died of an illness, and would only return as ashes. It is this, perhaps, that gives us Marco Polo's confused assumption of a Mongol victory in Annam. The Mongol records, after all, would only show that the attack on Annam had been a success, since it did eventually result in the paying of tribute from the locals. The captive generals were finally returned in

1289, although Hung Dao carefully ensured that Omar, whom the Annamese detested most of all, 'accidentally' drowned on the way home.[12]

Had Khubilai lived any longer, there would surely have been another invasion of Annam. The Annamese king promised to come to Beijing, but immediately postponed, pointedly claiming at first that he was in mourning, then sending two successive stand-ins. By the time Khubilai realized that the latest Annamese 'surrender' was yet another lie, his health was already fading. When Khubilai died in 1294, the next invasion was in the preparatory stages, although it was quietly shelved by his successor.

In the aftermath of the war, minor collaborators were pardoned by the Annamese, although those who had supported the royal pretenders were banished from their families and forced to take a new surname. The inhabitants of two particular villages, whose collaboration with the invaders had cost the Annamese dearly, were conscripted for life into the Annamese army.

One of the prisoners left behind was a Chinese actor Li Yuanqi, who went by the name Ly Nguyen Cat among the Annamese, and lingered in his place of captivity long enough to introduce the Annamese to Chinese drama. Thereafter, 'Peking Opera' thrived in Annamese garb – a strange coda to the Mongol invasions.[13]

To this day, Tran Hung Dao remains a cult figure among the modern Vietnamese. Folklore tells of a Mongol prisoner whose head magically regrew each time after he was decapitated. It was Tran Hung Dao and his magic sword that eventually beheaded the recalcitrant captive for good, although the victim was then reborn as a demon called Nhan the Criminal, who specialized in haunting expectant mothers. Prayers to Tran Hung Dao, the patron saint of warding off demons, pestilence and Mongols, is thought in Vietnamese popular belief to be the best way to thwart the predations of Nhan. Meanwhile, the former Annamese stronghold of Kiep Bac, a bastion against the Mongol invasions, remains a site with powerful links to Vietnamese folk religion, and the location of an annual ceremony designed to ward off evil spirits.[14]

12

DOWN TO A SUNLESS SEA

LAST YEARS

Vexing reports continued to arrive from the borders: Annam was up in arms again in the 1270s; Japan remained defiant. In 1273, envoys from Khubilai's realm were sent to Pagan (Burma)[1] to order the submission of the local king. In doing so, they entered a new realm of which they were almost entirely ignorant, as the vague pronouncements of the *History of the Yuan* make clear: 'The people live in cities and rural areas, in houses and crude huts; they ride on elephants and horses, and they cross rivers in boats and on bamboo rafts.'[2]

The local king, Narathihapate (1256–87), was a colourful character. He had been placed on the throne by his elder brothers, perhaps in imitation of the subterfuge also employed in Annam and Japan – the Mongols occupied the borderlands, which would surely have persuaded the smarter crown princes to avoid donning a crown in such dangerous times. He was an entertainingly arrogant despot, who once boasted that he commanded 36 *million* soldiers, (roughly the entire population of north China), ate 300 curries a day, and serviced 3,000 concubines – 'a puissant prince', comments Marco Polo. It is thus not all that surprising to hear that he had the Mongol ambassadors executed, and launched his own immediate counter-attack against the statelet of Kaungai on his own northern border. Kaungai had submitted to the Mongols to avoid an invasion, and paid the price ironically when it became a casualty of Narathihapate's vengeful strike.[3]

Narathihapate presumably attacked Kaungai because he knew it would be the conduit through which Mongol avengers would come. However, instead of then preparing for the inevitable Mongol counter-strike, Narathihapate put his subjects to work on the creation of a massive new temple: the towering Mingalezedi Pagoda, decorated with glazed terracotta tiles, with a series of terraces leading to a great curving stupa, topped in turn by an umbrella-like roof, encrusted with jewels. For a country already struggling with its own financial crisis, the pagoda was undoubtedly a bad idea, and there were already whispers that the completion of the pagoda would be accompanied by the death of the king.

If Narathihapate was hoping that religious devotion would save him, he was to get a rude awakening. In 1277, the Mongol army reached the edge of his realm, led by the new governor of Yunnan, Nasir al-Din, son of the famously competent Saiyid. Nasir's forces swiftly approached the Yunnan–Burma border, riding, in the words of Marco Polo, 'for two days and a half continually downhill' on the long descent out of the hills. There is a sense, in Polo's involved report of the Pagan campaign, that the Mongol and Chinese troops felt increasingly out of their depth, as if they had somehow left behind the familiar world of the Chinese, and, by crossing Khubilai's mountainous south-western border, had entered a region with markedly different climate, population and customs. Pagan itself, comments Marco Polo, begins with 'great woods abounding in elephants and unicorns and numbers of other wild beasts'.[4]

It was the elephants that were the problem – Chinese sources have nothing to say about the dangers of unicorns. On a plain called Ngasaunggyan, Nasir's army faced Narathihapate's massed troops. Narathihapate had been boasting for years that the Mongols were too preoccupied to come after him; he had doubtless already heard stories from nearby Annam of the difficulties that the invaders faced in the jungles and tropical heat. He also had elephants – 2,000 of them, if Polo is to be believed – each fitted with a howdah carrying archers. For Nasir's invaders, largely comprising lancers on horses, this was a problem:

> And when [Narathihapate's] army had arrived in the plain, and was within a mile of the enemy, he caused all the castles that were on the elephants to be ordered for battle, and the fighting-men to take up their posts on them, and he arrayed his horse and his foot with all skill, like a wise king as he was. And when he had completed all his arrangements he began to advance to engage the enemy. The Tartars, seeing the foe advance, showed no dismay, but came on likewise with good order and discipline to meet them. And when they were near and nought remained but to begin the fight, the horses of the Tartars took such fright at the sight of the elephants that they could not be got to face the foe, but always swerved and turned back; whilst all the time the king and his forces, and all his elephants, continued to advance upon them.[5]

With their horses petrified by the sight of the elephants, the Mongols were forced back into the treeline. Understanding that the Burmese were in fast pursuit, Nasir ordered his men to abandon their horses for the moment and line up with bows and arrows. Waiting until the approaching Burmese were perilously close, Nasir gave the order for his archers to fire directly at the unarmoured elephants.

Narathihapate, it seems, had not expected the valuable elephants to become targets. Their immense value in scaring the

Mongol horses was now reversed, as the wounded animals wheeled and stampeded back towards Narathihapate's foot-soldiers, who were forced to break ranks to save their own lives:

> Understand that when the elephants felt the smart of those arrows that pelted them like rain, they turned tail and fled, and nothing on earth would have induced them to turn and face the Tartars. So off they sped with such a noise and uproar that you would have thought the world was coming to an end. And then too they plunged into the wood and rushed this way and that, dashing the castles against the trees, bursting their harness and smashing and destroying everything that was on them.[6]

Victory belonged to the Mongols, although there was still a conspicuous number of hostile natives alive and uncaptured. Nasir's victorious report back to Beijing was misconstrued by some (including Polo) as notification that the whole region had been pacified. In fact, Nasir made no such claim. The contested border-march of Kaungai was back in Mongol hands, and Nasir extended the Mongol system of post-stations and garrisons a little way into Burmese territory.

Nevertheless, Narathihapate was still at large, and a second 'Mongol' expedition force arrived in Pagan in 1283. This time led by a Mongol prince Sangudar, it was typical of the melting pot armies that Khubilai liked to encourage newly occupied states to form, utilizing a large number of 'Miao' auxiliaries – that is to say the Hmong people from the borderlands. These people, it was surely hoped, would be better able to endure the forbidding southern heat and humidity about which Nasir had already complained. Under Sangudar, the invaders made it as far as the eponymous capital of Pagan itself. Narathihapate fled, earning himself the less impressive nickname among his people of 'Tarokpyemin', 'the king who ran from the Chinese'. The invaders offered him the opportunity to buy back his capital by taking an oath of fealty to Khubilai Khan – a humiliating climb-down for the man who once claimed to lead 36 million warriors.

Returning to the Burmese province of Prome to regroup and plot the resistance, Narathihapate was instead cornered by one of his sons, who threatened to have him executed unless he did the honourable thing and committed suicide. With a final kingly curse, Narathihapate proclaimed that he wanted no more boy children, in this life, the next or any of his many incarnations to come; he drank poison and died.

Such, at least, is the way that Burmese legend tells the story. It is oddly convenient that Narathihapate should die just at the point when he was rumoured to be seeking a peace deal with the Mongols. Centuries on, it is impossible to say for sure, but Pagan seems to have been torn apart by rival factions, some of which were ready to accept the Mongols, others determined to hold them off in the same obfuscatory manner that was working rather well in Annam.

However, the death of Narathihapate left Pagan with no leader at all – also depriving the Mongols of any authoritative figure with whom they could negotiate. In 1287, Khubilai's grandson Esen-Temur tried to lead a new force into the region to capitalize on the unrest. He planned to put one of Narathihapate's sons on the throne as a vassal king, but was unable to enforce the rule of a monarch whose capital was in ruins, and whose own subjects did not acknowledge his legitimacy.

Kyawswa, younger son of the ill-fated King Narathihapate, eventually proclaimed loyalty to the Mongols in 1297, initiating a brief period in which the disparate provinces of Burma were at least officially under Mongol suzerainty. However, Kyawswa was in no real position to proclaim himself the king of anything beyond the outer streets of his capital. His kingdom was already falling apart, and at the time he graciously offered to accept the Mongol yoke, he was already embroiled in a civil war against three of his viceroys. If the Mongols wanted to claim their new province, they would have to fight for it all over again against the various princelings and upstarts who had already proclaimed themselves as the true rulers of various parts of the state. Although the Mongols did make several attempts to assert their authority in the region of the Irrawaddy basin at the turn of the fourteenth century, the effort of establishing government in the area was regarded as too much like hard work, and Mongol forces retreated from Pagan/Burma entirely in 1303.[7]

One of the unexpected spin-offs of the Burma campaign was the Mongol acquisition of twelve elephants, some of which eventually made their way back to Beijing for the entertainment of Khubilai.[8]

Khubilai was already a very sick man by 1280. Grossly fat and gout-ridden, he put his engineers to work on an oddly ostentatious, imperial variant of the old, mobile tents of the steppe – an overblown parody of the legendarily portable 'pleasure dome' of his summer palace hunting grounds at Shangdu. The Chinese record refers to Khubilai's new transport simply as a *xiang-jiao* or 'elephant litter', a term that calls to mind something like a howdah or palanquin. In fact, as Marco Polo attested to generations of disbelieving Europeans, it was a far grander thing than that. It was a massive platform, easily matching the breadth of the wheelbase of the largest Mongol carts:

> mounted on a great wooden *bartizan*, which was borne by four well-trained elephants, and over him was hoisted his standard, so high aloft that it could be seen from all sides.[9]

Polo coins the term *bartizan*, from the same root that gives us 'bastion', and clearly regarded the *xiang-jiao* as less of an elephant-borne palanquin, and more of a mobile fort. Khubilai put his great transport to use in the field, when he took up arms to suppress yet another revolt. This time, the danger came from the north-east, where Nayan, another grandson of Temujin, raised a rebel standard against Khubilai for the usual reason – forgetting his Mongol roots. With the usual irony, Nayan was a Nestorian Christian, so hardly an old-school Mongol himself.

He was allied with Khaidu, who had somehow arranged for the pair of them to attack Khubilai's realm from opposing sides in order to spread chaos.

Bayan, the great general 'of a hundred eyes' who had once vanquished the Southern Song for Khubilai, was sent to Manchuria in 1287 to assess Nayan's supposed disloyalty. According to Marco Polo, he was invited to dine with Nayan, but sensed a trap and made a hasty exit. Khubilai himself led the army that followed to put Nayan back in his place. While a separate force headed west to prevent any aid arriving from Khaidu, Khubilai made innovative use of his much-derided fleet. Instead of marching north from Beijing, where he was sure to attract the attention of Nayan's scouts long before battle could commence, Khubilai used the fleet to jump from the coast near Beijing to the Liaodong peninsula, effectively attacking Nayan from an unexpected direction, and bypassing any traps that Nayan may have left on the mainland.

Assured by his soothsayers that victory would be his, Khubilai made his own luck with the landing at Liaodong – an effective transportation of the bulk of his force into the heart of Nayan's territory. When Nayan's guardsmen reported the approach of Khubilai, Nayan rushed to arms, heading out to a nearby plain where Khubilai, his teeming thousands of cavalrymen and his elephants lay in wait.

We do not have the doomed Nayan's version of events, but Khubilai's elephant litter must have been a sight to see. Marco Polo's description has it:

> full of cross-bow men and archers, with his flag above him bearing the figures of the sun and moon, and so high that it could be seen from all sides. The four elephants were covered with very stout boiled hides, overlaid with cloths of silk and gold.[10]

More controversially, the opposing standard of Nayan bore a massive crucifix – on that remote Manchurian plain, perhaps the easternmost sign of Christendom that would be seen for centuries, until missionaries came ashore in distant Japan in the late sixteenth century. Nayan saw himself as a Christian soldier, and Khubilai as a heathen to be trounced by the power of the Cross.

Then, if Marco Polo is to be believed, the opposing armies paused to sing at each other,

> for this is a custom of the Tartars, that before they join battle they all unite in singing and playing on a certain two-stringed instrument of theirs, a thing right pleasant to hear.[11]

The battle itself is described in all available sources in a cluster of clichés – the arrows, then the horsemen, then the clash of hand-to-hand combat. Suffice to say, by the afternoon, the day belonged to Khubilai, who observed from his elephant-borne platform as the captured Nayan was brought before him. Nayan's fate was predictable by the customs of the Mongols – no blood could be spilt of the line of Temujin, nor could it be seen beneath the eye of the sun. Consequently, Nayan was wrapped in a rug and beaten to death.

In the aftermath, the households and clans associated with Nayan's revolt declared loyalty to Khubilai, although a new form of unrest arose from an unexpected quarter. The last reported religious dispute of Khubilai's long life began as the victorious army returned to Beijing – reports reached Khubilai of arguments among his troops. This was because, as Marco Polo noted,

> different kinds of people who were present, Saracens and Idolaters and Jews, and many others that believed not in God, did gibe those that were Christians because of the cross that Nayan had borne on his standard, and that so grievously that there was no bearing it.[12]

Nayan had proclaimed himself to be a Christian, and had trusted, in the style of Saint Constantine the Great, in the power of the Cross to lead him to victory. When Khubilai had crushed him, quite literally, this had led to significant taunts among Khubilai's followers. Surely it had been proved that Christianity had no power? In a carefully worded rebuttal, Khubilai pointed out that it merely proved that Nayan had no power, and therefore no place calling on God to come to his aid in an unjust war:

'Nayan was a disloyal and traitorous Rebel against his Lord, and well deserved that which had befallen him. Wherefore the Cross of your God did well in that it gave him no help against [me].' And this he said so loud that everybody heard him. The Christians then replied to the Great Kaan: 'Great King, you say the truth indeed, for our Cross can render no one help in wrong-doing; and therefore it was that It aided not Nayan, who was guilty of crime and disloyalty, for it would take no part in his evil deeds.'[13]

This put an end to the anti-Christian whispers within Khubilai's entourage, although some might have speculated on the flipside on his argument. Khubilai still declared no preference for any one deity. If there were indeed a magical power that could be imparted to an army by invoking its true faith, then surely it would have been in Khubilai's interests to decide on that faith and proclaim where he stood. But he did not, and his last years were occupied with further futile attempts at extending the Mongol conquest.

The last great military endeavour of Khubilai's reign was yet another doomed expedition to the south, this time against Kertanagara, the King of Java (r.1268–92). When Khubilai's officials had arrived for the first time in Java in 1289, they had behaved in their customary manner, and ominously requested that the ruler submit to the distant Khan. Perhaps ignorant of the implications, perhaps emboldened by news of the resistance in other parts of south-east Asia, Kertanagara branded the face of Khubilai's envoy, a Chinese official called Meng Chi. If he had simply killed him, the reaction might have been swifter, but it seems that Meng Chi's particular indignity slowed down the usual speed of Mongol communications: it was three years before Meng Chi could return to Beijing, literally show his face, and hence get the Mongol retribution machine rolling. In 1290, Kertanagara extended his authority across into southern Sumatra, attacking the Muslim kingdom of Jambi, which already enjoyed a vassal status with Khubilai's China.

In 1292, a great fleet set out from China for the dual purpose of restoring Jambi and chastising Java. It was truly multi-racial, led by a triumvirate of Mongol, Chinese and Uighur officials, and carrying some 20,000 troops in 1,000 ships crewed by Chinese and Muslims. In an acknowledgement that the journey to Java was truly long and hard, the fleet also carried a number of Mongol envoys on an even longer mission. Among them, it is believed, was Marco Polo, whose itinerary for his homeward voyage suggests that he travelled first among the Java expedition force, before a flotilla peeled away for India and then Persia, where Polo was expected to deliver a Mongol princess bride to the ruler of the Ilkhanate.

Hence, Polo's last report of Khubilai's realm is a series of reminiscences of the Java expedition, which he left to continue his westward voyage when the Sino-Mongol army was still establishing its presence:

> This is how we spent our five months. We disembarked from our ships and for fear of these nasty and brutish folk who kill men for food we dug a big trench around our encampment, extending down to the shore of the harbour at either end. On the embankment of the trench we built five wooden towers or forts; and within these fortifications we lived for five months.[14]

Kertanagara cunningly decided to meet the Mongols halfway, sending invasion fleets of his own to Champa, where he was sure that the Mongol fleet would stop on its route. This could have caused great troubles for the Mongols, but backfired when Kertanagara's pro-active scheme over-stretched his limited forces. One of his own vassals, Jayakatwang, took the opportunity to turn on him, and killed Kertanagara in battle while the Mongols were still approaching.

Khubilai's generals were understandably surprised to discover that the political situation had changed so radically during their approach that they now faced a wholly new enemy. Jayakatwang was the new public enemy number one, whereas Kertanagara's replacement, his son-in-law Vijaya, had decided to defect to the Mongols in order to enlist their support in avenging his father's death.

If this sounded too good to be true, it was. King Vijaya and his newfound Mongol allies made short work of the rebellious Jayakatwang, killing the bulk of his army, and capturing and executing the rebellious vassal. However, Vijaya then turned on the Mongols, murdering his honour guard en route to his own ceremony of allegiance to Khubilai, and turning on nearby garrisons with vengeful fury.

One of Khubilai's generals barely escaped with his life, and joined a heated conference on the flagship. In a rehash of the debates among the invaders of Japan, the triumvirate bickered over whether their mission had been fulfilled. Kertanagara was dead, and a rebellion had been put down – surely that was good enough for dispatches home and a well-earned rest? At least one of Khubilai's generals argued that they had only fulfilled their mission by the letter of the law; in spirit, Java was demonstrably no more under Mongol rule than it had been before they arrived. Meanwhile, several thousand troops were dead, and fleet strength was presumably depleted by the scheduled departure of Marco Polo's India-bound squadron, which may have taken a significant proportion of the remaining provisions with it.

All things considered, it was time for the Mongol fleet to return home, and to report a guarded 'success' to their ruler. In what may have been an attempt to play down the appeal of Java as a future destination, the *History of the Yuan* added that:

'their people are ugly and strange, [and] their temperament and their speech cannot be understood in China.'[15]

They need not have worried. Marco Polo's decision to leave China, as well as the triumvirate's decision to return with their Java mission incomplete, all seem to have mirrored a more general sense of gloom in Beijing, and a general trepidation that Khubilai Khan, the architect of the Yuan dynasty, was fading, with little clue of what direction his state would take after his death.

In November 1293, the astronomers at Khubilai's Beijing observatory noted the appearance of a 'broom star' – a comet that lingered in the morning sky, crossing slowly across the apex of heaven. Towards the end of the year, it 'trespassed' against the Purple Forbidden Enclosure, the area of the sky that corresponded to the very centre of power. To the astrologically inclined, it was a sign of great upheaval at the very heart of the empire. Khubilai was dying.[16]

The eighty-year-old Khubilai did not need astrologers to tell him that. Drinking and eating in great imperial binges, he had swelled to gargantuan levels of obesity. Inconsolable in his Beijing palace, still grieving over the loss of Chabi and Zhenjin, he refused to go through the correct protocols for accepting the customary New Year's gifts. By mid-February 1294, shortly after the Chinese New Year, it was over.

13

THE ROMANCE OF THE GRAND KHAN

KHUBILAI'S LEGACY

Khubilai's funeral arrangements were in keeping with his life – a clash of Chinese and Mongol traditions. His grandson Temur, the most appropriate heir available, was proclaimed as his successor at a *kurultai*, although it had none of the lively debate and politicking of previous councils that had borne the name. Instead, the argument came down to which of the two candidates could best quote the words of the late Temujin. When Temur was able to reel off a few quotes from his ancestor, he was meekly ratified by the attendant nobles, who then initiated Chinese-style coronation proceedings that the majority present clearly thought were far more important.

Supposedly out of respect for the task ahead of him, Temur gave up alcohol. That, at least, is what Rashid al-Din was told to say, in the conclusion to the work he was probably writing while Temur was still alive:

God Almighty, when [Temur] became a great lord, removed the
love of wine from his heart, whereas Khubilai had been unable
to prevent his drinking either by pleas or by compulsion.[1]

The funeral ceremony was decidedly Mongol. There would
be no ostentatious mausoleum for the founder of the Yuan
dynasty. Instead, his body was carried in a procession towards
northern Mongolia, to the Khentii range, which included the
sacred mountain Burkhan Khaldun, the last resting place of
Temujin. There, like his grandfather, he was laid to rest in an
unknown location, all the better to evade grave robbers or evil
spirits.

Temur, the newly crowned second emperor of the Yuan
dynasty, put his stamp of approval on a more lasting memorial
to Khubilai closer to home. As June 1294 loomed, and the
dwindling Mongol presence headed north to Karakorum and
Shangdu for the summer, Temur ordered a great altar to be built
in Khubilai's honour, south of Beijing.

Despite the strife they had caused him when he was alive,
the feuding religious traditions of Khubilai's realm all found
something positive to say about him after he was gone. Rashid
al-Din, who put the finishing touches to his *Compendium of
Chronicles* during the reign of Temur, remembered Khubilai
Khan as a great friend of the Muslims, judiciously ignoring over
a decade of persecutions and anti-Muslim decrees that bore
Khubilai's personal seal. Giving him the benefit of the doubt,
Rashid al-Din assumed that the blame for anti-Muslim feeling
rested with others. Similarly the Tibetan Buddhists who had
witnessed Khubilai's soldiers destroy the 'Bri-gung Monastery
in 1285 were prepared to regard Khubilai not only as a wise
ruler, but as the epitome of wisdom – an incarnation of
Manjusri, the Bodhisattva of Wisdom. The Mongols remembered him as a great khan, and made no mention of his
troubling Chinese enculturation, which led him to spend so
much of his life away from the steppes, in the world of farmers
and merchants. Only the Taoists seemed to stay quiet about

him, although many of those people who claimed to have been Taoists had had their faith rudely annihilated by Khubilai's attempts to clamp down on superstition and charlatanry.

He was remembered by the Chinese Confucians as a wise, *Confucian* ruler, accepted as one of their own and as a dutiful adherent to principles of Chinese government, even though he had swamped the administration with foreigners and dismantled their Sinocentric examination system. It was Khubilai's great-grandson, the Renzong Emperor, who reinstituted the Confucian examinations in 1315, effectively drawing the lines of demarcation once more, and leaving China solely in the hands of the Chinese or the wholly Sinified. During the short reign of the Renzong Emperor's son, there was a brief flurry of excitement over forgotten wars. In Tibet, a monk in his fifties, who had led a quiet contemplative life translating Buddhist scriptures, suddenly discovered that he was really Gongdi, the sixteenth Emperor of the Song Dynasty, crowned as a child and disinherited scant weeks later by General Bayan. Whisked away to Tibet and exiled to a monastery, Gongdi appears to have been young enough at the time of his arrival to have completely forgotten his former life as the last hope of the defenders of Hangzhou. He was, in effect, one of the many recipients of Khubilai's mercy, permitted to live a good life instead of dying a summary death. With monastic resignation, he considered the wheel of fate, and wrote a small poem about the loss of the empire he never knew he once had. The result was predictable – there could not be two suns in the same sky, nor could there be two emperors. In even acknowledging the possibility that he had been a rallying point for the Song loyalists, Gongdi had signed his own death warrant, and he was swiftly executed after decades of non-interference.

One might be forgiven for thinking that Khubilai would enjoy better success in terms of his military legacy. He had, after all, done what no Mongol leader had ever accomplished before, the complete conquest of all China. In doing so, he had brought China back together again as a unified realm, restoring an order that had not been seen since the collapse of the Northern Song centuries earlier. However, his military record was arguably not his own. His generalship 'in the field' was largely confined to his figurehead status in the Dali campaign of his youth, and in several command positions in wars against his own people. He took the credit for the military successes of the great generals like Bayan and Uryangkhadai, but much of the Mongol war machine was built before Khubilai's birth, and had expended much of its force in campaigns undertaken in his youth. By the time 'Mongols' conquered the Southern Song, in a hard-fought campaign that took many years, the army they led comprised large numbers of Jurchens and Chinese defectors. An appraisal of Khubilai the great conqueror has to carefully avoid mentioning the huge military disasters that also happened on his watch – Japan and Annam, of course, but also Java and the abandonment of his footsoldiers in the desert during the campaign against Arigh Boke. Meanwhile, even his most loyal subjects, the Koreans, were not immune from uprisings and rebellions during his reign. Khubilai did, to be sure, unify China with its neighbouring cultures, but it was a unification that was already fraying at the edges by the time of his death. Despite ruling an empire that supposedly stretched all the way to Europe, Khubilai did not dare put the loyalty of his western vassals to the test. He fused China together, but claimed in his lifetime to have unified a lot more than that.

Undeniably, one of his enduring legacies was the establishment of powerful ties, for good or ill, between China and Mongolia. In adding China to Mongol possessions, Khubilai inadvertently created a recoil effect – in later years, it would become common for Mongolia, now part of the Chinese orbit, to be regarded as a *Chinese* possession, as it would be again under the Qing dynasty, which only ended in the twentieth century.

Khubilai's successors would carefully integrate the northern borders of China into the Chinese worldview, ironically by completing the long-delayed histories of former regimes. In the

1340s, scholars finally began compiling the records of the Yuan's predecessor regimes. This saw the completion in 1343 of a *History of the Liao*. Two years later, the Jurchens got their own chronicles, with the *History of the Jin*. The same year, 1345, also saw the *History of the Song*. The assembly of these chronicles not only closed the book on the former regimes, so to speak, but announced the Yuan dynasty's confidence that it was their true successor. Behind the scenes, it also sneakily helped further another of Khubilai's recurring obsessions – the desire to be taken seriously as a legitimate Chinese dynasty. Chinese orthodoxy had long held that neither the Liao nor the Jin deserved a history because they were regimes of 'barbarian' origin and hence not worthy of consideration. The Jurchens had already done a lot of the work on the *History of the Liao* themselves, but have never got round to publishing it.

By compiling them en masse with the Song dynasty, the Mongols inadvertently set a precedent. When their own dynasty itself eventually fell to be replaced by another, the issue of whether a non-Chinese regime was worthy had already been settled – the Jurchens were already on the record. Hence, when the Yuan dynasty was gone and the scholars of the Ming dynasty wrote the *History of the Yuan* in turn, it was established, without complaint, as another one of the procession of dynasties deemed worthy of a place in the Chinese record. What nobody working in 1345 could have admitted was that the Yuan's days were already numbered. It had taken them a century to write up the stories of their predecessors, but the *History of the Yuan* would be written by the victorious Ming dynasty only twenty-five years later.

The Yuan dynasty, for all its achievements, is one of the shortest in Chinese history, occupying less than a century before its fall. In the dozen years after the death of the Renzong Emperor, the Yuan dynasty somehow got through six successors, as Khubilai's descendants fought over the throne. The last of Khubilai's descendants to rule China, the Huizong Emperor, was crowned aged thirteen in 1332, and would die in exile, hounded out of China by the resistance movement. Hard times led to rebellions in the 1350s, with the leader of the rebels seizing Beijing itself in 1368. As the last of the Mongol aristocracy fled back to the north, the rebel leader claimed that China was once more in the hands of the Chinese, and proclaimed that the Yuan dynasty was over. Instead, with the dark days behind him, the new emperor announced the 'Ming': the 'dynasty of Brightness'. The new Ming dynasty soon overturned most Mongol influences in China, except one. Yunnan, the south-western province that Khubilai won in his early rise to power, was the last Mongol possession to fall in China. Another of Khubilai's descendants, Basalawarmi, the Prince of Liang, clung to Yunnan until the 1380s, but killed himself after losing a battle with resurgent Ming forces.

The Mongol innovations during the Yuan – the short-lived experiment in 'Phags-pa script, the sudden movement of isolated populations and traditions into close proximity – were soon buried beneath fervid Sinification once more. Khubilai's melting pot – when Arab merchants served as town councillors in Quanzhou, when the Venetian Marco Polo worked in local government in Yangzhou, and when a Tibetan monk oversaw temple restoration in Hangzhou – was never quite repeated in imperial China. The Ming dynasty learned from the Yuan dynasty's failures by reacting against them. The result was conservative, arguably repressive, but served to enforce harmony by trampling on difference. The first ruler of the Ming dynasty, rumoured in some quarters to have had Central Asian blood himself, soon grappled with the issue of the Muslims, ordering that they should 'marry, speak, and dress Chinese'.[2] In return for such assimilation, they were permitted religious and political freedom, a guarantee made infinitely easier by the removal of many of the superficial elements that marked them out as different from the hidebound Han Chinese.

The Chinese Muslims were given greater religious freedom under the Ming, at the expense of outward appearances – intriguingly opposite to their position under Khubilai, when they were permitted to dress in an identifiably Muslim way and often spoke languages that were not Chinese.[3] Others were simple removed from the gene pool. Zheng He, the famous mariner of the early Ming, had been captured as a boy by Ming soldiers during the fall of Yunnan, and castrated to serve as a palace slave. Eventually becoming the captain of the Ming Emperor's exploratory treasure fleet, he notably settled a large number of Chinese Muslims in south-east Asia, further reducing the number of *semuren* in what had once been Khubilai's realm.

However, not even these forcible relocations could undo the *genetic* changes wrought by the Mongols. According to the *American Journal of Human Genetics*, a certain pattern in DNA can be found all across Asia, indicating that some 16 million men, from Hungary to Korea, can count themselves as the descendants of a single ancestor. That man is likely to be Temujin, the Genghis Khan, whose many descendants, including Khubilai, enjoyed a brief tenure at the top of the food chain, and spread their DNA far and wide.

Such fertile, wild scattering of influences can also be seen in the art world. A landmark exhibition at the New York Metropolitan Museum of Art in 2010 argued for Khubilai as a great 'Chinese' emperor, and presented the early days of the Yuan dynasty not as a time of ruin and deprivation, but as the great beginnings of a period of unparalleled communication, art and culture. In artistic terms, Khubilai's Yuan dynasty . . .

> has become a vast dumping ground for connoisseur and archaeologist. Like Limbo, neither Heaven not Hell, it provided a resting place for the in-betweeners, those works considered too poor for the glorious Song and Ming dynasties, or for those curious objects which defied accurate classification.[4]

And yet we can easily see what makes an object characteristically Yuan – the sudden admixture of Arab porcelain with Chinese characteristics, Mongol themes on Chinese scrolls,

Muslim patterns on Chinese tiles, or odd materials from far-flung new provinces. The Yuan dynasty, in being so short, also created two closely situated generations of ousted officials, retiring from public life at both the end of the Song and the end of the Yuan, and devoting themselves instead to artistic pursuits. Khubilai's legacy among many ministers took the form of a vast outpouring of paintings, from former officials with nothing else to do.

Early attempts under the Ming to return to a southern-facing society began with a capital at Nanjing on the Yangtze. However, the capital was soon moved back to Beijing, in part as the result of politicking among the new imperial family, but also because the Mongols were, once again, a threat on the northern borders, and Beijing was a more efficient base from which to sally forth against them. From that time onwards, with only a couple of brief interregnums, Beijing has remained as the capital of China, even though it is peculiarly far to the north – its location reflecting the shadowy vestiges of the time of Khubilai, when it was more central within a combined Sino-Mongol realm.

The collapse of Mongol power, or rather its swift fade into local traditions, was similarly pronounced elsewhere in the world. In Persia, the new ruler Ghazan professed loyalty to the sons of Khubilai, as his title 'ilkhan' ('subordinate khan') implied, but he also turned away from the Buddhist faith that had been a preoccupation of most of his predecessors. In 1295, he converted to Islam, adopting the new name Mahmud, and turned his Mongol dynasty into a Muslim one. However, this, too was supplanted within a century, and fell in 1353.

In Korea, the removal of the Yuan dynasty removed the need for local rulers to pay lip service to the Mongols, even though they shared the same bloodline. Khubilai's descendant King Gongmin had spent much of his life in Beijing, and even had a Mongol wife, but he soon tried to distance himself from the old regime after the fall of the Yuan dynasty. He initiated reforms in Korea that met with protest and indignation from a bureaucracy largely sympathetic to the Mongols, and powerful enough to split the country in two, between factions loyal to the retreating Mongols and the new rising Ming dynasty of China. After Gongmin's assassination, regents attempted to hang on to control through his son, infant grandson, and one final relative. The subsequent Joseon dynasty, established by a rebellious general, would rule Korea until 1910.

Over in Japan, there was relief at the news that their great enemy Khubilai Khan – the 'highwayman of the world' – was gone. The after-effects of his invasions, however, would reverberate for centuries. Although the samurai had successfully repulsed the invasion, the military system of Japan required that victors be recompensed with spoils from the vanquished, and the departing Mongol invaders had left nothing but driftwood. Disenchantment over the lack of rewards was one of the contributing factors that led to the collapse of the Kamakura Shōgunate a generation after Khubilai's death, plunging Japan into a prolonged civil war. Two centuries later, when the warlord Hideyoshi managed to precariously unify the chaotic country, his first act was to launch an attack on Korea. This was plainly intended to give his idle troops something to do, and to push thousands of defeated local enemies into a distant war, in the hope that they might either die or win fiefdoms for themselves instead of causing trouble in Japan.

Hideyoshi's grand scheme was framed not as an invasion of Korea, but as an invasion of China – Korea was merely the road to Beijing. Tucked among the propaganda of Hideyoshi's Korean war is the outrageous assertion that he was avenging the insult delivered to Japan by Khubilai, by returning along the route of the Mongol armada to teach the Chinese Emperor a lesson. This was, of course, all news to the Chinese Emperor, who was a member of the same Ming dynasty that had thrown the Mongols out of China, and hence of no relation to them.

And what of Marco Polo, last seen on a slow boat from China, escorting a Mongol princess to Persia? He made it home, somewhat the worse for wear, having travelled across half the known world under the protection of Khubilai's law, only to be mugged soon after he returned to Christendom. Understanding that things would never quite be the same with Khubilai gone, Marco Polo stayed in Italy and never returned to the place he had made his home for twenty years. Thrust back into local trade with some questionable characters, Polo found himself enduring a brief period of house arrest, and took the opportunity to write down as much as he could remember about his travels, with the help of his ghost writer: the rakish former soldier and sometime troubadour Rustichello of Pisa. The resulting document, *The Description of the World*, also known simply as *The Travels*, circulated in several variant forms, which seem to have included a rather dull merchants' gazetteer, a racier private version that left in all the good bits, and possibly an outrageously fictionalised version recorded in one Burgundian library as *The Romance of the Grand Khan*.[5]

Although none of *The Romance of the Grand Khan* originals is extant, there were enough copies of *Description of the World* made for some to survive. It is through Marco Polo's eyes that Khubilai lives again for us. Polo's reports of banquets and councils, religious debates and court intrigues, introduced Khubilai to an entire continent of readers. Somehow, Polo's account was copied in the right places, saved from the right fires. Other souvenirs of Polo's life in China – a knight's belt, a lady's head-dress, a packet of rhubarb – are no longer with us, but for centuries, readers have been entranced by his stories of the man he called 'The Great Khan'.

And of a surety he hath good right to such a title, for all men know for a certain truth that he is the most potent man, as regards forces and lands and treasure, that existeth in the world, or ever hath existed from the time of our First Father Adam until this day. All this I will make clear to you for truth, in this book of ours, so that every one shall be fain to acknowledge that he is the greatest Lord that is now in the world, or ever hath been.[6]

Polo's account became part of the heritage of travel literature, reprinted and refashioned so that by the seventeenth century, in England, it had been summarized and somewhat tweaked by a man called Samuel Purchas. It was the Purchas spin on Polo's story that Samuel Taylor Coleridge had been reading more than a century later, one fateful night in 1796, at a remote farmhouse in Exmoor.

Coleridge collapsed into an opium-induced stupor, apparently soon after reading the passage in Purchas' book about Khubilai's summer residence in Shangdu:

> In Xamdu did Cublai Can build a stately Pallace, encompassing sixteen miles of plaine grounde within a wall, wherein are fertile Meddowes, pleasant Springs, delightful Streames, and all sorts of beasts of chase and game, and in the middest thereof a sumptuous house of pleasures, which may be removed from place to place.[7]

When he awoke, he did so with a great sense of creativity and poetry, with a great, epic account of Khubilai in his mind – a fever-dream of surreal images and powerful orientalist ideas. He immediately began jotting it down, only to be disturbed by a knock at the door – a visitor, widely believed to be the man who supplied him with much of his opium. An hour later, the visitor having been eventually sent packing, Coleridge returned to his Khubilai-themed writings, only to discover that his Muse had fled:

> with the exception of some eight or ten scattered lines and images, all the rest had passed away like the images on the surface of a stream into which a stone has been cast, but, alas! Without the after restoration of the latter![8]

The poem was not published until 1816, and remains Khubilai Khan's most famous appearance in Western literature. Little, however, of the historical Khubilai remains. True enough, there is the factual description of the pleasure dome itself, adhering closely to Polo, through Purchas. There is an allusion to the 'milk of Paradise', which is possibly a garbled reference to the *koumiss* known to be so beloved of the Mongols. If we stretch a point, we might believe that Coleridge mixed the section on Shangdu with the section on Beijing, and that his 'sacred river' was something to do with Marco Polo's description of a grated outflow channel that led from the lakes beside the Forbidden City. Other elements, though, are arbitrary and barely relevant. Coleridge's full text soon veers off into opium-addled burblings, with little relevance to the Mongol Emperor of China. And yet he lives on in the familiar metre and portentous declarations, familiar to people who know nothing of China, nothing of Mongolia, and nothing of Khubilai himself:

> In Xanadu did Kubla Khan
> A stately pleasure-dome decree:
> Where Alph, the sacred river, ran
> Through caverns measureless to man
> Down to a sunless sea.

CHRONOLOGY

1145	Rumours spread in Europe of the existence of 'Prester John', a Christian king of the orient.
1206	Mongol hordes conquer the Xixia, a Tangut empire to the west of China.
1215	Destruction of the Jurchen capital Zhongdu (Beijing). Birth of Khubilai.
1227	Death of Temujin (Genghis Khan).
1229	Ogodei proclaimed Khan. Establishment of the post-rider system.
1236	Sorghaghtani extends her domains into part of Hebei, China. Khubilai put in charge of the district of Xingzhou.
1241	Death of Ogodei.
1243	Birth of Khubilai's second son, Zhenjin.
1246	Guyuk proclaimed Khan.
1248	Death of Guyuk.
1251	Mongke proclaimed Khan.
1252	Death of Sorghaghtani.
1253	Khubilai commences operations against Dali (Yunnan).
1254	Marco Polo born.
1256	Khubilai starts building his summer capital at Kaiping.

1257	Officials from Mongke subject Khubilai's domain to an audit.
1258	Mongol forces pushed out of Annam.
	The ruler of Annam offers his submission.
	Khubilai and Mongke are reconciled.
	Khubilai presides at Kaiping religious debates.
	Taoist heretical texts are banned.
1259	Khubilai commences war against Southern Song.
	Death of Mongke Khan.
1260	Pope Alexander IV issues the Papal bull *Clamat in Auribus*.
	Khubilai and Arigh Boke are proclaimed Khan at rival councils.
	The future King Wonjong of Korea pledges allegiance to Khubilai.
	Khubilai's troops install Wonjong as King of Korea.
	The Southern Song detains Khubilai's ambassadors.
1261	Arigh Boke reneges on peace treaty with Khubilai.
	Khubilai abandons his footsoldiers in the desert.
	Li Tan's son sneaks out of Khubilai's court.
1262	Revolt of Li Tan in north China.
	Khubilai forbids nomads from grazing on Chinese farmland.
1263	Kaiping is renamed Shangdu ('Xanadu').
	Prince Zhenjin is made Prince of Yan – the ruler of Beijing.
1264	Arigh Boke surrenders.
	Khubilai reprimands his officers for executing defecting Song generals.
1265	Khubilai's men capture 120 ships from the Song – foundation of the Mongol fleet.
	Niccolo and Maffeo Polo arrive in Shangdu.
1266	Death of Arigh Boke in custody.
	Khubilai orders the Koreans to secure Japanese tribute.
1267	Khubilai recommences military operations against Song China.

	King Wonjong of Korea sends fish skins for Khubilai's bloated feet.
1268	Attack on the Song stronghold of Xiangyang.
	Mission to Japan delivers letter to the Shōgun.
1269	Niccolo and Maffeo Polo return to Europe.
	The 'Phags-pa Lama introduces his unified script.
1270–3	Revolts and unrest in Korea.
1271	Khubilai proclaims that the Yuan dynasty has begun.
	Prince Nomukhan appointed to pacify the west (i.e. Khaidu).
1272	Surrender of Xiangyang after prolonged siege.
1273	Mongol envoys demand the surrender of Pagan (Burma).
1274	First Mongol attempt to invade Japan.
1275	Marco Polo reaches Shangdu.
	Surrender of Hangzhou.
	The Mongol general Bayan captures the infant Song emperor, Gongdi.
	Khubilai sends a final warning to Japan.
	King Thanh Tong of Annam claims that his country requires no supervisors.
1276	The Polos reach Khanbalikh (modern Beijing).
	Khubilai authorizes the printing of extra money.
1277	Nasir al-Din invades Burma.
1278	Realizing all is lost at the Battle of Yamen, the minister Liu Xufu jumps into the sea with the child emperor. End of the Song dynasty.
	The White Pagoda is the tallest building in Beijing.
	In Annam, Thanh Tong 'abdicates' in favour of his son.
1280	Khubilai discovers that the Japanese have executed his ambassadors.
	A fire at a Beijing Buddhist temple is discovered to be arson.
	Death of the 'Phags-pa Lama.
	The 'Bri-gung Revolt in Tibet.
1281	Second Mongol attempt to invade Japan.

	Death of Khubilai's wife, Chabi.
1282	Murder of Ahmad Fanakati in Beijing.
	Failed Mongol seaborne assault on Champa.
1283	Second Mongol expedition force in Burma.
1285	Death of Zhenjin.
	Controversial temple restoration project in Hangzhou.
	Mongols take Hanoi.
1287	Nayan rises in revolt against Khubilai Khan.
	Sangha pleads with Khubilai to reverse anti-Muslim policies.
1289	Kertanagara, King of Java, insults Khubilai Khan by branding a Mongol ambassador.
	Mongols defeated by Annamese at battle of Bach Dang River.
1292	The Polos depart from Quanzhou.
	A Mongol invasion fleet departs Quanzhou for Java.
	Marco Polo spends five months in Sumatra.
1293	The Mongol invasion fleet commences operations in Java.
	Taking advantage of forces spread thinly to resist the invasion, Jayakatwang, King of Kediri, attacks and kills Kertanagara, King of Java.
	Kertanagara's son Vijaya surrenders to the Mongols, but double-crosses them.
	Beijing observatory reports a comet in the imperial sector of the sky.
1294	Death of Khubilai Khan.
	The Polos reach Persia and travel to Tabriz.
1295	The Polos reach Venice.
1298	Captured in a battle with Genoa, Marco Polo begins work on his book in collaboration with his fellow prisoner Rustichello of Pisa.
1312	A book called *The Romance of the Grand Khan* is reported in the possession of Mahaut, Countess of Burgundy.
1323	A monk in Tibet discovers that he is the former Song

child-emperor Gongdi. He publishes a poem about his lost destiny, and is subsequently executed by the Mongols.

1343–5   Yuan dynasty scribes compile the *History of the Song*, along with chronicles of the Liao and Jin dynasties.

1368   Ming rebels seize Beijing. Last of the Mongols retreat to their homeland.

NOTES ON NAMES

The subject of this book is *Hubilai* in Chinese, *Qubilai* in Mongol, *Kubirai* or *Fubirai* in Japanese, *Hot-Tat-Liet* in Vietnamese, and *Khubilai* in Russian. As a feature of the primacy of Chinese culture during the period, many of the sources are *Sinoxenic* texts – in which foreign nouns are written using approximate (sometimes barely relevant) Chinese characters. Hence, we must piece together, for example, that the figure recorded as 洪茶丘 is not Hong Chaqiu as a Chinese reader might first assume, nor Kō Chakyū, as the same characters are pronounced in Japanese, but Hong Dagu, a Korean name transposed into the Chinese language by chroniclers of the period.

For this work for the general reader, I have deliberately favoured romanizations that avoid the diacritic marks so beloved of Chinese, Mongol, Vietnamese and Korean orthographers. The subject of this book is referred to throughout as Khubilai, not as the Qubilai of many modern accounts, or the Kubla of some older ones. I largely avoid the multiplicity of honorifics used by his loyal subjects, who would often call him 'the Emperor' [of China] while he was alive, or 'Genesis Progenitor' (*Shizu*), his posthumous 'temple name' used in official chronicles such as the *Yuan-shi*.

Khubilai's grandfather is called Temujin here, not the Temüjin of older history books. Furthermore, I largely avoid the use of his grandfather's title of 'Great Leader', popularly rendered as Genghis Khan, but also as Činggis, Jinggis or Jenghiz. For Chinese, I have used Pinyin Romanization. For Korean, the Revised Romanization introduced in 2000, mercifully lacking in accents and apostrophes. In the case of the kingdom of Goryeo (Koryŏ) itself, I have simplified matters by simply referring to it as Korea. The city of Zhongdu (Middle Capital), razed to the ground by Temujin, rebuilt as Dadu (Great Capital) by Khubilai, known in Persian as Khanbalikh (the Khan's City), I have usually referred to anachronistically by its modern name of Beijing. I have employed similar anachronism where I think it aids the flow of the text.

When dealing with multiple individuals who share the same surname, such as Annam's Tran dynasty, I largely use their given names. Tran Hung Dao, for example, is usually identified as 'Hung Dao'. Although such familiarity might appear odd to Vietnamese speakers, I believe it is vastly preferable to having a dozen individuals all called Tran in my text.

SOURCES AND FURTHER READING

Sources on the Mongols in European languages are remarkably sparse. Scholars often seem drawn to Mongol studies as an annex to pre-existing disciplines, and often reflect a bias from their previous training. Many pursue an agenda of enculturation, assuming that the Mongols were barbarians who were uplifted and assimilated by their conquest of other cultures. This is not necessarily inaccurate, but for those of us whose nations were built by rapacious cowboys, axe-wielding Vikings, or tyrannous Romans, we should consider the dangers of throwing stones in glass houses. It is worth noting that such bias usually affects even primary sources, and we must walk a careful line between the disapproving sneers of Christian missionaries, the defiant recollections of Japanese warriors and the proud boasts of Chinese or Islamic successor states.

It is perhaps not surprising that the first truly comprehensive English-language study of Khubilai's life and times was not published until 1988 – Morris Rossabi's thoroughly annotated account remains the best available. For an overview of the entire Yuan dynasty, and how developments continued after Khubilai's death, George Lane's *Daily Life in the Mongol Empire* offers a richly annotated mix of primary sources and detailed argument. For an account of Khubilai that places him within the broader context of Mongolia and the Turkic realms, the reader is directed to René Grousset's *The Empire of the Steppes: A History of Central Asia*.

Khubilai is absent from *The Secret History of the Mongols*, which deals largely with the life and achievements of his grandfather, and tails off in 1228, when Khubilai was only thirteen years old. It is, however, a wonderful source for the Mongol world of Khubilai's youth – in Mongol, Japanese and Chinese versions, as well as editions in European languages, of which Rachewiltz's is easily the best. So that readers may zero in on the original text with greater ease, regardless of the version they consult, I have given references to the *Secret History* by the more widespread section number, not a specific page that will obviously vary from translation to translation.

Chinese sources are dominated by the mammoth dynastic histories. As a reigning 'Chinese' emperor, Khubilai appears as Genesis Progenitor (*Shizu*), the first true emperor in chapters 4–17 of the dynastic annals of the Yuan dynasty, the *History of the Yuan* or *Yuan-shi*. The preceding chapters are biographies of Temujin, Ogodei, Guyuk and Mongke, accorded honorary imperial status out of respect to Khubilai. Other relevant sections include the genealogies in *Yuan-shi* 57, the account of the invasion of Korea and Japan in *Yuan-shi* 208, of Annam in *Yuan-shi* 209, Burma, Champa, Java and the Ryūkyū Islands in *Yuan-shi* 210, and many potted biographies of minor officials in the later books. The Chinese original is freely available online at: <http://www.guoxue.com/shibu/24shi/yuanshi/yuasml.htm>

The Mongols also feature, of course, as the enemy in the chronicles of the Song dynasty, the *Song-shi*, which was compiled in 1345 under the auspices of one of Khubilai's descendants. The volumes on the reigns of the Lizong in *Song-shi* 41–5, the last true emperor Duzong in *Song-shi* 46, and the ill-fated claimants in *Song-shi* 47 cover the period of Khubilai's lifespan. A biography of Khubilai's great foe Jia Sidao can be found in *Song-shi* 474, and a fully annotated contents list, with

direct links to the original Chinese text online at: <http://zh.
wikisource.org/wiki/%E5%AE%8B%E5%8F%B2>

Khubilai also appears in the annals of Korea's Goryeo
dynasty, the *Goryeo-sa*, which details the various attempts of
the Koreans to delay the Mongol assimilation of their country,
and their fears of the disaster that would ensue when the
invasion of Japan finally commenced. This, too, is unavailable
in English, although there are editions in Chinese (the original,
since Koreans of the time used Chinese for their documents),
modern Korean and Japanese. Rashid al-Din's *Compendium of
Chronicles*, or *Jami' al-Tawarikh*, is a massive history of the
world, written at the behest of the Persian ruler Mahmud
Ghazan, ostensibly so that he and his descendants would not
forget their Mongol roots. Work on the book was likely to have
commenced while Khubilai was still alive, and completed
shortly after his death, leading to a detailed account of his reign
and deeds, most accessible in English in Boyle's *Successors of
Genghis Khan*. Another observer of events at which the young
Khubilai was surely present is Friar John of Plano Carpini,
whose affable and cynical account of the coronation of Guyuk
Khan, is freely available in a Latin/English online edition from
the University of Adelaide.

Of course, the best-known personal description is that of
Marco Polo, who met Khubilai Khan in the 1270s. I have
largely quoted from the Henry Yule translation, but instead of
using a scarce and antique original to be found in only a few
libraries, for ease of access I instead give section numbers from
the version to be found online at en.wikisource.org. Often
ridiculed for his claims about life in Khubilai's empire, Polo has
suffered varying fortunes in the centuries since. However,
despite assertions in the late twentieth century that he might
have made up most of his famous book, the trend in modern
scholarship (e.g. Larner's superb *Marco Polo and the Discovery
of the World*) is to acknowledge that his experiences as one of
the *semuren* were genuine, albeit not without methodological
issues such as his apparent failure to learn Chinese. *Marco Polo's*

China by Stephen Haw presents a compelling analysis of Polo's text, sufficient to persuade that Polo is a worthy source on Khubilai's realm. Komroff's *Contemporaries of Marco Polo* compiles the accounts of several other European observers, such as William of Rubruck, who may have found himself at the same occasions and banquets as Khubilai, although the future emperor was probably too young or anonymous at the time to attract such writers' direct attention.

With so many conflicting sources concerning the names and identities of Khubilai's children, I have usually consulted the nomenclature and classification system of Cawley's *Medieval Lands*, an online source that seems to present the most complete listings of Khubilai's many offspring and descendants. The Hambis and Pelliot work cited is an older print source summarizing *Yuan-shi* 57.

Aida, N., *Mōko Shūrai no Kenkyū* [*Studies in the Mongol Invasions*]. Tokyo: Yoshikawa Hirobumi-kan, 1958.

Arlington, L. and William Lewisohn, *In Search of Old Peking*. Hong Kong: Kelly and Walsh, 1935 (reprinted 1967).

Bell, J., *A Journey From St. Petersburg to Pekin 1719–22*. Edinburgh: Edinburgh University Press, 1965.

Berzin, A., *A Historical Sketch of the Muslims of China*, 1995. http://www.berzinarchives.com/web/en/archives/study/islam/historical_interaction/overviews/history_hui_muslims_china.html (Accessed 18 January 2010).

Biran, M., *Qaidu and the Rise of the Independent Mongol State in Central Asia*. Richmond: Curzon, 1997.

Boyle, J. (ed.), *The Successors of Genghis Khan: Translations from Rashid al-Din's Jami' al-Tavarikh, dealing with the years 1229–94*. New York: Columbia University Press, 1971.

Brose, M., 'Realism and Idealism in the *Yuanshi* Chapters on Foreign Relations', in *Asia Major*, vol. 19, Taipei: Academica Sinica, 2006. pp. 327–47.

Cahill, J., *The Art of Southern Sung China*. New York: Arno Press, 1976.

Cawley, C., *Medieval Lands: A Prosopography of Medieval European Noble and Royal Families*. Foundation for Medieval Genealogy, 2009.

http://fmg.ac/Projects/MedLands/Contents.htm (Accessed 5th December 2009).

Chan, H., *The Fall of the Jurchen Chin: Wang E's Memoir on Ts'ai Chou Under the Mongol Siege (1233–1234)*. Stuttgart: Franz Steiner Verlag, 1993.

Charbonnier, J., *Christians in China: AD 600 to 2000*. San Francisco: Ignatius Press, 2007.

Ch'en, P., *Chinese Legal Tradition Under the Mongols: The Code of 1291 as Reconstructed*. Princeton: Princeton University Press, 1979.

Cleaves, F., *The Secret History of the Mongols, for the first time done into English out of the Original Tongue and Provided with an Exegetical Commentary*. Cambridge: Harvard University Press, 1982.

Clements, J., *Pirate King: Coxinga and the Fall of the Ming Dynasty*. Stroud: Sutton Publishing, 2004.

— *Wu: The Chinese Empress Who Schemed, Seduced and Murdered Her Way to Become a Living God*. Stroud: Sutton Publishing, 2007.

— *Marco Polo*. London: Haus Publishing, 2007.

— *Beijing: The Biography of a City*. Stroud: Sutton Publishing, 2008.

— *A Brief History of the Samurai*. London: Robinson, 2010.

Cobbing, A., *Kyūshū: Gateway to Japan – A Concise History*. Folkestone: Global Oriental, 2009.

Conlan, T., *In Little Need of Divine Intervention: Takezaki Suenaga's Scrolls of the Mongol Invasion of Japan*. Ithaca: East Asia Program, Cornell University, 2001.

di Cosmo, N. et al. *The Cambridge History of Inner Asia: The Chinggisid Age*. Cambridge: Cambridge University Press, 2009.

Crump, J., *Chinese Theater in the Days of Kublai Khan*. Tucson: University of Arizona Press, 1980.

Deal, W., *Handbook to Life in Medieval and Early Modern Japan*. Oxford: Oxford University Press, 2006.

Delgado, J., *Khubilai Khan's Lost Fleet: History's Greatest Naval Disaster*. London: Bodley Head, 2009.

Ebrey, P. and Maggie Bickford (eds), *Emperor Huizong and Late Northern Song China: The Politics of Culture and the Culture of Politics*. Cambridge, MA: Harvard University Press, 2006.

Farris, W., *Heavenly Warriors: The Evolution of Japan's Military, 500–1300*. Cambridge, MA: Harvard University Press, 1995.

— *Japan to 1600: A Social and Economic History*. Honolulu: University of Hawaii Press, 2009.

Franke, H., *China Under Mongol Rule*. Aldershot: Variorum Reprints, 1994.

Gernet, J., *A History of Chinese Civilization*. Cambridge: Cambridge University Press, 1990.

Golden, P., 'Migrations, ethnogenesis', in di Cosmo et al., *The Cambridge History of Inner Asia: The Chinggisid Age*. Cambridge: Cambridge University Press, 2009. pp. 109–19.

Grousset, R., *The Empire of the Steppes: A History of Central Asia*. New Brunswick: Rutgers University Press, 1970.

van Gulik, R., *Sexual Life in Ancient China: A Preliminary Survey of Chinese Sex and Society from ca. 1500 BC till 1644 AD*. Leiden: E.J. Brill, 1974.

[Hakluyt Society], *The Long and Wonderful Voyage of Frier Iohn de Plano Carpini*. Adelaide: University of Adelaide Library, 2004. eBook edition:
http://ebooks.adelaide.edu.au/h/hakluyt/voyages/carpini/complete.ht ml (Accessed 19 December 2009).

— *The Iournal of Frier William de Rubruquis, a French man of the order of the minorite friers, vnto the East parts of the worlde*. Adelaide: University of Adelaide Library, 2004. eBook edition: http://ebooks.adelaide.edu.au/h/hakluyt/voyages/rubruquis/ (Accessed 21 December 2009).

Halén, H., *Biliktu Bakshi: The Knowledgeable Teacher – G.J. Ramstedt's Career as a Scholar*. Helsinki: Finno-Ugrian Society, 1998.

Hambis, L. and Paul Pelliot, *Le Chapitre CVII du Yuan Che: Les Généalogies Impériales Mongoles dans L'Historie Chinoise Officielle de la Dynastie Mongole*. Leiden: E.J. Brill, 1945.

Haw, S., *Marco Polo's China: A Venetian in the realm of Khubilai Khan*. London: Routledge, 2006.

— *Beijing: A Concise History*. London: Routledge, 2007.

Hearn, M. and Judith Smith, *Arts of the Sung and Yüan: papers prepared for an international symposium organized by the Metropolitan Museum of Art in conjunction with the exhibition Splendors of Imperial China: Treasures from the National Palace Museum, Taipei*. New York: Metropolitan Museum of Art, 1996.

Henthorn, W., *Korea: The Mongol Invasions*. Leiden: E.J. Brill, 1963.

Hsiao, C., *The Military Establishment of the Yuan Dynasty*. Cambridge, MA: Harvard University Press, 1978.

Htin Aung, M., *A History of Burma*. New York: Columbia University Press, 1967.

Huu, N., *Wandering Through Vietnamese Culture*. Hanoi: The Gioi Publishers, 2008.

Jay, J., *A Change in Dynasties: Loyalism in Thirteenth-Century China*. Bellingham, WA: Western Washington University, 1991.

Kaplonski, C., 'The Mongolian Impact on Eurasia: A Reassessment', in Andrew Bell-Fialkoff (ed.), *The Role of Migration in the History of the Eurasian Steppe: Sedentary Civilization versus 'Barbarian' and Nomad*. New York: St Martin's Press, 2000. pp. 251–74.

Kawagoe, S., *Hōjō Tokimune*. Tokyo: Yoshikawa Hirobumi-kan, 2001.

Keach, W. (ed.), *Samuel Taylor Coleridge: Complete Poems*. Harmondsworth: Penguin, 1997.

[Kokusho Kankokai], *Kōrai-shi* [*The History of Goryeo (Goryeo-sa)*].Tokyo: Kokusho Kankokai, 1909.

Komroff, M., *Contemporaries of Marco Polo, consisting of the travel records to the eastern parts of the world of William of Rubruck (1253–1255), the Journey of John of Pian de Carpini (1245–1247), the journal of Friar Odoric (1318–1330) and the Oriental Travels of Rabi Benjamin of Tudela (1160–1173)*. London: Jonathan Cape, 1928.

Kronk, G., *Cometography: Volume 1, Ancient–1799*. Cambridge: Cambridge University Press, 1999.

Lane, G., *Daily Life in the Mongol Empire*. Indianapolis: Hackett, 2009.

Langlois, J. (ed.), *China Under Mongol Rule*. Princeton: Princeton University Press, 1981.

Larner, J., *Marco Polo and the Discovery of the World*. New Haven: Yale University Press, 1999.

Latham, R., *Marco Polo: The Travels*. Harmondsworth: Penguin, 1958.

Lee, S. and Ho Wai-kam, *Chinese Art Under the Mongols*. Cleveland: Museum of Art, 1968.

Lorge, P., *War, Politics and Society in Early Modern China 900–1795*. London: Routledge, 2005.

Man, J., *Genghis Khan: Life, Death and Resurrection*. London: Bantam, 2004.

— *Kublai Khan: From Xanadu to Superpower*. London: Bantam, 2006.

Martinez, A., 'Institutional development, revenues and trade', in di Cosmo et al., *The Cambridge History of Inner Asia: The Chinggisid Age*. Cambridge: Cambridge University Press, 2009. pp. 89–108.

Ngyuen, V. and Nguyen Van-mung, *A Short History of Vietnam*. Saigon: The Times of Vietnam, 1958.

Oppert, E., *A Forbidden Land: Voyages to the Corea*. London: Sampson, Low, Marston, Seale and Rivington, 1880.

Paludan, A., *Chronicle of the Chinese Emperors: The Reign-by-Reign Record of the Rulers of Imperial China*. London: Thames & Hudson, 1998.

Pelliot, P., *Histoire Secrète des Mongoles: Restitution du Texte Mongole et Traduction Française des Chapitres I a VI*. Paris: Libraire d'Amérique et de l'Orient, 1949.

Rachewiltz, I., *Papal Envoys to the Great Khans*. London: Faber & Faber, 1971.

— (ed.) *The Secret History of the Mongols: A Mongolian Epic Chronicle of the Thirteenth Century*. Leiden: E.J. Brill, 2004.

Rossabi, M., *Khubilai Khan: His Life and Times*. Berkeley: University of California Press, 1988.

Sasaki, R., 'Not So Divine Wind'. College Station: Texas A&M Nautical Archaeology Institute, 2005. http://nautarch.tamu.edu/shiplab/randall/Upgrade2005/Notsodivinewind.htm (Accessed 20 December 2009).

— 'Making Sense of Piles of Junks: Archaeology of the Lost Fleet of Kublai Khan.' College Station: Texas A&M Nautical Archaeology Institute, 2004. http://nautarch.tamu.edu/shiplab/randall/ (Accessed 20 December 2009).

Satō, K. and Higuchi Kunio (eds), *Hōjō Tokimune no Subete* [*All About Hōjō Tokimune*]. Tokyo: Shin Jinbutsu ōraisha, 2000.

Saunders, J., *A History of Medieval Islam*. London: Routledge, 2003.

Schultz, G., *Tran Hung Dao's Proclamation to His Officers*. www.vietspring.org/history/tranhungdao.html (Accessed 8 December 2009).

Schweyer, A., *Le Viêtnam Ancien*. Paris: Société d'édition Les Belles Lettres, 2008.

Silhol, R. '"Kubla Khan" – genesis of an archetype', in *PsyArt: An Online Journal for the Psychological Study of the Arts*, 2006. http://www.clas.ufl.edu/ipsa/journal/2006_silhol01.shtml (Accessed 2 March 2010).

Skelton, R. et al, *The Vinland Map and the Tartar Relation*. New Haven: Yale University Press, 1965.

Soumaré, M., *Japan in Five Ancient Chinese Chronicles: Wo, the Land of Yamatai, and Queen Himiko*. Fukuoka: Kurodahan Press, 2009.

Tsunoda, R. and L. Carrington Goodrich, *Japan in the Chinese Dynastic*

Histories: Later Han Through Ming Dynasties. South Pasadena: P.D. and I. Perkins, 1951.

Varley, P., *Warriors of Japan as Portrayed in the War Tales*. Honolulu: University of Hawaii Press, 1992.

von Verschuer, C., *Across the Perilous Sea: Japanese Trade with China and Korea from the Seventh to the Sixteenth Centuries*. Ithaca: Cornell University East Asia Program, 2006.

Walker, B. and Ni Hua Ching, *Hua Hu Ching: The Later Teachings of Lao Tzu*. Boston: Shambhala, 1995.

Wei, J., *Gen-Nichi Kankei-shi no Kenkyū* [*Studies in Yuan–Japanese Relations*]. Tokyo: Kyoiku Shuppan Centre, 1993.

Wood, F., *Did Marco Polo Go To China?* London: Secker & Warburg, 1995.

Yamada, N., *Ghenkō: The Mongol Invasion of Japan*. London: Smith, Elder and Co., 1916.

Yule, H., *The Book of Ser Marco Polo the Venetian, Concerning the Kingdoms and Marvels of the East*. 2 vols. London: John Murray, 1871.

Zerjal, T. et al, 'The genetic legacy of the Mongols', in the *American Journal of Human Genetics*, 72, March 2003, pp. 717–21.

NOTES

Introduction

1. Pope Alexander IV, *Clamat in Auribus*, quoted in Latham, *Marco Polo*, p. xi.

2. Boyle, *Successors of Genghis Khan*, p. 241. The wet-nurse, Saruq, would eventually be richly rewarded for her efforts. When she duly gave birth to her own two months later, she gave him up to a wet-nurse of her own, and continued to feed the infant Khubilai. For this, Khubilai came to regard her as a second mother, accorded her great respect in adulthood, and honoured her even after her death.

3. It has been pointed out, for example by Kaplonski, 'The Mongolian Impact on Eurasia,' p. 252, that the Mongol experience in China was far from unique. Like other rapacious regimes, such as the Vikings, they were soon assimilated by the peoples they conquered. By the time Khubilai was being sinified, his cousins in the Kipchak Khanate were already speaking more Turkish than Mongol.

4. William of Rubruck, quoted in Komroff, *Contemporaries of Marco Polo*, pp. 80–1.

5. John of Plano Carpini, quoted in Komroff, *Contemporaries of Marco Polo*, p. 33.

6. Back in prehistory, there may have been a proto-Indo-European word in the middle of Asia, something like **ker*, meaning a fire, that ultimately gave us *hearth*, *herd* and *horde*, and quite possibly the *ger* of a Mongol tent, that entered European languages through Turkish

as *yurt*. Under the reforms of Temujin, a legion of Mongols was called a *tuman* – 'ten thousand'. A group of several *tuman* was a *hordu*.

Chapter 1: Conquered by Wine

1. William of Rubruck, quoted in Komroff, *Contemporaries of Marco Polo*, p. 83.
2. Charbonnier, *Christians in China*, p. 98.
3. Grousset, *Empire of the Steppes*, p. 253.
4. *Secret History of the Mongols*, Section 255.
5. Golden, 'Migrations, ethnogenesis,' p. 110.
6. Grousset, *Empire of the Steppes*, p. 254.
7. Man, *Kublai Khan*, p. 53.
8. Rossabi, *Khubilai Khan*, p. 18; see also Man, *Kublai Khan*, pp. 38–9.
9. *Secret History of the Mongols*, Section 270.
10. Ibid., Section 272.
11. Ibid., Section 272.
12. John of Plano Carpini, quoted in Komroff, *Contemporaries of Marco Polo*, p. 32. Friar John is very specific that the incident happened 'at the time of our abode in this country' and names the 'duke' as 'Andreas', although neither Andrey I nor Andrey II of Vladimir would fit the time period. Combined with the fate of the poisoned Yaroslav at the hands of Toregene, it would appear that the Mongols were meddling directly in the affairs of many Russian leaders. It should be noted that 'leader' and 'duke' in Latin are both written as *dux*. Hence, Friar John could have easily been speaking of a mere horse-rustler rather than the landed gentry implied by the English translation. The original Latin text is online, and listed in the bibliography under Hakluyt, although Komroff's chapter four is chapter *six* in Hakluyt: *De Legibus et Consuetudinibus Eorum* – 'Of Their Laws and Customs'.
13. [Hakluyt Society], *The Long and Wonderful Voyage*, XIII. '*Huius Mengu mater Seroctan est, Domina magna inter Tartaros, excepta Imperatoris matre plus nominata, omnibusque potentior, excepto Bathy.*'
14. Man, *Kublai Khan*, p. 40.
15. Rossabi, *Khubilai Khan*, p. 14.
16. Cawley, *Medieval Lands*, claims Khubilai's first children were born in the 1230s. Although this is probably true, Rossabi, *Khubilai Khan*, p. 16 notes that his first son, Dorji, was born in 1240.

17. Secret History of the Mongols, Sections 275–7.
18. Ibid., Section 281.
19. Grousset, *Empire of the Steppes*, pp. 268–9.

Chapter 2: Voices Prophesying War

 1. Rossabi, *Khubilai Khan*, p. 15. Zhenjin predeceased his father.
 2. John of Plano Carpini, quoted in Komroff, *Contemporaries of Marco Polo*, p. 61. I have altered the archaic spelling on his 'divers', and also his spelling of the Latinized *Turakina* for Toregene.
 3. John of Plano Carpini, quoted in Komroff, *Contemporaries of Marco Polo*, p. 62. I have altered his spelling of Jeroslav for Yaroslav, i.e. Yaroslav II of Vladimir (1191–1246), the father of the famous Alexander Nevsky.
 4. John of Plano Carpini, quoted in Komroff, *Contemporaries of Marco Polo*, pp. 62–3. I have altered his spelling of Kuyuk for Guyuk.
 5. Ibid., p. 28.
 6. Ibid., p. 63.
 7. Grousset, *Empire of the Steppes*, pp. 269–70.
 8. John Plano de Carpini, quoted in Komroff, *Contemporaries of Marco Polo*, p. 67.
 9. William of Rubruck, quoted in Komroff, *Contemporaries of Marco Polo*, p. 139.
10. Ibid., p. 139.
11. Ibid., p. 127.
12. Ibid., p. 140.
13. Ibid., p. 140.
14. Gernet, *A History of Chinese Civilization*, p. 368.
15. William of Rubruck, quoted in Komroff, *Contemporaries of Marco Polo*, p. 148.
16. The name Yunnan was in use for areas within Dali for many centuries, but it is only from the time of the Mongol conquest that it is applied to the entire region. It retains the name to this day.

Chapter 3: In Xanadu

 1. See, for example, Clements, *Beijing: The Biography of a City*, pp. 39–40.
 2. Yule, *The Book of Ser Marco Polo*, I: 61.
 3. Ibid.
 4. Samuel Taylor Coleridge, who most famously wrote of Xanadu in his

poem *Kubla Khan*, was the son of a clergyman and grammar school headmaster, and hence would have been steeped in Latin like any other late-eighteenth-century schoolboy. However, the echo of *domus* in his 'pleasure dome' is largely lost on modern English readers.

5. Boyle, *The Successors of Genghis Khan*, p. 247.

6. *Yuan-shi* 209.

7. Rossabi, *Khubilai Khan*, p. 38. The book's full title is *Taishang Lingbao Laozi Huahu Miaojing*, or *The Supreme Numinous Treasures Sublime Classic on Laozi's Conversion of the Barbarians*. Purportedly the work of Laozi itself, it is widely understood to be a forgery from the fourth century AD or later, and to be the work of Wang Fu, an embittered Taoist who had been repeatedly trounced in debates by a prominent Buddhist. A complete edition of the book, appearing to contain additional chapters added by many hands over many centuries, was catalogued in the findings from the Mogao caves at Dunhuang in 1997.

8. Walker and Ni, *Hua Hu Ching*, sections 54, 58, 59 and 79.

9. Rossabi, *Khubilai Khan*, p. 243, n. 62.

Chapter 4: The Revolution of Fate

1. Rashid al-Din, quoted in Boyle, *Successors of Genghis Khan*, p. 248.

2. Ibid., p. 249.

3. Ibid., p. 250.

4. Ibid., p. 250. I have changed Boyle's Wade-Giles romanization of 'Ochou' to the Pinyin 'Ezhou'.

5. *Yuan-shi* 4.

6. *Goryeo-sa*, quoted in Henthorn, *Korea: The Mongol Invasions*, pp. 153–4.

7. *Goryeo-sa*, quoted in Henthorn, *Korea: The Mongol Invasions*, p. 152.

8. Henthorn, *Korea: The Mongol Invasions*, p.152. Henthorn doubts the validity of such statements, and suspects that they are reminders added by Korean scribes, in an attempt to put off other would-be invaders.

9. *Goryeo-sa*, quoted in Henthorn, *Korea: The Mongol Invasions*, p. 152. See also Oppert, *A Forbidden Land*, pp. 65–6 for an appraisal of conditions in Korea, which remained defiant because Mongke had refused to accept anything except an unconditional surrender after previous betrayals during the reign of Ogodei.

10. Rashid al-Din, quoted in Boyle, *The Successors of Genghis Khan*, p. 253.

11. Ibid., p. 256.
12. Ibid., p. 257. Italics are author's emphasis.
13. Ibid., p. 260.
14. Ibid., p. 262.
15. Ibid., p. 263.
16. Ibid., p. 266.

Chapter 5: A Plague upon the Throne

1. Rossabi, *Khubilai Khan*, p. 68. For more on the young Taizong, see Clements, *Wu*, pp. 14–27. Surely his appeal to Chabi would have also come from the fact that one of his concubines, the future Empress Wu, would eventually become the only reigning female sovereign in Chinese history. She would achieve this, at least in part, by marrying her stepson, which was scandalous to the Chinese, but a perfectly normal occurrence for the Mongols.
2. Yule, *The Book of Ser Marco Polo*, II: 61.
3. Ibid.
4. I choose these terms deliberately, in order to acknowledge the influence of Brose, 'Realism and Idealism in the *Yuanshi* chapters on Foreign Relations,' p. 330.
5. Rossabi, *Khubilai Khan*, p. 84, mentions 'joining the ramparts'. We might also assume that the river platforms were also joined together by barrages or chains to impede the progress of ships. Although this is not specifically mentioned in the sources, it is a logical idea. Considering that, in the seventeenth century, the Chinese would blockade the Yangtze River itself with linked platforms called the 'Boiling River Dragon', it seems likely that something similar was tried here. For the Boiling River Dragon, see Clements, *Pirate King*, p. 146.
6. Larner, *Marco Polo and the Discovery of the World*, p. 63.
7. Yule, *The Book of Ser Marco Polo*, II: 70.
8. Rashid al-Din, quoted in Boyle, *The Successors of Genghis Khan*, p. 271.
9. Proclamation of the Empress Dowager Xie, 1275, quoted in Jay, *A Change in Dynasties*, pp. 29–30.

Chapter 6: Beginning

1. Yule, *The Book of Ser Marco Polo*, Preface: 12.
2. Ibid., II: 8; see also Rossabi, *Khubilai Khan*, p. 151.

3. *Goryeo-sa*, quoted in Rossabi, *Khubilai Khan*, p. 98.

4. Yule, *The Book of Ser Marco Polo*, II: 33.

5. Ibid., II: 11.

6. Ibid., II: 10.

7. Friar Odoric of Pordonone, quoted in Komroff, *Contemporaries of Marco Polo*, p. 242.

8. Arlington and Lewisohn, *In Search of Old Peking*, p. 209.

9. Ibid., p. 297. It was renamed the Temple of Everlasting Peace in 1465, and changed again to the Temple of the Sleeping Buddha (*Wofo-si*) in 1734. It is still there today, although the city of Beijing has expanded so far that anonymous suburbs now surround the temple.

10. Ibid., p. 316. At least, Miaoyan's portrait was still there in 1935, when the authors wrote their guide to the old town.

11. Lane, *Daily Life in the Mongol Empire*, p. 78.

12. Rossabi, *Khubilai Khan*, p. 93. For remarkable historical parallels with a later fugitive dynasty, see Clements, *Pirate King*, pp. 109–11.

Chapter 7: Samurai

1. Clements, *Marco Polo*, p. 137. Columbus may not have been following Polo directly on his first mission, but appears to have deliberately returned in his later voyages in search of a passage to 'Cipangu'.

2. See, for example, Clements, *A Brief History of the Samurai*, pp. 129–48, which tells the story largely from the Japanese point of view.

3. Letter of Khubilai Khan to King Wonjong, in *Xin Yuan-shi* 250, quoted in Tsunoda and Carrington Goodrich, *Japan in the Chinese Dynastic Histories*, pp. 73–4. The *Xin Yuan-shi* is a new version of the *Yuan-shi*, compiled in the nineteenth century in 257 books.

4. Conlan, *In Little Need of Divine Intervention*, p. 256.

5. King Wonjong to Khubilai Khan, in *Xin Yuan-shi* 250, quoted in Tsunoda, *Japan in the Chinese Dynastic Histories*, p. 75. Soumaré, *Japan in Five Ancient Chinese Chronicles*, p. 53, notes that several Chinese annals refer to Japan as being many thousands of leagues distant, mixing up the large *li* of Chinese measurement with the *duanli* used in Korea, a tenth of the size. By accident or design, this translation 'error' was retained in many accounts, making Japan appear to be much further away than it really was.

6. Khubilai Khan to King Wonjong in *Xin Yuan-shi* 250, quoted in

Tsunoda, *Japan in the Chinese Dynastic Histories*, p. 75.

7. Khubilai Khan to the 'Ruler of Japan', 1268, quoted in Yamada, *Ghenkō*, p. 83.

8. Yamada, *Ghenkō*, p. 91.

9. Ibid., p. 92.

10. Ibid.

11. Ibid., pp. 99–100. Choyonpil is listed in the *Yuan-shi* biographies under his Chinese name Zhao Liangbi – cf. *Yuan-shi* 159 and *Xin Yuan-shi* 158. Yamada erroneously calls him a Tartar, whereas strictly speaking he was actually a minister of the old Jurchen regime. See Tsunoda, *Japan in the Chinese Dynastic Histories*, p. 90, n. 20.

12. Tsunoda, *Japan in the Chinese Dynastic Histories*, p. 79.

13. Yamada, *Ghenkō*, p. 102.

14. Tsunoda, *Japan in the Chinese Dynastic Histories*, p. 79.

15. History would repeat itself in the sixteenth century, when the Japanese warlord Hideyoshi and the Chinese Emperor of Ten Thousand Experiences were strung along for years, each convinced that the other had offered his submission. Both were carefully manipulated by Korean intermediaries, who knew once again that in the event of an outbreak of hostilities, it would be Korea that bore the brunt of the damage. See Clements, *A Brief History of the Samurai*, pp. 214–16.

16. Henthorn, *Korea: The Mongol Invasions*, p. 205.

17. Kronk, *Cometography*, p. 223.

18. Yamada, *Ghenkō*, p. 106; Tsunoda, *Japan in the Chinese Dynastic Histories*, p. 80. Tsunoda's reading of the *Xin Yuan-shi* goes on to include a confusing passage that essentially repeats Choyonpil's previous mission. 'Your subject visited the Dazaifu a number of times and reprimanded the Japanese for their impoliteness, admonishing them in regard to a correct sense of propriety. The official of the Dazaifu, somewhat ashamed, asked for his credentials. Your subject told him that they could only be submitted in the presence of the ruler. [The Japanese] went away and came back four times, even going so far as to threaten your subject at the point of arms. Still we did not give them the credentials, but showed them instead a duplicate. Later they announced that the Shōgun was coming at the head of a force of one hundred thousand to demand the letter. Then your subject said as long as I do not see the ruler of the country, even if you take my head, you will be unable to get the letter. The Japanese realised that your

subject could not be intimidated and they therefore sent those twelve men to the court to pay homage.' This all seems to be a retelling of his embassy in 1271, unless events in 1273 played out in exactly the same way. Still, it is churlish to doubt one element of a story that is already understood to be false.

19. Henthorn, *Korea: The Mongol Invasions*, p. 183.

20. Yamada, *Ghenkō*, p. 114–15. The claim in Yamada that the Mongol arrows were 'poisoned' is a strange one. It is not impossible that the Mongols, Chinese or Koreans had decided to improve the odds a little by poisoning their arrows, but just as likely that Japanese accounts refused to believe that enemy arrows could ever be effective without some sort of additional attribute.

21. Ibid., p. 116. The *Yuan-shi* account of the taking of Tsushima is considerably briefer: 'Sō Sukekuni, Japanese provincial commander, went to defend the island at the head of a force of eight thousand horsemen. He sent an interpreter to visit the fleet and ask the reason for its coming. Without giving any answer, [Hol-Ton] landed his army and advanced on on the Japanese. Sukekuni fell in the battle. [Hol-Ton] then turned to attack the island of Iki. He landed on the beach and planted a crimson flag.' Tsunoda, *Japan in the Chinese Dynastic Histories*, p. 81.

22. Tsunoda, *Japan in the Chinese Dynastic Histories*, p. 81.

23. Yamada, *Ghenkō*, p. 142. Hol-Ton's name was originally Hindu. He was Khubilai's distant cousin, a fifth-generation descendant of Temujin's younger brother. He does not have a biography in the *Yuan-shi*, but is mentioned in the list of high officials in *Yuan-shi*112. Hong Dagu is called Hung Tsa-Kiu in Yamada's manuscript, reflecting the Japanese version of his name, Kō Chakyū. He has a biographical entry in *Yuan-shi* 154 (*Xin Yuan-shi* 176), and is also mentioned in the Korean annals, *Goryeo-sa* 43, which describes him as a refugee in Mongol service. For a different version of the conversation, which replays the arguments but with the Mongol counselling retreat while the wounded Koreans inexplicably call for a renewed assault, see Tsunoda, *Japan in the Chinese Dynastic Histories*, p. 81.

24. Delgado, *Khubilai Khan's Lost Fleet*, p. 97.

25. Tsunoda, *Japan in the Chinese Dynastic Histories*, p. 82. For the Japanese perspective and historiographical problems arising, see Clements, *A Brief History of the Samurai*, pp. 140–1.

Chapter 8: The Miscellaneous Aliens

1. Rossabi, *Khubilai Khan*, p. 118. For the Tang parallels, see Clements, *Wu*, p. 118.
2. Rossabi, *Khubilai Khan*, p. 71.
3. Lane, *Daily Life in the Mongol Empire*, p. 212.
4. Ch'en, *Chinese Legal Tradition Under the Mongols*, p. 46.
5. Yule, *The Book of Ser Marco Polo*, II: 26.
6. Ibid., II: 24.
7. Ibid., II: 24.
8. van Gulik, *Sexual Life in Ancient China*, pp. 245–6.
9. Latham, *Marco Polo*, p. 119.
10. Yule, *The Book of Ser Marco Polo*, IV: 2.
11. Ibid., IV: 4. Rossabi, *Khubilai Khan*, p. 104, does not doubt the story at all, but notes that her name was more likely to have been Khutulun.
12. Yule, *The Book of Ser Marco Polo*, IV: 4.
13. Rashid al-Din, quoted in Boyle, *Successors of Genghis Khan*, pp. 26–7.
14. Puccini, *Turandot*, Act II, Scene 2.

Chapter 9: Dragons in the Water

1. Yamada, *Ghenkō,* p. 152.
2. Ibid., p. 153.
3. Ibid., pp. 169–71.
4. Ibid., p. 173.
5. Tsunoda, *Japan in the Chinese Dynastic Histories*, p. 84.
6. Latham, *Marco Polo*, p. 201.
7. Yule, *The Book of Ser Marco Polo*, III: 2.
8. Tsunoda, *Japan in Chinese Dynastic Histories*, p. 85.
9. Ibid., p. 86.
10. Yule, *The Book of Ser Marco Polo*, III: 2.
11. Tsunoda, *Japan in Chinese Dynastic Histories*, p. 86.
12. Ibid., p.88.
13. Conlan, *In Little Need of Divine Intervention*, p. 113.
14. Takezaki, quoted in Conlan, *In Little Need of Divine Intervention*, p. 154.
15. Yamada, *Ghenkō*, pp. 188–91.
16. Yule, *The Book of Ser Marco Polo*, III: 2.
17. Delgado, *Khubilai Khan's Lost Fleet*, p. 146.
18. Sasaki, 'Not So Divine Wind'.

19. Ibid.
20. Ibid. Sasaki concedes that his hypothesis remains to be fully tested, but holds out hope that somewhere in the waters off Takashima is a wreck in better condition, at least partially intact, so that he and his colleagues can truly test their ideas.
21. Tsunoda, *Japan in Chinese Dynastic Histories*, p. 89.
22. Yule, *The Book of Ser Marco Polo*, III: 2.
23. Yamada, *Ghenkō*, p. 200.
24. A brief note in *Yuan-shi* 210 has the Mongols securing the Ryūkyū Islands to the south of Japan as a separate tributary, perhaps as the opening moves of a new assault on Japan from the south, but Khubilai was dead two years later, and thereafter the planned invasion was quietly shelved.

Chapter 10: The Accursed Doctrines

1. Latham, *Marco Polo*, pp. 198–9.
2. Bell, *A Journey from St. Petersburg to Pekin*, p. 115. Bell observed this method of butchery still in use in Mongolia, just north of the Gobi Desert, in October 1720. I choose to repeat his account here because every other seems to be based on hearsay. Marco Polo, for example, talks of a Mongol ritual that calls for 'ripping the stomach', while Rashid al-Din is even vaguer, merely noting that Mongols 'split open the breast and side.' Rossabi, *Khubilai Khan*, p. 200, remains faithful to the *Yuan-shi*, thereby noting only that the Muslim fashion was criminalized, not explaining what the Mongol alternative would have been.
3. Rashid al-Din, quoted in Boyle, *The Successors of Genghis Khan*, p. 294.
4. Yule, *The Book of Ser Marco Polo*, II: 23.
5. Rashid al-Din, quoted in Boyle, *The Successors of Genghis Khan*, p. 295.
6. It is, however, difficult to reconcile the precise order of events, as Rashid has Ahmad's reign coming *after* that of Sangha (Sengge in his text). My version of events steers the best course between a few contradictions in the rival accounts cited.
7. Yule, *The Book of Ser Marco Polo*, II: 23.
8. Ibid., II: 23.
9. Rossabi, *Khubilai Khan*, p. 179; Boyle, *Successors of Genghis Khan*, pp. 289–93.

10. Yule, *The Book of Ser Marco Polo*, II: 23. For an analysis of Marco Polo's account, and a comparison with the *History of the Yuan* account of the same incident, see Haw, *Marco Polo's China*, pp.160–1.

11. Yule, *The Book of Ser Marco Polo*, II: 27.

12. Rossabi, *Khubilai Khan*, p. 197.

13. Ibid., p. 198.

14. Rashid al-Din, quoted in Boyle, *The Successors of Genghis Khan*, pp. 296–7. My 'donkey-load' is a literal translation of the measure reported in Rashid: a *kharvār*.

15. Latham, *Marco Polo*, p. 237.

16. Yule, *The Book of Ser Marco Polo*, II: 9.

17. Rashid al-Din, quoted in Boyle, *Successors of Genghis Khan*, p. 301.

Chapter 11: Death to the Mongols

1. *Yuan-shi* 209. Nguyen and Nguyen, *A Short History of Vietnam*, p. 97, draws on Tran Trong-kim's *Vietnam Suluoc* and refers to 'Emperor Ngot-Luong-Hop-Thai', giving his Chinese name as Wouleangotai. This is clearly a reference to Uryangkhadai although his position in the Mongol hierarchy has been seriously misread.

2. Huu, *Wandering Through Vietnamese Culture*, p. 873, claims that the Mongol army 'invaded the country and set its capital afire after the Court and the population had left it', whereas Nguyen and Nguyen's *Short History of Vietnam* claims that the fall of Hanoi was 'a general slaughter'.

3. Nguyen and Nguyen, *A Short History of Vietnam*, p. 98. The Nguyens do not appear to realise that their 'Konbilai' on p.98 is the same man as the 'Chinese Emperor Hot-Tat-Liet' on p.101. Both, of course, are Khubilai Khan.

4. Nguyen and Nguyen, *A Short History of Vietnam*, p. 100, call this official a *Chuong-An*, which seems to be the Vietnamese reading for the Mandarin *Zhiguan*, 'duty official'.

5. Nguyen and Nguyen, *A Short History of Vietnam*, p. 101, call the Chinese hero by his Vietnamese pronunciation, 'Ma-Vien'. Ma Yuan's expedition in the AD 40s was against an uprising legendarily led by two ladies, the Trung sisters. Their story remains a popular Vietnamese national epic to this day.

6. Schultz, *Tran Hung Dao's Proclamation to His Officers*.

7. Tran Trong-kim, *Vietnam Suluoc*, quoted in Nguyen and Nguyen, *A Short History of Vietnam*, p.107.

8. Nguyen and Nguyen, *A Short History of Vietnam*, p. 110. The Nguyens' text actually has 'king', a literal translation of the Chinese *wang*, although it is more properly translated as 'prince' in this period.
9. Yule, *The Book of Ser Marco Polo*, III: 5.
10. Schweyer, *Le Viêtnam Ancien*, p. 32.
11. Nguyen and Nguyen, *A Short History of Vietnam*, p. 119. The Bach Dang River has long since silted up, but was dredged in 1953 to reveal many of the legendary stakes still in place. See Man, *Kublai Khan*, p. 353.
12. Nguyen and Nguyen, *A Short History of Vietnam*, pp. 121–2.
13. Huu, *Wandering Through Vietnamese Culture*, pp. 667–71.
14. Ibid., p. 874.

Chapter 12: Down to a Sunless Sea

1. *Yuan-shi* 210 refers to Burma or Myanmar, known at the time as Pagan or more properly Bagan after its capital, using the Chinese term *Mian*.
2. *Yuan-shi* 210, quoted in Brose, 'Realism and Idealism in the *Yuanshi* Chapters on Foreign Relations,' p. 327.
3. The first expedition is dated to Khubilai's reign period Zhiyuan 8 (1273).
4. Yule, *The Book of Ser Marco Polo*, II: 53.
5. Ibid., II: 52.
6. Ibid., II: 52.
7. *Yuan-shi* 210 has an entry for the second year of the reign of Khubilai's successor, Temur Khan, also known as the Chengzong Emperor, outlining the attempt to rule through Kyawswa. Pointedly, it is the last mention of Burma in the entire *History of the Yuan*.
8. *Yuan-shi* 210; Marco Polo claims that there were 200, but then again, he also claimed that there were unicorns in the forest.
9. Yule, *The Book of Ser Marco Polo*, II: 4.
10. Boyle, *Successors of Genghis Khan*, p. 298, n. 227.
11. Yule, *The Book of Ser Marco Polo*, II: 4.
12. Ibid., II: 5.
13. Ibid., II: 5.
14. Latham, *Marco Polo*, p. 254.
15. *Yuan-shi* 210, quoted in Brose, 'Realism and Idealism in the *Yuanshi* Chapters on Foreign Relations,' p. 340.
16. Kronk, *Cometography*, p. 224.

Chapter 13: The Romance of the Grand Khan

1. Rashid al-Din, quoted in Boyle, *Successors of Genghis Khan*, p. 302.
2. Berzin, *A Historical Sketch of the Muslims of China*.
3. Ibid.
4. Lee and Ho, *Chinese Art Under the Mongols*, p. 1.
5. Larner, *Marco Polo and the Discovery of the World*, p. 106.
6. Yule, *The Book of Ser Marco Polo*, II: 1.
7. Silhol, '"Kubla Khan" – genesis of an archetype'.
8. Keach, *Samuel Taylor Coleridge: Complete Poems*, p. 250.

INDEX

Abaqa Khan 93, 180 *see also*
    Persia
Abd al-Rahman: tax collector 30
    see also Toregene
Ahmad, Fanakati 182, 184
    death and dishonour of 176–9
Aiyaruk (Bright Moon) 149–51
    legendary reputation of 150–51
Ajiqi, Prince 77
Alandar (Mongol official) 53
alcohol/alcohol abuse 9, 22, 27,
    36, 40, 54, 182, 191, 219–20
    see also gout *and* koumiss
Alghu, Prince 76–7, 79
*American Journal of Human
    Genetics* 225
Ananda, Prince 180
    converts to Islam 180
Annam/Annamese 3, 6, 55, 62,
    169, 181, 192–206, 222 *see
    also* Thanh Tong *and* Tran
    Hung Dao
    and death to the Mongols
    tattoos 202–3
    fanatical resistance of 202
    lay waste to
        countryside/villages 199–200
    nominal submission of 195
    resistance to Khubilai in
        192–206
    rulers of 55–6, 102 *see* Di Ai;
        Nhan Tong; Thai Tong;
        Thanh Tong *and* Tran Ich Tac
    stronghold: Kiep Bac 205–6
Antong (finance minister) 182,
    184
Arakhan (Mongol general) 157–8
    replaced by General Atahai 159
Arigh Boke 2, 4, 24, 63–4, 67–71,
    73–9, 82–3, 84, 87, 101, 222
    decree trap of 69
    defections from cause of 76–7
    makes overtures of peace to
        Kubilai 74
    trial, confinement and death of
        78–9
Art of War (Sun Tzu) 197
artisans/craftsmen 34, 41, 142,
    187
Atahai, General 159, 167–8
atrocities 122, 130–32
    as insurance against resistance
        203

Baha al-Din, punishment of 190
Banggyeong, Kim 160

Basalawarmi, Prince of Liang 224
battle to be Khan 62–80
battles 75–7, 84, 91 see also
    Annam; Hakata Bay; Khaidu;
    sieges and Tsushima island
at Bach Dang River/Halong
    Bay 203–4
between Khubilai and Nayan
    213–14
Elet 75–6
on Ngasaunggyan plain 209
Batu 2, 9, 23–4, 27, 31–2, 36–40
    see also Golden Horde and
    kurultai
and accounts of death of
    Guyuk 36
convenes own kurultai 37
death of 39
refuses to attend kurultai 31
Bayan, General 43–4, 55, 95–7,
    99, 148, 221, 222
besieges Yangzhou 96–7
sent to assess Nayan's
    disloyalty 213
takes Hangzhou 97
Beijing 52, 112, 139, 148, 167,
    176, 201, 210, 226
construction of 104–9
observatory 105, 218
rebel seizure of 224
and restoration of White
    Pagoda 108
Berke 69–70, 74, 79 see also
    Golden Horde
Book of Barbarian Conversions
    (Huahu Jing) 57, 59, 60, 171
Book of Changes (Yijing) 51, 70,
    101
Bouchier, William 41

Buddhism/Buddhists 15, 56–8,
    103, 120, 147, 170–72,
    180–81, 220, 226 see also
    Tibet
Chan (Zen) 57–8, 154
and mediation 58
Nichiren 154
Tibetan vs local 56–7
Buddhist–Taoist conflicts 171–2
Buddhist–Taoist debate at Kaiping
    59–60, 68
Burma 5, 169, 207–12 see also
    Narathihapate, King of
    Burma
final retreat of Mongol forces
    from 212
Kyawswa proclaims loyalty to
    Mongols 211–12
Nasir al-Din leads first force
    into 208–10
Sangudar leads second force
    into 210–11

Catholicism 15, 180
Chabi (favourite wife of Khubilai)
    60, 67, 81–2, 108, 218
death of 175
Chaghadai 76, 79
Khanate 87, 147
Champa 196–202, 216 see also
    Annam and Zhang Shijie
Sogetu's army in 200
China, North 12, 17–18, 20, 22,
    86, 112, 138 see also Li Tan
    and Northern Song
conscripts from 76
depopulated 141
taxation in 30–31, 87
China/Chinese 6, 11, 18, 41, 89,

138 *see also* Dali *and* Southern Song
anti-Muslim feeling in 172–81
civil examination system 47–8, 88, 138, 185, 221
culture 7–8
education system 47–8
Great Wall of 11
provinces, government of 139
rebellions 224
reunification of 112–13
sources on Khubilai 4
superstitions 9
Cho-I (interpreter): brings Japan to Khubilai's attention 116
Choyonpil (Jurchen minister) 71, 123–6, 135 *see also* Japan
Christian/ity 5, 40, 147 *see also* Catholicism *and* Nestorian Christians
and Christian–Muslim tension 31
and anti-Christian rumours 215
missionaries 2, 40, 57, 107, 214, 238 *see also main entry*
Chungnyeol, King of Korea 157
betrothed/married to Quduluq Kalmish 73, 114, 126
civilization
Chinese 90, 184
concepts of 7–8, 21
climate and effect on Mongol armies 62, 91, 194 *see also* disease
Coleridge, Samuel Taylor 53, 229–30
communication 33, 216, 225
lines of 202

post-rider system 19, 72, 142–3
and problems of distance 6
problems with Annamese 193
Confucians/Confucian scholars 47–50, 176, 186–7, 189
advisers 70, 88–9, 185
and civil service exam system 47–8, 138, 185, 221
Liu Bingzhong 47
registration of 46–7
Confucius 47, 48, 58, 88
conscription/conscripts 5, 42, 76, 112, 116, 125, 156, 158, 167, 195, 205
corruption 5, 7, 44, 53, 139, 140, 154, 189, 196
accusations of sexual 178–9, 185
cosmopolitan empire 137–51
crime 179 *see also* punishment(s)
classification of 140
Taoist 171

Daily Life in the Mongol Empire 140
Dali 4, 48, 50, 56, 169–70, 193, 222
becomes Mongol province of Yunnan 45
and execution of Khubilai's envoys 43
Khubilai attacks 43–4
King Duan Xingzhi of 43, 44–5
siege and surrender of 44–5
Daode Jing (Book of the Path and the Power) 57
darughachi/viceroys 73, 139, 195
Daughter of Turan, The 150
Dazaifu 123, 133, 152, 159

death sentence(s) 75, 158 *see also* execution(s)
  commuted 140, 158
Depictions of the Eighty-One Conversions (Bashiyi Huatu) 60
Description of the World, The 228
Dharmapalaraksita: regarded as Mongol stooge 181
disease 16, 62, 64–5, 91, 105, 162, 194
  on Mongol ships 159
Di Ai (ruler of Annam) 196–7
'divine wind'/*kamikaze* 135, 162–3, 165
doctors/physicians 142, 194
Dorje (Ogodei's grandson) 67
Dragon's Mouth 152, 154
Drogön Chögyal Phagpa *see* 'Phags-pa Lama
dynasties
  Annamese Tran 193
  Han 100–101, 170, 224
  histories of 49–50
  Jin 12
  Joseon 227
  Liao 17, 50, 223
  Ming 223–4, 226
  Qing 222
  Song 5, 43–4, 86, 99, 155, 158, 187, 223
  Sui 123
  Tang 71–2, 81–2, 98, 101, 108, 18
  Yuan 7, 100–13, 146, 223, 225–6

East Coast Office of Reconciliation in Yangzhou 155

eldest sons, traditional duties of 20–21
elephants 207–10
  Mongol acquisition and use of 212, 213–14
  as tributes 201–2
  used by Narathihapate 209–10
Elet, consequences of battle at 75–6
execution(s) 140–41, 170, 171, 175, 185
  averted 154
  of envoys to Burma 208
  of envoys to Japan 153–5
  for forgery 144
  of Lu Shizhong 183
  and pardons 141
  of Sangha 190
  of traitors 86–7

Fan Wenhu, General 157–60, 165–7
  indicted for dereliction of duty 167
  leaves men to their fate 166–7
farmers 27, 41, 125, 187, 220
  and clashes with nomads 10–11
Fatima: tax collector 30, 35–6 *see also* Toregene
feng shui/geomancy 50, 106
finance ministers *see also* Lu Shizhong
Friar John of Plano Carpini 32–5, 52
  reports on *kurultai* and enthronement of Guyuk 32–5

Ganghwa Island 71–3, 119–20

Gao Taixiang 43–4 *see also* Dali
Genghis Khan *see* Temujin
Ghazan, ruler of Persia 226, 240
Golden Horde 39–40, 87, 147
Gongmin, King 226–7
    assassination of 227
    and reforms in Korea 226–7
gout 24, 54–5, 104, 191, 212
Grand Canal, renovation of 105,
        109, 122, 144
Grand Empress Dowager Xie
        (Song Dynasty) 97–9
    capitulates to General Bayan 99
Guyuk (son of Ogodei) 23, 27,
        29–36, 69, 100, 144 *see also*
        Toregene
    crowned Great Khan 33–4
    death of 36
    disowned by Ogodei 27
    executes relatives and officials
        35–6

Hakata Bay 115, 154, 157, 159,
        160, 165
Hamid al-Din, interpreter of
        Quran 175
Han dynasty/Chinese 100–101,
        170, 224
Hangzhou 7, 63, 64, 97, 109, 185,
        224 *see also* Southern Song
    fall of 100, 102
    restoration programme for
        186–9
Hanoi 193–4, 199–200, 203
Hao Jing (adviser to Khubilai) 89
Hirado Island 158–9, 165
History of the Jin 223
History of the Liao 223
History of the Yuan 3, 55, 140,

166, 169, 178, 183, 184, 207,
        217–18, 223
Hol-Ton 133, 157–9
    missing in action 165
Hong Dagu (Korean general)
        133, 157, 158–9
Huizong Emperor 223–4
Hulagu (leader of khanate of
        Persia) 2, 65, 69–70, 74, 79,
        93

Iki Island 157–9
    atrocities on 130–31, 132
    resistance by samurai on 159
Iran, attacked by Ogodei 21–22
Islam 2, 15, 70, 178–80, 226 *see
        also* Muslim(s)
    and Mohammed 58

Japan (and) 5–7, 44, 102, 113, 181,
        192, 222 *see also* Tsushima
        island
    atrocities on Iki island 130–31,
        132
    attacks, burns and sinks
        Mongol fleet 133–5
    battles in Hakata Bay 115,
        131–2
    Hōjō Tokimune (shōgunal
        regent) *see* Tokimune
    Japanese pirates/raiders in
        Korea 116, 126
    Mongol invasions of 114–36,
        152–68
    relief at death of Khubilai 227
    warlord Hideyoshi 227
Java 215–18 *see also* Kertanagara,
        King of Java
Jeju island (Korean) 126–7

Jesus the Christian (Isa Tarsa
    Kelemechi) 174–5
  interprets Quran to Khubilai
    174
Jia Sidao (Southern Song minister)
    66–7, 70, 83
  death of 96
  and defence of Xiangyang
    92–3
  detains Hao Jing's emissaries
    89–90
  taxes Buddhist Taoist
    monasteries 95
Jochi 15–16, 68
  descendants/sons of 16, 21, 24,
    39
Jurchen(s) 5, 12, 17, 21–2, 48–50,
    104, 106, 108, 138, 190, 222–3

Kaiping 50, 53, 59, 67, 69, 77 see
    also Shangdu
Kamakura Shōgunate, collapse of
    227
kamikaze 135, 162–3, 193
Karakorum 19–21, 30, 47, 53–4,
    63–4, 68, 69, 73, 103, 142,
    148, 220 see also Ogodei and
    Tolui
  as first secure Mongol city 21
  foreign residents in 40–41
  Khaidu's failed strike at 151
  Muslim and Christian
    communities in 76
Kertanagara, King of Java
    215–18
  attacks Jambi 216
  brands Khubilai's envoy
    215–16
  killed by Jayakatwang 217

replaced by Vijaya 217
Khaidu, Prince 79–80, 87, 112,
    147–9, 180
  death of 151
  as protector of old Mongol
    values 149–50
Khubilai Khan 2–6, 13, 24, 32,
    46–61, 79, 81–99 see also
    Annam; cosmopolitan empire;
    Japan; Java; Khubilai's legacy;
    Korea; Mongke; Nayan;
    political intrigues and
    religious persecutions;
    Sorghaghtani; Southern Song;
    Yangtze campaign; Yuan
    dynasty and Zhenjin
  has accounts audited 53–4
  accused of 'going native' 5, 68,
    141, 212
  afflicted with gout 24, 54–5,
    104, 191, 212
  appearance of 104
  appoints 'pacification
    commissioners' 26–7
  asks Thanh Tong for skilled
    workers 194–5
  attacks Java 216–17
  attitude to non-farmers 142
  authorizes printing of paper
    money 42
  besieges Xiangyang 64
  betrayed by Wang Wendong
    85–6
  boasts of being Emperor of
    China 7
  boasts of unifying China 138
  builds Shangdu (Xanadu) see
    Xanadu
  and Chinese way of life 53

Chinese/Confucian advisers to 31, 39, 70, 88

death/funeral of 218, 219–20

early policies of 86–7

education of 24

and elephant litter/*xiang-jiao* 212, 213

as Emperor of China 13, 82, 87, 100, 114

endeavours to unify Mongols and Chinese 4

falls out/reconciliation with Mongke 53–6

as fan of early Tang dynasty 81–2

and feud with Khaidu 80, 147–50, 168

given mission to rule more of China 41–2

as Great Khan

as high priest of Chinese state religion 146

and hostility towards Muslims 172–5, 190 *see also* legislation

institutes suggestion box 137

invades Champa 196–7

invades Japan 113, 114–36, 152–68

last years of 207–18

losing touch with Mongol roots 5

mid-reign foreign relations of 193

and mobile palace/tent 52–3

navy and fleets of 91–2, 155, 157, 163

neglects Xingzhou 26–7, 141

no longer unquestioned ruler of China 168

orders Thanh Tong to Beijing 195

orders third expedition to Japan 167

and power struggles with Nhan Tong 196–7

and preservation of true Taoism 171–2

proclaims new dynasty 100

proclaims Tokimune king of Japan 152–3

purges heresies 171–2

renames Monastery of Manifestation of Filial Piety 109

renovates Grand Canal 105, 109, 122, 144

restores religious order 61

sends Thanh Tong Mongol demands for vassal behaviour 195

shows mercy to Chinese 64

as Sinophile 47–8, 149

and Southern Song 43, 63–80

swayed by foreign advisers 5–6

as symbol of transformation 4

undeclared religion of 180

urged to abandon invasion of Japan 121–2

vetoes writing of dynastic histories 49–50

wages propaganda war against Arigh Boke 70

as Zhongtong/Moderate Rule 70, 101

Khubilai's legacy 219–30

in art and culture 225–6

as friend of Muslims 220

genetic changes 225
unification of China 221–2
Kono-Michiari (samurai): attacks
    Mongol fleet 161
Korea 3, 5, 71–4, 227 see also
    Wongjong, King of Korea
attacked by Ogodei 21
and dynastic marriages/heirs
    raised in Beijing 126–7
famine in 72
and Goryeo-sa (chronicles of
    ruling house) 185
involved in invasion of Japan
    114–25
Japanese pirates/raiders in 116,
    126
proclaims fealty to Khubilai
    71–2, 81, 102
Korea Strait 115, 120 , 122, 127,
    156
koumiss 11, 40, 182, 230
kurultai(s) 29–38, 65, 67, 79, 101,
    149, 219 see also Batu and
    Friar John of Plano Carpini
four-day ceremonies of 33
at Kaiping: Khubilai declared
    Great Khan 69
at Karakorum: Arigh Boke
    declared Great Khan 69
Kyawswa, son of Narathihapate
    211–12

Lane, George 140
language, unification of 144–6
Laozi, founder of Taoism 57–8,
    60, 171
and Book of the Path and the
    Power 171, 172
law/legal code 141

capital 144
'latter days of 154
on liquor 182
martial 138
Mongol yasa 139–40
on ritual (Muslim) slaughter
    173–4
Li Tan 82–6
deceives Khubilai 83–4
'defends' borders at Lingzhou
    83–4
execution of 85
Liao dynasty 17, 50, 223
and Emperor Shoulong 108
and History of the Liao 50, 223
Lian Xixian (Uighur official) 64
Liu Bingzhong (adviser to
    Khubilai) 39, 47, 50–51, 101
Lu Shizhong 182–4
angers merchants, landowners
    and Mongols 182–3
execution of 183
increases tax on import duty
    182
prints money 183

Mandate of Heaven 88, 98, 153
mangonels 93–4 see also siege(s)
Miaoyan, Princess 109
missionaries 2, 40, 57, 107, 120,
    146–7, 214, 238
Mongke 23, 35–9, 46–66, 68, 75,
    77, 78, 82, 100, 193, 194
death of 65, 91
decree for mourning for 69
falling-out/reconciliation with
    Khubilai 53–4
ignores warnings of disease
    64–5

kills conspirators 38
as new Great Khan 39
reign of 46–61
and religious conflict 57–9
and Southern Song 62–5
Mongol Armada: the first 114–36
    see also Japan
Mongol Armada: the second
    152–68 see also Japan
defeat of 161–2
modern-day evidence of
    wrecking of 162–5
Mongol(s)
code of conduct: Yasa 139–40
crafts 142
customs 9, 43
destructiveness 39
and genetic changes across Asia
    225
homes/transport 8–9
horsemen 10–11
ordo(s) 10, 75
shamans 22
siege tactics 42, 44, 63, 96–7 see
    also siege(s)
superstitions 9
westward advance of 39
Mongol Pacification Bureau 42
Muslim(s) 5, 57, 103, 138, 162–80,
    190, 220
advisers 30–31
and anti-Muslim feeling in
    China 172–80
freedom for Chinese 224–5
and halal legislation/scandal
    173–4, 177
and Quran 174–5
siege engineers 157
tax collectors 30–31, 48

Nambi (wife of Khubilai) 175
Narathihapate, King of Burma
    207–11 see also Kyawswa
attacks Kaungai 208
commits suicide 211
Nasir al-Din (governor of
    Yunnan) 208–10
leads Mongol army into Burma
    208
Nayan 212–15
allied with Khaidu 213
disloyalty of 213
Mongol execution of 214
as Nestorian Christian 212,
    214–15
rebels against Khubilai 212–14
Nestorian Christians 14–15, 31,
    39, 48, 94, 103, 174, 180, 189,
    212, 213–14
Nhan Tong, ruler of Annam
    196–8
appoints Tran Hung Dao as
    army leader 197–8
sends Di Ai to Khubilai's court
    196–7
nomads/nomadic life 7–11, 20,
    41, 50, 67
forbidden to graze stock 141
Nomukhan, Prince 147–8
appointed as pacification officer
    147
kidnapping of 148
Northern Song 67, 85, 222
Noyan, General Bahadur 64, 69
Noyan, Tumen 78

Odoric, Friar 107
Ogodei (and) 5, 13–30, 67, 68, 69,
    79, 87, 88, 100, 147, 176

accession as Great Khan 17
alcohol abuse 22–3, 27
creation of Karakorum 19–20
death after hunting 27–8
death proclaimed as murder 35
disowns Guyuk 27
illness and Tolui's 'sacrificial
    death' 22–3
Jurchen people/government
    17–18 see also Yelu Chucai
nominates Shiremun as
    successor 27, 29
retreat of Mongol army from
    Hungary 28
Omar, Muslim General 203
'accidentally' drowns 205

paper money 42, 87, 112, 143–4,
    170, 178, 187
abuse of 144
Pagan see Burma
Persia 2, 12, 17, 27, 40, 43, 143,
    145, 226 see also Bayan,
    General and Rashid al-Din
Ilkhanate of 87
khanate of 69
siege engineers from 93–4
'Phags-pa Lama 59–60, 144–5,
    180, 183
death of 181
and What One Should Know
    176
'Phags-pa script 224
political intrigues 169–91 see also
    religious conflict(s)/debate
Polo, Maffeo 102–3, 180
Polo, Marco 3–4, 6, 13, 51–3, 57,
    86, 94–5, 102–7, 109, 112,
    137–8,143, 144, 146–7, 149,

150, 155–6, 158, 163–4, 166,
    171–2, 175, 176–9, 185–6, 190,
    192, 201–2, 204, 208–9, 212,
    213, 214, 216, 224, 227–9, 230
on deceptions of Li Tan 84–5
and departure for India 217–18
describes palace at Xanadu 51
describes Khubilai's
    observatory 105
and Description of the World 3
describes city of Beijing 105–6
on invasion of Japan 115
and Rustichello of Pisa 228
and Samuel Purchas 229, 230
Polo, Niccolo 102–3, 180
Pope Alexander IV 1–2
prisoners 97, 141
and imprisonment with hard
    labour 140
of war 104, 126, 130, 181, 203,
    205
punishment(s) 43, 96, 137, 140,
    203

Qin Shihuangdi (emperor of
    China) 98, 100
Quanzhou 190, 224
and Pu Shougeng 110
Quduluq Kalmish (daughter of
    Khubilai) 73, 114, 126

Rashid al-Din 54, 65, 68, 75, 94,
    97, 150, 176, 178, 185,
    190–91, 219–20
and Compendium of Chronicles
    3, 220
religious conflict(s)/persecutions
    31, 169–91, 181, 214–15
religious debate 56–9, 138, 228

Renzong Emperor reinstates Confucian exams 221
revenge killings/suspicious deaths 35–6, 38–9
rivers
  Bach Dang 203
  at Beijing 106
  Han 92–3
  Huai 64
  Red 193, 202
  Yangtze 41, 43, 49, 61, 63, 65–7, 90–91, 96–8, 109, 155, 157, 163, 167, 226
Romance of the Grand Khan, The 228
ruling from horseback 39, 47, 88, 184

Saiyid Ajall Shams al-Din (Yunnan governor) 169–70, 177, 208
  'golden age' of 170
samurai *see* Kono-Michiari *and* Takezaki Suenaga
Sangha (or Sengge/Sangko) 183–5
  accused (by Mubarak Shah) of hoarding gifts 189–90
  execution of 189–90
  puts down 'Brig-gung revolt 183–4
Sasaki, Randall 163, 164–5
Secret History of the Mongols 13, 22–3, 27, 32
semuren 5, 107, 155, 169–70, 178, 183–5, 19, 225, 240–41
  definition of 138–9
  system 183
settled and pastoral cultures, antagonism between 10

Shandong 82–4 *see also* Li Tan
Shangdu 20, 50–52, 54–5, 61, 77, 104, 137, 212, 220, 229–30
Shiremun 27
  attempts to take khanship by force 37–8
  confesses to Mongke 38
  execution of 39
  takes refuge with Khubilai 38–9
Shulita (*darughachi*/viceroy) 73
siege(s) (of) 64
  Chinese parable of 44
  Dali 44–5
  engineers (Muslim) 157
  Ezhou 66–7, 69
  tactics 42
  trebuchets/mangonels for 92–4
  Xiangyang 91–5, 100, 101, 178
  Yangzhou 96–7
slavery 5, 19, 34, 90, 106, 112, 140–42, 167, 177, 182, 225 *see also* prisoners
Sogetu (Mongol governor of Canton) 197
Song dynasty 5, 43–4, 86, 99, 155, 158, 187, 223 *see also* Northern Song *and* Southern Song
  and deaths of last Song rulers 110–11
  fugitives 109–10
  and Grand Empress Dowager Xie 97–9, 101
  merchants 89–90
Sorghaghtani 3, 13–15, 23–7, 31–2, 35, 37, 38, 64
  as acting queen of Mongolia 23
  as chief wife of Tolui 14

death of 39
gives Khubilai own estate:
    Xingzhou 26–7
honours all religions 25
interrogates and kills Guyuk's
    widow 38
as Nestorian Christian 14–15,
    25
offers support for Guyuk 32
power of 14
refuses to remarry 23–4
settles in Zending 25–6
sons of 14, 35
Southern Song (and) 25, 43,
    49–50, 54, 56, 61, 62–80,
    82–4, 87–90, 95, 138, 185,
    186–7, 195, 222 see also
    Khubilai Khan and Mongke
    Emperor of 89, 97
fall of 100, 142, 144, 155, 181,
    186
involvement in attack on Japan
    155
Jia Sidao 66–7, 70, 89, 96
legal code of 140
legend of 'Hundred Eyes' 95–6
outnumbering of Mongols in
    88
regency of Empress Dowager
    Quan/GrandEmpress
    Dowager Xie 97–8
repossession of lands: given to
    Buddhists 187–8
reunification of China 112
shipbuilding/fleet in 91, 110
Stican 36 see also Batu and Guyuk

Taizong (Tang emperor) 81–2,
    108, 120

Takashima Island 162, 164–7
Takezaki Suenaga (and) 160–61
    account of battle of Hakata Bay
        131–2
    captures crew members of
        Mongol fleet 161
Tang dynasty 71–2, 81–2, 98, 101,
    108, 18
Taoism/Taoists 57–8, 60, 103,
    170–72, 220
    accumulated wealth of 57
    Chang-zhun 57
    inflammatory texts of 171–2
    vs Buddhists 57–8, 171–2
taxation 19, 26–7, 30–31, 53, 57,
    87, 112, 141, 142, 148, 182–3,
    187–8
    avoidance and religious land
        188
    and import duty 182, 190
    of monasteries 95
    on salt 182
Temuge 31
    executed by Guyuk 35
Temujin 2–3, 10–12, 13, 15–17,
    24, 49, 53, 57, 62, 64, 76, 79,
    88, 100, 121, 122, 139, 176,
    190, 212–13, 219, 220 see also
    Arigh Boke; Batu and
    Hulagu
    campaigns against Jurchens 12
    conquests of 4–5, 12
    death of 12, 16
    and decree of succession 16–17
    and destruction of Xixia and
        the Tanguts 11–12
    settlement of estates of 17
Temur 190–91
    addicted to alcohol 191

gives up alcohol 219–20
signs of gout in 191
succeeds Khubilai 219–20
Thai Tong, ruler of Annam 193–4
abdicates in favour of Thanh
Tong 194
Thanh Tong, ruler of Annam
194–6
abdicates in favour of Nhan
Tong 196
Tibet/Tibetans 56–7, 138, 179–5,
185
and 'Bri-gung Monastery 181,
220
'Brig-gung revolt in 181, 183–4
and execution of Gongdi, 'lost'
16th Song Emperor 221
traditions 188
Toghan, Prince 198–204
captures and executes Marquis
Bao-Nghia 200
leads army against Champa
198–9
threatens Nhan Tong 199
and troops routed 204
Toghrul (leader of Keraits) 14
Tokimune 119, 123–4, 152–6
and execution of Khubilai's
envoys 153–4, 155
Tolui 21–3, 64, 148, 149
death of 22–3, 27
sons of 21, 23, 29–45
Toregene, wife of Ogodei 24,
29–32, 35–6
as regent 30–31
replaces officials with Muslim
advisers 30–31
and taxation crises 30–31
unexplained death of 36

Tran Hung Dao 200–205
addresses Annamese soldiers
198–9
counter-attacks 200–201
destroys Mongol fleet 203–4
as modern cult figure 205
Tran Ich Tac 200–201
cowardice of 201
as nominal ruler of Annam
200
Tsushima island 117–18, 157–8
battle on/fall of 127–30, 132
massacre of survivors on 129
new massacre on 158
Sō Sukekuni, lord of 122,
127–9

Uighur(s) 86, 138
Uryangkhadai, General 46, 55,
63, 66, 193–4, 222

Vietnam see Annam

Wang E (adviser to Khubilai) 70
Wang Wendong, sentencing and
execution of 85–6
wars against Xixia and Jurchens
21
widows, remarriage of 23–4
William of Rubruck 8–9, 36–7,
57, 142
at Mongke's winter court
40–41
reports to Pope on death of
Guyuk 36
Wongjong, King of Korea 71–3,
102, 104, 120, 126
death of 114
and invasion of Japan 114–18

Xanadu 50–61
Xiangyang, siege of 91–5, 100,
    101, 178
Xingzhou 26–7, 41
Xinjiang (Chinese Turkestan) 147

Yang Lianzhenjia (Buddhist
    monk) 185–9
  desecrates/plunders tombs of
    song emperors 187–8
  restoration programme in
    Southern Song 185–8
  settles scores with Taoists and
    Confucians 189
  takes land and gives to
    Buddhists 187–8
Yangtze campaign 81–99
Yangzhou 109, 155, 224
Yaraslav, (Russian) Duke 35
Yasa 139–40
Yelu Chucai 17–20, 28, 30–31
  as adviser to Ogodei 17–20
  as adviser to Sorghaghtani 25–6
  death of 31
  given responsibility for north
    China 20

and Jurchen regime 17–18
Yesungge, General 75
youngest sons, traditional duties
    of 21, 63
Yuan dynasty (and) 7, 100–113,
    146, 223, 225–6
  and art 225–6
  tributes to new emperor 101–2
Yunnan 55, 169–70, 194, 224
  border with Burma 208
  'golden age' government of
    170
  and Nasir al-Din 208–10

Zhang Shijie (Song admiral) 111,
    197
Zhang Xi 165–6
  given posthumous decoration
    167
Zheng He 225
Zhenjin 31,183, 184, 190, 218
  has enemies at court 180
  as heir apparent 175–6
  made Prince of Yan 176
Zhongdu 104
  curse on rebuilding of 106–7